Populations at Risk in America

A publication of the Nelson A. Rockefeller Center
for the Social Sciences at Dartmouth College,
Hanover, New Hampshire

Populations at Risk in America

Vulnerable Groups at the End of the Twentieth Century

EDITED BY

George J. Demko
and Michael C. Jackson

WestviewPress

A Division of HarperCollinsPublishers

Published in 1995 in the United States of America by Westview Press, Inc., 5500 Central Avenue, Boulder, Colorado 80301-2877, and in the United Kingdom by Westview Press, 12 Hid's Copse Road, Cumnor Hill, Oxford OX2 9JJ

A CIP catalog record for this book is available from the Library of Congress.
ISBN 0-8133-8946-1

The paper used in this publication meets the requirements of the American National Standard for Permanence of Paper for Printed Library Materials Z39.48-1984.

10   9   8   7   6   5   4   3   2   1

Contents

Tables and Figures

Preface

At this time, near the end of the twentieth century—the end of the second millennium, *anno Domini*—the United States has not reached the period of euphoria described in Revelations (20). The end of the current thousand-year period was to be a time when great happiness prevailed and human perfection achieved. Indeed, around the globe as well as in the United States, the century has been plagued by great and small wars (all vicious), intolerance, injustice, inequality, global and local environmental threats, and the ominous danger imposed by weapons of mass destruction. Here at the end of the second millennium there even appears to be an upsurge in ugly, inhumane and malevolent events and processes—the scourge of AIDS, virulent and violent nationalisms, increasing inequality, and constantly increasing poverty.

Given the above, it is very important to attempt to understand the processes and problems afflicting our globe and it is especially important to examine the problems within our own boundaries. To comprehend these issues is important for a number of reasons—in order to increase public awareness of the issues; in order to understand the root causes of these problems; and in order to impel us to seek solutions and measures to ameliorate these problems.

On the occasion of the tenth anniversary of the creation of the Nelson A. Rockefeller Center for the Social Sciences at Dartmouth College, a series of lectures by distinguished scholars was organized to focus on populations at risk in America at the end of the twentieth century. The chapters that follow are the product of that lecture series and reflect a broad range of views from a wide array of social sciences. Obviously the series could not cover every group at risk in America. A close examination of the American demographic landscape with its dizzying array of ethnic, economic, social, political, and other special interest groups clearly obviates complete coverage. Even consideration of the primary groups proved difficult because expertise was not available to provide an appropriate, dispassionate and analytical paper on some. Other groups are very recent additions to the vulnerable list such as male homosexuals and others at risk of AIDS and a clear perspective is not possible at this time.

The papers collected here are an attempt to cover the most visible and numerous groups that have been marginalized or afflicted and whose plight will undoubtedly continue into the twenty-first century. Some groups that are covered, such as Native Americans, are well documented and have long been disenfranchised. Others, such as the homeless, are a relatively newly recognized problem. Others, such as mothers and children, are groups viewed from a different and somewhat radical perspective. Some of the papers view the underclass as a whole and address the problems from an historical or a public policy perspective.

Professor Jones focuses attention on the proliferation of distressed communities throughout the United States and the poverty-stricken populations in them. The focus is on *place* rather than race and ethnic group, and the point is made that the poor are ethnically and racially diverse. She rejects the concepts of *underclass* and *cultures of poverty* often associated with African Americans and explores and clarifies the composition of the poor and near-poor. She concludes with possible measures to alleviate distress in these communities.

Professor Perrow argues that the entire United States population is at risk, endangered by the replacement of a civil society and culture by a society of huge organizations. His ominous fear is that we all stand to lose our egalitarian and democratic culture as a result of the imposition of large and intrusive bureaucratic organizations into our lives.

The paper by Professor Gordon focuses on U.S. welfare programs which are designed to mitigate poverty and inequality. She argues that these efforts often actually exacerbate existing problems. She begins with the Social Security Act of 1935 and proceeds to trace the impact of social insurance on the development of an "underclass" which is deeply gendered and disproportionately ethnic/racial minority in composition.

Professor Blank notes that the nature and causes of poverty in America have changed over the past thirty years. The major changes have been the feminization and urban concentration of poverty and the growing wage inequality. She then reviews the most promising new ideas in the public policy arena designed to alleviate poverty and assesses their prospects for success.

The paper by Professor Wolch describes the problem of homelessness in America and argues that we are all at risk of homelessness in all settings—the central city, the suburbs, the exurbs. She posits that we have a polarized situation which pits people on the inside (domiciled) against those on the outside (homeless) for control of public space and community resources.

James Q. Wilson explores two populations at risk—the general public at risk of exploitation by criminals and, in more detail, that subset of the population that may have a serious genetic predisposition to criminal behavior. The latter group and the genetic basis of deviance is the primary focus of his essay. Some of the treacherous ground of group differences in criminal behavior is examined in detail.

Jetter, Orleck and Taylor explore in an imaginative way the underlying myths and stereotypes we have about the poor, especially women and children. The basic argument they make is that racism, sexism and fear of the poor exacerbate these societal problems and interfere in the search for solutions. In a related paper, the Rameys focus their attention on impoverished children of low I.Q. mothers and stress the value of early and continued intervention. They identify six types of experiences which lead to positive outcomes via intervention programs.

Professor Russell Thornton describes the prolonged demographic disaster experienced by Native Americans which began with the arrival of the Europeans. He notes that even today, Native Americans are trying to cope with the demographic impacts of European contact. He concludes with a discussion of future trends of the population and emphasizes the importance of tribal membership and new types of tribalism.

Finally, Professor Carol Stack focuses attention on rural-urban contrasts and tensions in the lives of African Americans who return to the South. She describes the return by this group as "emancipatory, gendered and dangerous."

The overall goal of this volume is to provide a number of disciplinary perspectives on those in our society who are at great risk as we near the next century, the third millennium. We hope the view provided herein moves our readers to a greater awareness of the ills of our country and stimulates discussion and even action to move toward solutions to these persistent ills and societal failures. As most of our contributors point out, these problems are ours—in fact *we* are the population at risk.

George J. Demko and Michael C. Jackson

About the Contributors

Rebecca M. Blank, Professor of Economics at Northwestern University.

Linda Gordon, Professor of History and Women's Studies at the University of Wisconsin.

Alexis Jetter, a former reporter for New York's *Newsday* and a freelance journalist living in Vermont.

Jacqueline Jones, Professor of History at Brandeis University.

Annelise Orleck, Assistant Professor of History at Dartmouth College.

Charles B. Perrow, Professor of Sociology at Yale University.

Craig T. Ramey, Professor of Psychology, Pediatrics, and Public Health at the University of Alabama at Birmingham.

Sharon Landesman Ramey, Professor of Psychiatry, Psychology, Pediatrics, and Public Health at the University of Alabama at Birmingham.

Carol B. Stack, Professor of Education and Women's Studies at the University of California at Berkeley.

Russell Thornton, The Samson Occom Professor of Native American Studies and Professor of Sociology at Dartmouth College.

Diana Taylor, Professor of Spanish and Comparative Literature at Dartmouth College.

James Q. Wilson, Professor of Political Science at the University of California at Los Angeles.

Jennifer R. Wolch, Professor of Geography at the University of Southern California.

1

Beyond "Race and Culture": American Underclasses in the Late Twentieth Century

Jacqueline Jones

For all the media sound-bites and partisan-political fury unleashed by the 1992 presidential campaign, that campaign represented a failure of politics in the broadest sense of the word. It is true that, toward the end of the contest, the three major candidates engaged in spirited rhetorical fisticuffs, and brief cameo appearances by Murphy Brown and Harry Truman helped to enliven evening broadcasts and front-page news stories. As a result, apparently, after election day the journalists and politicians alike claimed that the American people had witnessed, and participated in, a thorough airing of the issues confronting the nation in the late twentieth century. Unfortunately, this display of self-congratulation was misguided, to say the least. In fact, I would argue that the campaign was notable in general for its almost exclusive attention to the beleaguered middle class, and in particular for the failure of all three candidates to address in any direct or compelling way the major domestic problem plaguing the nation today—the proliferation of distressed communities throughout the country.

Absent from the 1992 national political agenda, then, poverty-stricken populations remained inconspicuous throughout debates over the federal deficit, foreign policy, abortion, and taxes. As some observers noted, the Presidential campaign took the form of the "Battle of the Malls"—a term I take to mean that the overall prosperity of America was given as fact. The larger question was thus framed this way: Where would the American people be doing their shopping in the years to come, at a Wal-Mart or at a Bloomingdales? Few bothered to worry whether some folks might not have the resources to do much shopping at all. By successfully deflecting attention from the growing numbers of the poor in this country, and by catering to the anxieties of the middle class, candidates Bush, Clinton and Perot expressed their collective contempt for the needs of the men, women, and children who remained on the margins of the political process, without a voice, without an advocate—and too often, without hope.

In order to explore the histories of these different distressed communities, and their similar structures today, I would like to depart from two well-worn paths followed by many social scientists who write about poverty. First, I would like to suggest that the term "underclass" actually hinders our attempt to understand the global political and economic forces creating a large number of ethnically and racially diverse poverty-stricken populations all over the country, and not just in the black ghettoes of the largest northern cities. All this is to say that I want to distance myself from the academic equivalent of racial politics, which I define as the manipulation of images, code words and statistics to create the impression that all black people are poor, and that all poor people are black.[1]

Second, I would argue that this misguided, exclusive association of African-Americans with poverty fuels the notion that there is a "culture of poverty"[2]—a present-minded, live-for-the-day kind of life that prevents the poor from climbing out of poor neighborhoods, and that this way of life is roughly congruent with African-American culture.[3] All too frequently sociologists and political scientists, as well as journalists and policy makers, create the impression that the black culture is somehow exotic, outside the "mainstream" of white, middle-class American life.[4] Along these lines, a respected and widely quoted political scientist has declared unequivocally that whites and blacks "don't have a common culture. We have two nations and two cultures."[5] In fact, of course, over the generations, the vast majority of black people have wanted for themselves and their children the same blessings of American life that white middle-class families have claimed as their own—the right to a good job and a good education, the right to participate in the political process and move to a new place in search of a better life.[6]

A myopic focus on race will continue to blind us to the fact the United States is in the midst of worldwide transformations that are rendering increasing numbers of people, and increasing numbers of whole communities, economically superfluous. By my conservative estimate, these communities include about twenty-five percent of the total American population, and that proportion will continue to grow in the absence of major federal initiatives in the areas of housing, employment, and education.

Distressed populations consist of men and women who are in the paid labor force, as well as their neighbors who are outside of it. The 1990 census lists 36 million poor in the United States, about fourteen percent of the total population. To this figure I would add the near-poor, all of the people who just barely clear the poverty line (defined as an annual income of $13,920 for a family of four). This near-poor, or working poor, population includes an additional 26 million men and women who work at one or more jobs, at seasonal or part-time jobs, and live only one paycheck, or one health-care crisis, away from complete and utter disaster.[7]

Though analytically superior to certain race-based and culture-based theories of poverty, the concept of the distressed community is not comprehensive. For example, we might argue that the homeless constitute a counter-community of sorts, a group of poor people who remain scattered throughout towns and cities. Some municipalities have taken stern measures to prevent the homeless from coming together in any public or permanent way; in their aloneness, or in groups of three of four, the homeless remain a mere nuisance, in contrast to concentrations of homeless people who might become an obvious, and an obviously political, presence, in the life of a city.[8] Or we might focus on particular demographic, racial and labor groups particularly vulnerable to long-term changes in the American economy—African-American civil servants disproportionately hurt by public-sector layoffs and cutbacks in government spending at the local, state, and national levels; wives and mothers of small children, pulled in growing numbers into the work force to make up for the joblessness and decreased income suffered by the men in their lives; young adults without seniority in the workplace; and children, now called upon to begin wage-earning at an ever earlier age, after school and on weekends, in order to help their households make ends meet. To cite a final example of ways to eschew an exclusive focus on African-Americans in northern cities, we might concentrate on a single indicator of poverty like hunger. Measuring distress in terms of actual physical want, a team of researchers in the mid-1980s pointed to the plight of people living in Texas, South Dakota, and Missouri, which together accounted for one-half of the nation's worst "hunger counties," where malnutrition was a fact of everyday life for large numbers of men, women, and children.[9]

Regardless of the limitations of distressed communities as a lens into the causes and consequences of poverty in the United States, such communities do offer a dramatic revelation of the failure of the American economy and the American social-welfare system to meet the needs of a nation in the midst of global restructuring.[10] Representative communities include industrial workers displaced by advanced technology and foreign imports; migratory agricultural workers; rural folk in areas dominated by seasonal tourist industries; Appalachian migrant communities in the Midwest; single-industry towns that have lost their economic mainstays; Native American reservations throughout the country; big-city concentrations of poor people; and enclaves of refugees from Central America and Southeast Asia. From this list it is clear that these communities include a wide range of ethnic and religious groups, and that they are located all over the United States, not just in the ghettoes of the largest northern cities.

The steel workers of Indiana, auto workers of Michigan, rubber workers of Ohio, and textile workers of Georgia and the Carolinas are representative of a segment of the American labor force that has fallen victim to certain advanced, and logical, economic processes and business practices. Over the last two decades, worldwide market competition has forced heavy industries to streamline, consolidate, and mechanize their operations. The increased use of robotics and computers has produced smaller, more efficient work forces. In the process, hundreds of thousands of workers of both sexes and all races have lost their jobs. For example, out of the devastation of the midwestern steel industry has arisen the triumphant mini-mill. Within the last decade or so, the industry has invested more than $20 billion in new machinery and other forms of modernization, and in the process cut the average man-hour per ton of steel produced from 10.2 in 1980 to 4.4 in 1990. These smaller mills rely primarily on nonunion work forces; not only do they employ far fewer people than the largest mills needed not so long ago; they pay those people less, as well. [11]

This then, is the end of the American dream for the children of blue-collar workers who came to enjoy the comforts of a middle-class way of life in the 1950s and 1960s, a way of life sustained by protectionist tariff policies and, in some cases, the power and political clout wielded by labor unions.[12] Though differentiated by size, region and industry, towns like Eden, North Carolina; Barberton, Ohio; Gary, Indiana; and Flint, Michigan began to suffer a similar fate of declining population and decaying infrastructure. The residents of these towns of course include blacks as well as whites. [13]

Communities of displaced heavy-industry workers began to decline under the pressure of a global marketplace in the 1970s. In contrast, poor communities of agricultural migrant laborers have a history that stretches back to the early twentieth century, when commercial fruit and vegetable growers emerged to respond to the year-round demand for fresh produce in major urban areas. Located on both coasts, and in the Midwest as well, communities of migrants today still consist of men, women and children who follow the crops "on the season." They toil under an exploitative labor-management system that has remained intact over the last seventy-five years or so, though various streams of workers have undergone striking changes in terms of their racial and ethnic composition. For example, the East Coast stream, based in Belle Glade, Florida, originated in the 1920s as a destination-of-last-resort for Georgia sharecroppers pushed off the land by the declining price of cotton and the appearance of tractors on the southern countryside. Joining these African-American workers were Mexican immigrants fleeing from revolution and poverty in their own land, and a few native-born southern whites. World War II drew whites out of the migrant force and into war industry work, and agricultural employers sought to replace them with off-shore workers from Puerto Rico and the Bahamas.[14]

Today, the East Coast stream stretching from Lake Okeechobee in Florida up to the blueberry fields of Maine claims the energies of African Americans, Haitians, Laotians, Mexicans, and Native Americans. These workers, who earn meager wages for back-breaking toil in the fields, remain outside the welfare system created through New Deal measures in the 1930s. They are largely unaffected by measures that other kinds of workers take for granted, including federal minimum wage laws and health and safety standards established by the Occupational Safety and Health Act. Migrant laborers are at risk for tuberculosis and a whole host of diseases stemming from the increased use of pesticides in the fields. Their families are routinely separated as children stay in the care of elderly kin while parents and older siblings go up the coast for part of every year.[15]

The plight of agricultural workers serves as a stark reminder that rural poverty is pervasive throughout the United States. Within some of the most scenic areas of the country, not far from the interstate highway, rustic campground, or upscale resort, lie scattered distressed communities. In parts of New England—the back country of Maine, New Hampshire, Vermont, and western Massachusetts—in upstate New York and down through the southern Appalachians, households struggle to make do during annual depressions, each winter time. With the decline of commercial farming in New England in the early nineteenth century, and with the decline of coal mining in the Appalachians beginning in the 1920s, some rural folk migrated to other farm areas, or city-ward, while others, along with their children and grandchildren, stayed behind.[16] Today, communities in these areas are sustained by service jobs in motels, fast-food restaurants, and gift shops, and in some cases by part-time crafts that are marketed to skiers in the winter and hikers and sunbathers in the summer. In some counties, the public school system is the largest employer.[17] From the back roads of Maine to the hills and hollows of Kentucky, these (mostly white) rural folk continue to forage, hunt, fish, and rely on the goodwill of kin and neighbors in times of need.[18]

In his 1933 book, *Machine Age in the Hills*, Malcolm Ross described the historical process which would link the subsistence farms of Appalachia to the big-city factories of Chicago and Detroit. Ross noted the tendency of large farm families to leave the land and seek out steady work and wages in the coal mines; beginning in the 1920s, a downturn in the coal industry, combined with mechanical innovations, pushed miners and their families out of these towns and into the Midwest. Wrote Ross, "Here, in miniature, is a cycle which seems to be working out in America at large. Some of the children must be the next generation of coal miners; the rest will be surplus hands in a region which has no other ways to use their energies."[19] Many of these young "surplus hands" eagerly took jobs in the rubber factories of Ohio and the auto plants of Detroit, and it is their children today who are suffering the consequences of economic and social dislocation in the Rust Belt. Throughout the twentieth century, some white southern migrants could not commit themselves to city life, and remained in limbo, neither in the North nor at home in the mountains; today, clusters of Appalachian migrants in Uptown Chicago and the Lower Price Hill area of Cincinnati (for example) remain dependent on day work because of local and state residency requirements, outside the purview of public assistance programs.[20]

Although Appalachia attracted a great deal of attention in the mid-1960s, when writers and policy makers "discovered" widespread poverty there, the forces that created distress in that region are the sources of affliction for communities in other regions of the country today. With increasing frequency, apparently stable communities, some in America's heartland, disappear almost overnight, their steady jobs eliminated, along with plants that close and shops that "run away" to the South, to Mexico, to off-shore islands, or to South East Asia. In the late 1980s, Waterloo, Iowa, lost its Rath meat packing plant and its John Deere farm machinery factory cut its work force in half. Within a few years this town of 70,000 had to grapple with the loss of 7,000 jobs. Unemployed workers took positions in nearby malls, nursing homes, and restaurants. A new meat packing plant opened in the area, but it boasted state-of-the-art machinery and employed only a small work force.[21] Similarly, the fire that swept through the Imperial Food Products plant in Hamlet, North Carolina in 1991 killed 25 workers, blacks and whites, and injured 56 more. The fire also consumed Hamlet's mainstay. According to a *New York Times* reporter who visited the town two months later, "the loss of a major employer, compounded by the deaths, exposes an industrial backwater. ... Hamlet's economy is sinking, and its people are too poor, too locked to their unsalable trailers and weather-scarred houses, or too bound to their families to leave."[22]

The blacks and whites in Waterloo and Hamlet lost more than jobs when they lost their livelihood; they lost the infrastructure that supported traditional patterns of family and community life. In its place appeared the forms of fragmented social organization created by the irregular hours of low-paying jobs, the increased pressure on children to enter the paid labor force, and the insecurity of service-sector work. The dispossessed of rural America may choose to stay in their communities, or to leave, but either way their families register the effects of such choices in dramatic ways. Some men and women decide to cast their lot with tight-knit webs of kin and community support, thereby continuing to honor those bonds of mutual dependence and obligation that have characterized their families—in a certain place—through the generations. Some workers who own their own homes, modest though they might be, are committed to preserving their stake in society, and realize that an attempt to sell off such a stake will result in further financial loss, if indeed it can be accomplished at all. People who choose not to move face the prospect of taking part-time jobs at the local Wal-Mart or Burger King, or commuting long distances to find better paying work. As we have seen, in this new service economy, young people from poor families are pressured to enter the work force early, and the father's bread-winning role gives way to a multiplicity of wage-earners within any one household.

Though often ignored in most historical and contemporary accounts of American life, the plight of Native Americans is emblematic of larger themes of distressed populations in the late twentieth century. On the East Coast and in the Southwest, on the Great Plains and in the Northwest, Indian reservations are home to a proud people, now suffering from all the ills that policy analysts and social scientists associate exclusively with northern, urban blacks. For example, the Pine Ridge Reservation of South Dakota, is "as poor as America gets." In 1989, nearly two-thirds of the Reservation's 16,000 Sioux Indians lived in poverty, making Shannon County, South Dakota, the poorest county in the United States. By any measure of distress—alcoholism, mortality, suicide, and homicide rates; broken families, demoralized mothers and fathers, poor housing and joblessness—Pine Ridge was a "prototype of rural poverty," its inhabitants isolated from good jobs, its young people eager to leave forever, breaking the bonds of a centuries-old culture in the process.[23]

Just as Indian reservations were created by the national government to confine and isolate a specific population, so the big-city northern ghettoes were the product of institutional and political forces designed to prevent southern migrants from encroaching into all-white suburbs and working-class neighborhoods. As it developed in the early twentieth century, the black ghetto was home to African Americans of various classes; but now, this kind of community is overwhelmingly poor. Yet even here it is difficult to generalize about poverty in racial terms, for inner-city neighborhoods also play host to various groups of immigrants from the far-flung corners of the world. This theme of the multiethnic ghetto characterized the April, 1992, civil disorders in South Central Los Angeles, a community with a poverty rate of 33 percent. The conflict that resulted in 60 deaths, 10,000 businesses destroyed and 10,000 people arrested, was less a clash between blacks against whites, than between poor blacks and Hispanics against recent Korean immigrants. To a large extent, middle-class blacks no longer live in South-Central Los Angeles; they have moved to suburbs like Inglewood, leaving only a subset of the migrant community—the very poorest people, behind. [24]

It is clear, then, that American communities of all sizes and divergent regions are increasingly playing host to immigrant groups whose homelands chart the course of revolution, repression and economic upheaval abroad during the last generation. Refugees from South East Asia and Central America in particular seek out their kin and cultural compatriots, creating enclaves of Laotians, Cambodians, Filipinos, and Vietnamese as well as Salvadorans, Haitians, Hondurans and Ecuadorians in American small towns and big cities. In the process of settling with kinfolk who can offer them support in the form of a vital religious and associational life, and help in finding jobs and sending their children to schools, these new immigrants overwhelm neighborhoods unable to provide them decent jobs and housing. For example, unemployment runs high within those large communities of Cambodians who have settled in the decaying mill towns of Massachusetts and Rhode Island; as these refugee communities grow, they attract new immigrants from a still war-torn Cambodia, and consequently, they exacerbate already critical housing and job shortages.

Like the riot in South Central Los Angeles, the civil disturbances in the Mount Pleasant neighborhood of Washington, D.C., in the spring of 1991, highlighted the poverty and resentment of enclaves of "new immigrants." Residents of the Mt. Pleasant area include middle-class whites as well as poor African-Americans, and immigrants from El Salvador, Guatemala, Nicaragua, and Honduras—immigrants who live in cramped apartments and rely on menial jobs that require long hours and pay very little. [25]

Clearly, then, it is impossible to generalize about the ethnic or racial composition of distressed communities. Moreover, these different types of communities have different histories. The black ghettoes of the big-city North grew because of the determination of the former slaves and their children and grandchildren to flee Jim Crow, lynching, and disfranchisement in the South. Mexican immigrants began to come to this country in large numbers in the 1920s, in response to poverty and political upheaval at home. The stranded communities of displaced workers in the Midwest and elsewhere began to reel under the pressures of a global economy beginning in the 1970s. During the heady days on Wall Street, in the years of Ronald Reagan's presidency, corporate takeovers and firm consolidations wiped out plants in small towns all over America, producing growing numbers of people new to a life of poverty.

Nevertheless, despite the fact that these distressed communities have followed different historical trajectories, they exhibit certain structural features regardless of their racial or ethnic composition, regardless of whether they are located in the rural South or urban North, on the East Coast or West Coast. In listing these features, we might consider as our model the Native American reservation, or the post-bellum cotton plantation, places where poor people might move around within a narrowly circumscribed area, but find it difficult to move out, by virtue of their straited economic circumstances and a lack of favorable opportunities (for people of their color or class) elsewhere, nearby or far away.

Whether these communities originated in the conquest of an indigenous people (the Navajo Nation in Arizona) in the institution of slavery (the Mississippi Delta), in the collapse of the coal-mining industry (Cranks Creek, Kentucky), in the great migrations of the twentieth century (inner-city Detroit), or in the repression and civil strife in the Caribbean (enclaves of Haitians in Miami), they all lack good jobs for unskilled and relatively uneducated workers within commuting distance. It is a commonsensical fact that the poor today confront a national economy qualitatively different from the one that greeted the Eastern European immigrants who came to these shores in the late nineteenth and early twentieth century. Though confined to arduous, dangerous, and ill-paid jobs, those immigrants found a ready place within an industrializing economy that had a seemingly insatiable need for unskilled workers, whether or not they could speak English.[26] By the 1920s, transformations in the economy—the large-scale mechanization of heavy industry, for example—meant that fewer and fewer eager workers could be absorbed so readily into the manufacturing sector. Cutbacks and layoffs in the 1980s and 1990s threw increasing numbers of workers into service jobs; in one week in early 1993, for example, Boeing, McDonnell Douglas, United Technologies, and Sears Roebuck announced cutbacks in their labor forces totaling 100,000 jobs—"most of them 'good' ones, meaning full-time work with health and pension benefits."[27] Only infrequently, now, do factory jobs hold out the promise of a foothold in the industrial sector, the promise of a living wage, or the promise of residential upward mobility that will enable one's children to go to better schools. Brockton, Massachusetts, Wichita, Kansas, and Memphis, Tennessee, for example, have all shared a similar, and a similarly painful fate; they now offer their workers "jobs without hope."[28]

The American public education system reminds us that the personal welfare of all Americans is tied to the places where they live; the schools are a dramatic example of this fact, since local schools rely to a great degree on funding raised through the property tax.[29] Yet in addition to this particular form of structural inequality, regardless of whether poor people live in the South Bronx or in a Texas barrio, in Belle Glade, Florida, or in Lower Price Hill in Cincinnati, they also lack access to adequate medical care (because they have no health insurance), and to quality, reliable police and fire protection. The fact of the matter is that the delivery of basic human services depends less on citizenship rights than on a family's relation to the labor market; residential location, based on income level, determines a family's collective fate, and the children's individual futures.

All families in distressed communities suffer from the effects of national and international political and economic transformations. Chronic unemployment and underemployment, seasonal jobs and unpredictable working hours put stress on husband-wife, parent-child, and male-female relationships within households. Men, women, and children follow time-honored adaptive strategies by relying on networks of kin and neighbors; they barter, trade, and exchange services like cooking and baby-sitting, they do odd jobs for one another and take their pay "off the books" and "under the table"; and some might engage in illegal activities that range from the mundane (using a forged Social Security card to get a job) to the overtly violent (selling guns or drugs illegally).[30] In this respect—on a scale of family fragmentation and social pathology—small towns and rural areas affected by economic distress are coming increasingly to resemble the inner cities. In the 1990s, the South Bronx—or any other northern, urban African-American community for that matter—has no monopoly on drive-by shootings, consumers of crack cocaine or predatory street gangs armed with automatic weapons.[31]

And finally, all of these communities illustrate, in their own ways, the tension between migration and residential stability—the conflict in the collective life of almost all groups about whether to go or to stay, whether to cling to the place of one's forbears or to strike out for territory unknown. Some groups have had less choice than others in the matter, and the forces of dispersal and displacement are many, from the brutal country sheriff to the mechanical cotton picker in the rural South of the 1950s, from the closing of a textile mill and the raiding of an employee pension fund in the Piedmont of North Carolina during the 1980s. Yet all households so affected have had to sort out their priorities related to honoring the past and responding to the promise of the future; they have to weigh the welfare of dependent grandparents living nearby with the best interests of children in the long run.

When we go to search for the root cause of these many communities, we are struck by causes that are as obvious as they are intractable. First, the American economy of industrial capitalism produces poverty as well as prosperity. In the late twentieth century global market, businesses either succeed or fail; either way, workers lose their jobs when work forces become "leaner and meaner," and hence more competitive, or plants fail or go elsewhere, closing their doors forever. Larger changes in the structure of the work force—the decline in heavy manufacturing, the shrinking of middle-level white collar and managerial jobs, and the rise of the service sector—all contribute to the marginalization of whole communities of people. In the absence of countervailing forces—a strong labor union movement, or aggressive government regulatory mandates, for example—these communities will continue to grow and multiply.[32]

Also, the end of the Cold War will wipe out whole cities built on the formerly rock-solid foundation of the military-industrial complex; for some regions, army base closings spell disaster as the need for a whole host of support services, from restaurants to dry-cleaning establishments, from movie theaters to department stores, withers away. To cite one dramatic example: the relatively affluent state of Connecticut will bear a disproportionate burden inflicted by the "peace penalty" in the coming years. From 1989 to 1993 the state lost one-eighth of its total nonagricultural jobs, with more plant closings in sight. Stripped of their military-based livelihoods, workers in formerly well-to-do towns like Groton and New London began to confront the hard choices faced by people in distressed communities everywhere—how to survive a medical crisis without health insurance, how to piece together a living through a series of short-term jobs.[33]

The classic answer to these problems, and the answer put forth by classical economists, has always been out-migration. In the early 1960s, jobless auto workers tried their luck in the Sun Belt, only to fall victim to a region-wide depression in the oil industry at the end of the decade. Since that time, no other area of the country has beckoned folk out of work and down on their luck with the possibility of good jobs that pay a living wage. Indeed, the 1980s and the early 1990s have been characterized by a national depressed-wage economy; a family hard hit by textile plant layoffs in Kannapolis, North Carolina, or steel mill closings in Aliquippa, Pennsylvania might well contemplate whether any other area of the country could offer them opportunities over and above the service sector jobs in their respective regions of the country.

And finally, as a nation, even the most powerful nation in the world, the United States possesses little control over forces of upheaval abroad—the civil wars and campaigns of religious or political persecution that have produced so many new immigrants, and ultimately, new Americans, over the generations. In sum then the economic forces of "progress" and the political forces of reaction will continue to displace workers, and dispossess whole cultural groups, into the foreseeable future.

This analysis paints a picture of American poverty that differs considerably from the one advanced by theorists of the "underclass." The term itself refers to the poor who are first spatially concentrated, and second, the product of long-term, intergenerational poverty.[34] By virtue of its definition, then, the term ignores rural poor populations altogether. In the early 1990s, welfare case rates were rising at the fastest rate in New Hampshire, and also in Arizona, North Carolina, and Kentucky, states noteworthy for their lack of large urban areas.[35] "Underclass" studies also ignore communities that have been reduced to poverty relatively recently—areas like Barberton, Ohio, for example, once the home of a strong rubber workers union and now a shell of its former self;[36] and neighborhoods of recent immigrants from Mexico, Vietnam, and China.

Moreover, the word underclass evokes certain stereotypes about poverty, stereotypes that rely more on sensationalistic media images— the headlines that trumpet a recent drug bust, the nightly newscast that features a family ravaged by crack addiction—and distracts us from the more modest, mundane struggles of the working poor. Theorists of the underclass imply that the poor are naturally, and overwhelmingly, criminally inclined. In fact, the underground economies of many distressed neighborhoods more often than not involve the production and distribution of a variety of services—baby-sitting or preparing food for friends and neighbors for instance, services that do not in any case rely on the use of violence or physical force. Journalists promote the idea of black distinctiveness by categorizing a wide variety of social-welfare indicators—from infant mortality statistics to tuberculosis rates—by race, rather than income level, perpetuating the idea that blacks inhabit a realm outside the mainstream of American life. Tuberculosis is not a "black" disease, the result of a distinctive black (and supposedly pathological) culture, but rather a poor person's disease.

As a matter of practical politics, we might also argue that blatant racial prejudices equating African Americans with poverty have inhibited efforts to eradicate poverty in this country over the last half century or so. Politicians have done little to disabuse the white middle-class electorate of the mistaken idea that anti-poverty measures will, and do, target the black population exclusively. In sum, a narrow-minded focus on the black underclass blinds us to the historical forces that have produced a variety of distressed communities, and blinds us to the multi-racial, multiethnic nature of those communities.

This is not to suggest that racism has played, or plays, no part in keeping African Americans poor. To the contrary, the history of poverty in America shows clearly that black men and women were consistently at a disadvantage in trying to enter, or remain in, the paid labor force, in contrast to (for example) equally poor or unskilled white people. A comparison of black and white migrants from the South—blacks from the Mississippi Delta and whites from the hills and hollows of Appalachia—reveals that white workers benefited from the racial preferences of employers, and also enjoyed a measure of residential mobility denied to all black migrants no matter how hard-working or talented. Whites managed to gain a foothold in the industrial sector *via* semiskilled wage work, and they managed to move to better areas which could insure their children greater educational opportunity, and hence, upward social mobility.[37] The personal predilections of personnel officials still shape hiring policy to a large degree; and connections based on kin relations and ethnic affiliation continue to determine the social composition of work forces in all kinds of settings. And the bottom line, so to speak, is the fact that proportionately, black people are twice as likely to be poor compared to white people. We historians bear at least some of the responsibility, some of the blame, for the lack of historical consciousness in the "United States of Amnesia." As scholars, we tend to write only for our colleagues, for journal referees and university press editors, for book reviewers and tenure and promotions committees. We scramble to publish our findings in expensive, specialized monographs and in inaccessible periodicals and working paper series. We have little to say about, little light to shed on, modern political and social issues, because we are quick to dismiss such endeavors as worthy only of journalists, and not historians.

A particularly unfortunate consequence of this collective, historical amnesia is the perpetuation of a form of racial politics practiced on both sides of the political aisle, and in the halls of academe. Too many politicians, policy analysts, social scientists, and journalists see in the African-American experience only a history of poverty and degradation, whether on the slave plantation or in the inner-city ghetto. Missing from this popular account of history are the efforts of black people, through their kin networks and households, through voluntary associations and self-help organizations, through churches and political clubs, to provide for themselves and challenge discrimination and prejudice in all areas of American life.

Meanwhile, more and more Americans are coming to realize that a white skin is no guarantee of freedom from poverty, or freedom from the fear of poverty. "The declining middle" is not an irrational nightmare on the part of middle-class Americans; indeed, in the late twentieth century, that class maintains only a tenuous hold on economic stability. It is up to political leaders, then, to draw the connection between the historic suffering of African Americans and the more recent plight of white displaced workers around the country.[38]

Above all, we must keep in mind the symbiotic relationship among jobs, schools, and housing—in other words, the significance of place for any study of poverty (or wealth for that matter). In the 1970s and 1980s the community of South Central Los Angeles lost several large plants belonging to Firestone, General Motors, Goodyear, and Bethlehem Steel; these companies had provided the jobs that lured migrants all over the country to that area, beginning in the World War II period. Today, of course, similarly large corporations are laying off workers elsewhere, and the chances that good blue-collar jobs will rise from the ashes of the 1991 conflagration are remote indeed. The empowerment of the black electorate has not been able to stem this long-term trend; the first black mayor of the city, Tom Bradley could do little but watch the dismantling of South Central's job structure.[39] Nevertheless, most Americans continued to derive their visual impressions of the city from the dramatic opening shots that accompanied the credits to the weekly television show "LA Law"; the glittering downtown skyline was the habitat of high-powered deal makers by day, but the workplace of South Central residents—custodians and maintenance staffs—by night. We have become inured to the juxtaposition of skyscrapers and burned out empty lots; such is the inequality of places in America.[40]

Solutions to these problems will not come in the form of piecemeal social-welfare programs or local, small-scale political initiatives. A few obvious sources of economic distress beg for attention, and radical change. We could, for example, equalize public school financing and extricate this key to equal opportunity from the clutches of the local tax base. We might consider measures that would guarantee to all American workers jobs that pay enough to support a family; this effort would require the bolstering of the minimum wage, and extension of minimum-wage provisions to seasonal and part-time work. A public, federally supported system of worker retraining would rescue displaced workers from the fly-by-night vocational schools that advertise so aggressively and then either fail to deliver promised services to students, or close their doors and abscond with tuition money. A national system of health insurance, in addition to subsidies that would enable all Americans to afford decent housing, would be imperative were health and economic well-being to rank with political equality as a measure of American citizenship.

We return finally to the image of the shopping mall, that repository of a dazzling array of consumer goods, the new public space of late twentieth century America. For almost half a century, the American free enterprise system stood in symbiotic relation to the Cold War, waged at home and abroad; the domestic economy was a machine that would go of its own, without tinkering or intrusion, leaving chief executives free to spend their time and energy monitoring the various foreign hot spots and international crises that cropped up so suddenly and unpredictably. Harry S. Truman, John F. Kennedy, and Lyndon B. Johnson are good examples of presidents who possessed at least the semblance of a will to tackle the problems of poverty and discrimination, and other domestic issues; but they found themselves distracted, side-tracked, into foreign affairs in an effort to halt the spread of communism in Latin America and Southeast Asia. Meanwhile, no matter how heated the arms race, and no matter how high the body count, American consumers (at least those with the requisite amount of cash or credit) could fulfill their hearts' desires at the mall. The backdrop for this burgeoning consumer culture was the proliferation of distressed communities.

Faced with the prospect of a "jobless" economic recovery from the recession of the early 1990s, the poor will continue to provide for themselves; and the depth of their hardship will serve as strident testimony to the pathetic shallowness of the 1992 Presidential campaign.

Notes

1. For discussions of racial politics, see Thomas Byrne Edsall with Mary D. Edsall, *Chain Reaction* (New York: Norton, 1991); Jim Sleeper, *The Closest of Strangers: Liberalism and the Politics of Race in New York* (New York: Norton, 1990).

2. For early uses of the term see Oscar Lewis, *La Vida: A Puerto Rican Family in the Culture of Poverty* (New York: Random House, 1965); Michael Harrington, *The Other America: Poverty in the United States* (New York: Macmillan, 1962).

3. See for example "Breakthrough Books on Poverty in America," *Lingua Franca* Vol. 3, March–April, 1993, p. 11.

4. See for example Ze'ev Chafets, *Devil's Night: And Other True Tales of Detroit* (New York: Random House, 1990), p. 6.

5. "On Inequality, Race, and a Nation Divided" [Interview with Andrew Hacker], *Boston Sunday Globe* March 29, 1992, p. 72. See also Hacker's fuller argument of his position, *Two Nations: Black and White, Separate, Hostile, Unequal* (New York: Scribners, 1992).

6. Jacqueline Jones, *The Dispossessed: America's Underclasses from the Civil War to the Present* (New York: Basic Books, 1992).

7. John E. Schwarz and Thomas J. Volgy, *The Forgotten Americans: Thirty Million Working Poor in the Land of Opportunity* (New York: W. W. Norton, 1992); Mary H. Cooper, "Help Wanted: Why Jobs Are Hard to Fill," *Editorial Research Reports,* Washington, D.C., September 9, 1988, pp. 442–451.

8. See for example Isabel Wilkerson, "Shift in Feelings on the Homeless: Empathy Turns into Frustration," *New York Times,* September 2, 1991; Joel Blau, *The Visible Poor: Homelessness in the United States* (New York: Oxford University Press, 1992).

9. Physician Task Force on Hunger in America, "Hunger Counties 1986: The Distribution of America's High–Risk Areas," Harvard University School of Public Health, Cambridge, Massachusetts, January, 1986.

10. Paul Kennedy, *Preparing for the Twenty-First Century* (New York: Random House, 1993).

11. William E. Schmidt, "A Steel City Still Needs Help Despite Big Steel's Comeback," *New York Times,* September 4, 1989, p. 1; Jonathan P. Hicks, "An Industrial Comeback Story: U.S. Is Competing Again in Steel," *New York Times,* March 31, 1992, p. 1.

12. Richard Feldman and Michael Betzold, eds., *End of the Line: Autoworkers and the American Dream: An Oral History* (Urbana: University of Illinois Press, 1990).

13. Ibid.

14. Jones, *The Dispossessed,* pp. 167–201.

15. Ronald Smothers, "Life as Migrant Worker Is Found to Nurture TB," *New York Times,* April 3, 1991, p. 16; Peter T. Kilborn, "Tide of Migrant Labor Tells of a Law's Failure," *New York Times,* November 4, 1992, p. 24.

16. Hal S. Barron, *Those Who Stayed Behind: Rural Society in Nineteenth Century New England* (New York: Cambridge University Press, 1984); Steven Hahn and Jonathan Prude, eds., *The Countryside in the Age of Capitalist Transformation: Essays in the Social History of Rural America* (Chapel Hill: University of North Carolina Press, 1985); Ronald D. Eller, *Miners, Millhands, and Mountaineers: The Modernization of the Appalachian South, 1880–1930* (Knoxville: University of Tennessee Press, 1982).

17. *Women of the Rural South: Economic Status and Prospects* (Lexington, Kentucky: Southeast Women's Employment Coalition, 1985).

18. See for example Rhoda Halperin, *The Livelihood of Kin: Making Ends Meet 'The Kentucky Way'* (Austin: University of Texas Press, 1990).

19. Malcolm Ross, *Machine Age in the Hills* (New York: Macmillan, 1933), pp. 3, 128.

20. Todd Gitlin and Nanci Hollander, *Uptown: Poor Whites in Chicago* (New York: Harper and Row, 1970); Michael E. Maloney, "The Social Areas of Cincinnati: An Analysis of Social Needs" (Cincinnati: Cincinnati Human Relations Commission, 1985); Harry K. Schwarzweller, et al., *Mountain Families in Transition: A Case Study of Appalachian Migration* (University Park: Pennsylvania State University Press, 1971); Kathryn Borman with Elaine Mueninghoff, "Lower Price Hill's Children: Family, School and Neighborhood," in Allen Batteau, ed., *Appalachia and America: Autonomy and Regional Dependence* (Lexington: University Press of Kentucky), 1983.

21. William E. Schmidt, "Hard Work Can't Stop Hard Times," *New York Times,* November 25, 1990, p. 1; Osha Gray Davidson, *Broken Heartland: The Rise of America's Rural Ghetto* (New York: Free Press, 1990).

22. Peter T. Kilborn, "In Aftermath of Deadly Fire, a Poor Town Struggles Back," *New York Times,* November 25, 1991. See also Linda Flowers, *Throwed Away: Failures of Progress in Eastern North Carolina* (Knoxville: University of Tennessee Press, 1990).

23. Peter T. Kilborn, "Sad Distinction for the Sioux: Homeland Is No. 1 in Poverty," *New York Times,* September 20, 1992, p. 1.

24. Peter Kwong, "The First Multicultural Riots," *Village Voice,* June 9, 1992, p. 29; Felicity Barringer, "Census Reveals City of Displacement," *New York Times,* May 15, 1992.

25. See news and feature stories in the *Washington Post* for May 9–11, 1991.

26. Stanley Lieberson, *A Piece of the Pie: Blacks and White Immigrants Since 1880* (Berkeley: University of California Press, 1980).

27. Louis Uchitelle, "Stanching the Loss of Good Jobs," *New York Times*, Sunday, January 31, 1993, Section 3, p. 1; Lieberson, op. cit.

28. Peter T. Kilborn, "A Disrupting Change Hits Workers After Recession," *New York Times*, December 26, 1992, p. 1.

29. Jonathan Kozol, *Savage Inequalities: Children in America's Schools* (New York: Crown, 1991).

30. Jagna Wojcicka Sharff, "The Underground Economy of a Poor Neighborhood," in Leith Mullings, ed., *Cities of the United States: Studies in Urban Anthroplogy* (New York: Columbia University Press, 1987), pp. 19–50; Marta Tienda and Haya Stier, "Joblessness and Shiftlessness: Labor Force Activity in Chicago's Inner City," in Christopher Jencks and Paul Peterson, eds., *The Urban Underclass* (Washington, D.C.: The Brookings Institute, 1991), pp. 135–154.

31. Erik Eckholm, "Teen-Age Gangs Are Inflicting Lethal Violence on Small Cities," *New York Times*, January 31, 1993, p. 1; Jane Mayer, "Seaford, Delaware Shows How Crack Can Savage Small-Town America," *Wall Street Journal* May 4, 1989, p. A1.

32. Lester Thurow, *Head to Head: The Coming Economic Battle Among Japan, Europe, and America* (New York: William Morrow, 1992); Kevin Phillips, *The Politics of Rich and Poor: Wealth and the American Electorate in the Reagan Aftermath* (New York: Random House, 1990).

33. Kirk Johnson, "Winning the Cold War and Losing a Job," *New York Times*, February 9, 1993, p. 1.

34. Erol R. Ricketts and Isabel V. Sawhill, "Defining and Measuring the Underclass," *Journal of Policy Analysis and Management*, Winter, 1988, pp. 316–325. For a critique of the term, see Herbert J. Gans, *People, Plans and Policies: Essays on Poverty, Racism, and Other National Urban Problems* (New York: Columbia University Press, 1991).

35. Jason DeParle, "Fueled by Social Trends, Welfare Cases Are Rising," *New York Times*, January 10, 1992, p. 1.

36. Gregory Pappas, *The Magic City: Unemployment in a Working-Class Community* (Ithaca, New York: Cornell University Press, 1989).

37. Jones, *Dispossessed*, pp. 205–265.

38. See for example James Lardner, "The Declining Middle," *The New Yorker*, May 3, 1993, pp. 108–114, a review of, among other books, Kevin Phillips, op. cit.; and *Boiling Point: Republicans, Democrats, and the Decline of Middle-Class Prosperity* (New York: Random House, 1993); Katherine S. Newman, *Falling From Grace: The Experience of Downward Mobility in the American Middle Class* (New York: Free Press, 1988); and Katherine S. Newman, *Declining Fortunes: The Withering of the American Dream* (New York, Basic Books, 1993). See also Barbara Ehrenreich, *Fear of Falling: The Inner Life of the Middle Class* (New York: Pantheon, 1989).

39. For discussions of the inadequacy of (local) black political power to relieve economic distress in black communities, see for example Melissa Fay Greene, *Praying For Sheetrock: A Work of Nonfiction* (New York: Addison-Wesley, 1992); David R. Goldfield, *Black, White, and Southern: Race Relations and Southern Culture*

1940 to the Present (Baton Rouge: Louisiana State University Press, 1990), pp. 199–255.

40. Douglas S. Massey and Nancy A. Denton, *American Apartheid: Segregation and the Making of the Underclass* (Cambridge: Harvard University Press, 1993); John Paul Jones and Janet E. Kodras, "Restructured Regions and Families: The Feminization of Poverty in the United States," *Annals of the Association of American Geographers,* Vol. 80, June, 1990, pp. 163–183.

2

Society at Risk
in a Society of Organizations

Charles B. Perrow[1]

The endangered population I wish to discuss is the U.S. population as a whole, as it is realized as a form of society, as a way of governing its affairs. Its form has been endangered for over a century, since it first appeared, but the form has been disappearing most rapidly since the end of World War II. Our nineteenth century heritage of a civil society and culture is being replaced by a twentieth century organizational society, and we are ambivalent about it. On one hand, we have the commonplace generalities about the evils of mass culture, the loss of community and powerlessness in the face of big business and big government. We romanticize part of our past and use it to critique the present. But at the same time we value employment in the big, secure, benefit-rich organizations, devour their mass cultural products, practice class and other discriminations, and guard our privacy and avoid community entanglements. Thus, while we deplore the loss of some of the civil society of the past, and we know something is wrong, we have already changed so much that we hardly would welcome that past society and willingly pay its dues.

I want you to take our present society, even with all your reservations about it, not "for granted," but take it "for constructed," as artifice, enacted, male-made, and far from inevitable, and certainly not natural. Though we may fuss about some of its faults, we tend to think of it as inevitable. It isn't.

Where We Are

Put most simply, in the nineteenth century, the U.S. developed a strong, decentralized and moderately democratic civil society and culture. The U.S. as a new nation was not cursed with European social forms and was blessed with unspoiled land and extraordinary natural resources, just at the time the industrial revolution was taking place. We still invoke this civil culture and expect it to function. But steadily, from the middle of the nineteenth century on, another form of governance unwittingly grew and increasingly absorbed and changed the civil culture.

I refer to the growth of organizations that employ large numbers of people—big organizations, both public and private. These organizations have taken over many of the tasks and structures of our civil society, made them a condition of employee status, and left that civil society weak. *Large organizations have in effect absorbed society.*

The civil society that grew in the democratic abundance of the late eighteenth and early nineteenth centuries was local, decentralized, loosely coupled, moderately egalitarian, adaptive and flexible. But its very success fostered another novel form, the large bureaucratized organization, and as these multiplied we developed an organizational society that is national, centralized, tightly coupled, enacting rather than adapting, and change resistant rather than flexible.

We still prize the elements of civil society and think of them as natural, if vulnerable. These elements are family, neighborhood, small and relatively autonomous religious and ethnic communities with their churches and small businesses and particularized educational systems, small, independent unions and professional associations, diverse do-it-yourself recreations, localized newspaper and communication networks and a weak government. This is a society where your relations with others that you knew on a personal basis determined a large part of your life. It has been replaced by one where your life chances and experiences are much more mediated by remote "elites"—the heads of large employing organizations.

As a new society emerges we are beginning to define some of its characteristics as goods that we always desired and people everywhere should desire, such as steady employment, consumption on an extravagantly wasteful scale, unobtrusive controls, the domination of the market, and an entertainment culture.

In 1780 it is estimated that 80 percent of the working population was self-employed; by 1880 it had dropped to 37 percent; by 1974 it was only 8 percent. This is a dramatic increase in the proportion of people working for someone else's power, wealth or privilege. And these are increasingly large organizations. In the private sector, 65 percent of all employees in

1986 worked in firms of 100 or more employees; 50 percent in firms of over 500,[2] and it is much the same in government organizations. About 95 percent of those employed work in establishments of under 50 people, but this includes all the franchises, where there may be only 10 people. Citibank or Burger King are the giant firms that tell them what to do and increasingly how to live. In fact, even in eating and drinking places, a site of small business if there ever was one, 35 percent of employees work in firms of over 500 persons.[3] Small, independent organizations, numerous as grains of sand among the boulders on a beach, are nestled in the trivial and largely unprofitable niches of the economy.

What kind of a society is being created within the large employing organizations, or through the dense clusters of smaller organizations that attach themselves to the big ones and are dependent upon big ones for their existence? It is a rationalized, controlled, surrogate society.[4] For employees of the large organizations the bureaucracy has increasingly become more than a source of wages and salaries, which can then be freely spent on the products that other bureaucracies choose to produce. The big bureaucracy is increasingly a source of benefits that can only be obtained by being an employee.

In 1985 executive remuneration already consisted of only 44 percent in base pay, with the other 56 percent in organizationally determined and controlled perks, long-term incentives, bonuses and benefits. In 1990 it was down from 44 percent to only 34 percent in base pay that you could count upon and spend as you choose, and fully 66 percent in company determined rewards. For employees in general, employee benefits went from 3 percent of wages and salary back in 1929 to 35.5 percent by 1986.[5] People get only two-thirds of their presumed worth in free dollars. Many of the benefits are not freely chosen and if not used, are lost to the employee.

I think it makes a difference in the relative strength of society as opposed to organizations if the organization is the source of the following services, or the arbiter of their availability, a list gleaned from personnel journals and business reports.

Of course, **health care** leads the list; without a job with a decent sized company health care for most is unaffordable, and comprehensive medical care has become a necessity, largely because of the pollution, addictions, diets and accidents our organizations generate. Think of the advertisements for dangerous life styles. Your ability to change employers is drastically limited by health care provisions; people stick in low level jobs because of vested health coverage. But some also provide, with the complicity of the IRS, pretax accounts for hearing aids, glasses, health-related travel, and fifteen-minute massages on-site.

But the company goes further, with nutritional counseling, programs in back care, substance abuse and stress control—And what helps create the stress?—by providing financial incentives for wellness, by rewarding the life styles that other companies draw one away from, and by taxing smokers, the overweight, those with high blood pressure, and by firing or not hiring those suspected of genetic traits the company's processes might fatally stimulate.

Recreation is essential and the firms shape that, as well, with vacation planning services, vacation resorts, travel services, and sports facilities and sports programs. Resort hotels flourish, gratifying the company convention; other employees in your firm or bureau provide you with the cues as to the appropriate kind of vacation and even its location. **Financial services** are shaped with financial planning, investment and tax advice, house and auto insurance at reduced rates, and special rewards for voluntary savings plans to instill rationality. Employees retire or are laid off of course, so there are retirement counseling, out-placement services, and incentives to save for retirement, and since employees are often required to move, relocation services to find a house in the right suburb. **Education** is encouraged through tuition reimbursement programs, time off, loan assistance, and grants to schools where employees do volunteer work. Educational services bring into the organization what were once local, independent facilities.

Extending the organization into the community is furthered by time off for parent-teacher conferences or for the first day of school for kids, summer camp options, programs for public schools to develop company-related curriculums and discuss aspects of corporate life with students, and on-site before-school and after-school programs, as one company says, to "show kids they are going to work just as their parents do," a key socialization task in an organizational society.

Many of the above services provided by the company touch the family, but there is more. There are eldercare referral services, employee benefits for what are now called "domestic partners," adoption assistance, high school graduation gifts, not just day-care centers but summer camps with bus transport for employee children, lunch time child development seminars, special phones to call home to latchkey kids if you don't have a phone on your desk, programs for kids to fill those organizational gaps on holidays and the first week of school vacation, Saturday child care during the tax-season rush at an accounting firm, maternal and also paternal medical leave, parenting courses, courses on balancing family and your organizational career, or the development of family goals, and, to round it out, the provision of religious facilities *and* funeral services.

Finally, the area of **personal services** is not neglected, with on-site beauty parlors and department store branches, sensitivity training and conflict resolution for managers, gays and lesbians, sex therapy, and, of course, all forms of psychological counseling.[6] Where you live, who you socialize with, make friends with and even mate with are influenced by organizations, and not so indirectly.

We applaud these; we count as progressive the employer, the firm or university that addresses our needs through these services, some of them tax-avoiding devices that are thus financed by the less fortunate employees in the marginal organizations that don't provide them. But they are *not* gifts; they are payments in *lieu* of wages or salary, and as such will be devised to shape our behavior and our consciousness in unobtrusive ways, taking a bit of choice that once was outside of the employment contract, and embedded in local and personal relations, and giving it to the bosses. Our choice is less subject to family and kin, neighbors, peer groups, religious or ethnic ties, or local government. It may even be a compassionate organizational gesture, to be welcomed in a society where compassion, like child care, seems harder and harder to find. But that is just the point. What happened to the source of that compassion? The groups that had provided it in the past are too weak to carry the burden, are on contract to the organization, or have disappeared entirely.

My long list of services that the enlightened employer provides was poorly performed in 1820, if at all. But most of these services now exist to redress the social costs of large-scale organizations that hardly existed before organizations appeared to generate these social costs. And with the wealth of this nation we might expect these and other services to be available either as a right of citizenship in a civil society, and thus provided collectively, by government, if they cannot be generated by small voluntary or familial units. Instead, they are a condition of employment at a progressive organization.

The choice need not be between either the large central government or the large employer as the source. If they cannot be generated by voluntary or familial units they could be generated by local government, which would be far more democratic and responsive than the employer, and considerably more responsive than a state or national government. But large organizations beget large government and that tends to usurp local government. We have big government because we have big corporations, and once had big unions. Big government organizations not only absorb society just as much as do big corporations, but they develop powerful self-interests in controlling the extra-organizational behavior of their employees because their size gives them the resources to do so.

All these societal services could come from small, local and more or less autonomous groups and organizations, what we once thought of as making up the community, but not in the face of large organizations. It's true we have many small organizations and especially small voluntary organizations (there has been an explosion of NPOs—non-profit organizations), but they are weak and vulnerable, and if successful, often quietly sponsored by big organizations. Mothers Against Drunk Driving could be described as a profitable scam financed by the auto and liquor industries to blame drivers rather than the organizational products— beer ads to encourage drinking and dangerous cars to get to the tavern or beach party.

If the services I have enumerated are a condition of employment, rather than citizenship, the logic of profit maximization in the private sector, and power and job security in the public sector, will distort the choices available to employees. If, in contrast the services are a condition of citizenship, then citizens can shape the choices, independent of who they work for, and have a say even if they are not part of the labor force.

How We Got Here

What has brought about the absorption of civil society by organization? I do not think it is the inevitable logic of history, or the implacable rationalization of the world that Max Weber saw, for there were choice points in our U.S. history; and other nations try alternatives and still reflect some of those decisions. Nor is it wholly our distinctive culture, that somehow sprung from our enterprise as citizens and our new political institutions, though that is a part of it. It is, rather, a confluence of unique and exceptional conditions that made possible a new social form, modern bureaucracy, that once unleashed by the leading economic power on the planet, is still spreading throughout it. In the nineteenth century, the U.S. went from dependency upon mother England to becoming the world's greatest economic power; from an economy where an organization with over 10 employees was rare to one where firms employing thousands was commonplace; from substantial economic equality to a plateau of inequality higher than almost all other industrialized nations, a plateau which would persist through 1992 despite unions and progressive reforms.[7] To achieve this growth, organizations needed resources, and the natural resources were abundant and easily claimed, from nature and the native Americans. The human resources flowed out of crowded Europe with the population explosion that so frightened Malthus and created attendant social dislocations. America's greatest product in the nineteenth century, one historian remarked, was people, and most of that product was imported, though often in an unfinished state.

There are three components that make our society of organizations possible: wage dependency, which made citizens available for organizations; the externalization of the social costs of extensive organized activity, which hid the costs from citizens; and the development and spread of a novel form of bureaucracy, "factory bureaucracy," which made controls unobtrusive.

Wage Dependency

With the first textile mill towns we had our first large organizations of hundreds of employees. It took new towns with five-story buildings in order to concentrate and service 500 or 1,000 employees within walking distance of work. These were the first instances of a society of organizations. The owners built the housing, stores, schools and churches because there was no infrastructure present, and without some minimal civil society they could not attract workers. This was repeated in the company towns of the mining industry later in the century. The textile mills also carefully supervised the free time of the largely female labor force in order to convince farmers in the area that it was safe to send their daughters to work in the mills. But those mills that were built in the decaying coastal towns needed to provide neither infrastructure nor supervision; the employees were immigrants and unemployed families, rather than farmer's daughters. Once the company town mills had a good labor supply of French Canadian and then Irish immigrants, they abandoned any supervisory role, and the towns were sufficiently established that company-sponsored housing, churches and schools were not necessary.[8]

Until cheap electric trolley lines appeared in the 1880s, the growth of most organizations was capped at a couple of hundred employees. Mill towns simply were clusters of small enterprises and each ward had its own bakeries, breweries, cobblers and stables.[9]

Fortunes were made from trade, where organizational size was very low, five or ten people; but few fortunes could be made from the new industrial revolution until mass transport of workers and goods allowed mass organizations.

Even firms of moderate size, with 50 or 100 employees, had another obstacle to overcome: workers resisted complete dependency upon a wage as a means of survival. Wage work, people felt, should supplement farming or other trades during slack seasons, and even those largely dependent upon wages should be able to hunt, fish, gather fuel and garden to maintain some independence.[10] The first factories, all small, in England, and some of those in the U.S., had to draw upon paupers and prisoners.[11] The U.S. recruited abroad and a significant proportion of our early factory labor was indentured. In contrast to the wage dependency of large organizations, employment in a small business or craft was considered a temporary state, until one could strike out on one's own, and of course 70 to 80 percent of the population lived and worked on family farms before the Civil War. But, steadily, a fully wage-dependent population was created from the waves of immigrants and the offspring of farmers.

The new large organizations that lived off the wage-dependent population drove the small ones out with their market power and scale economies, or swallowed them up under one gigantic roof, gradually substituting machines and unskilled tasks for the craft skills the workers had entered with.[12] A large service industry grew up to feed, clothe and house the dependent workforce that could no longer do these things for itself.

We take it for granted today that 90 percent of us will work for someone else, and be fully dependent upon wages and salaries for our living. But this idea was so foreign to the nineteenth century that it was called "wage slavery," making the telling connection to the only precedent, other than the military, they knew of for such an unwholesome state of dependency.

Externalities

The new organizations were immensely productive and the society benefited from industrialization, from the discipline created by having a wage-dependent population, and from the mass production economies of large organizations. But there were also substantial costs that need not have been born. Most were obvious and noted at the time, but they were "externalized," as we say. That is, the costs were not included in the price of the goods or services, which would make rational choice among alternatives possible, but were passed on in a hidden form to the society, and generally to the weaker parts of it. For example, the cost of producing goods or services in ever larger organizations meant more money had to be spent on transportation and more time en route to work than if organizations remained small; urban crowding increased and living spaces grew smaller; sewage and pollution problems multiplied; and freedom to change employers, seeking the best or the fairest, had to decline as a smaller number of organizations employed a larger percentage of the non-agricultural labor force. Blacklisting employees who quit one firm and tried to join another began with the first textile mills in Lowell, and while difficult to maintain in economically diverse cities, the practice persisted well into the twentieth century.[13] The notion that the organization owns you, and you must work for it and for it alone actually goes back to the Statute of Laborers formulated during the labor shortage occasioned by the Black Death in the Middle Ages. The English issued an ordinance in 1349 requiring everyone to work for the same pay as they had in 1347, and established penalties for refusing to work, for leaving for a job that paid more, or even for employers who tempted workers away from another with the offer of a raise.[14] Such legislation was rarely invoked except in times of labor shortages, but the whole nineteenth century was one such time, despite periods of unemployment and desperate hardship. For those who came to seek their fortune, the notion that the organization owns you and the state enforces that ownership prompted cries of "wage slavery."

The scale of production probably contributed to the fearful rise in accidents. As late as 1910 nearly one quarter of the full-time workers in the iron and steel industries suffered some type of injury each year. In one Carnegie mill alone one-quarter of recent immigrants were injured or killed each year between 1907 and 1910, 3,723 for a total of in these three years.[15] Indeed, externalities such as pollution and crowding perversely became business opportunities and spawned ever more large organizations, such that a good part of what we declare as progress today is only cleaning up the externalities that our large organizations create as they make progress. Big organizations grew up to handle these externalities, which expanded to include transportation costs, industrial accidents, the dislocations of business cycles, and the exhaustion of natural resources.

A significant consequence of passing off on the rest of society, generally its weaker parts, the social costs, resource costs, and environmental costs of organized activity on a large scale was a transfer of wealth from the weaker parts to the elites that ran the big organizations. Profits rose in the private sector and new fortunes were made. In the government sector, needed services became numerous and more costly, requiring more taxes and more employees, and thus raising managers' salaries and increasing their power.

Gradually some of the costs were internalized through workman's compensation, unemployment insurance, and some government-mandated fringe benefits. But it is only in the last ten years, after nearly two centuries of industrialization, that we are seriously beginning to measure these costs and require that the price of goods and services reflect them, as in effluent charges, environmental impact assessments, restrictions on auto commuting and so on. By and large, the nineteenth century and a good part of the twentieth has been a free ride for organizations that has contributed to our growth in income inequality and then its persistence. Most other industrialized countries have long internalized many more of the social, environmental and resource costs of industrialization. With all the advantages we had in resources and a nearly empty continent, the U.S. could have done much better than it did. With a weak central government during the first 120 or so years of industrialization, it is not surprising that business and industry could so easily remain untaxed in these areas.

Bureaucracy

We have reviewed the two important sources of organizational growth—wage dependency and externalization of the cost of business and industry and then government. Large organizations also created the problem of control, especially with an untrained workforce and one that began realizing that its dependency upon wages was lasting. The direct method of control, direct supervision, was costly except with the most visible, routine, and non interdependent tasks. Another method, decentralization with a skilled work force that could coordinate itself, was utilized in the high technology sectors such as arms, sewing machines, and certain parts of the iron- and steel-making processes. But these workers were expensive and had enough bargaining power to limit owners profits and increase the worker's share of it through higher wages.

A third form of control, neither direct nor delegated to professionals, proved to be as important as any new technology the nineteenth century produced: bureaucracy. It was an unobtrusive form of control, ran alternative to the reactive approach of giving direct orders. It was vested in rules and regulations and product surveillance rather than the process. It was also more exquisite and detailed than delegation to professionals, and offered minimum bases for employee bargaining.

Large-scale organizations have been around for centuries, building the pyramids or Venetian ships, establishing religions, fighting wars, administering kingdoms. Some had a core of permanent employees—that is wage-dependent individuals—or were total institutions such as the Catholic Church. But only with industrialization, initially with the factory and then the railroads, did the elements of factory bureaucracy come together in a large number of organizations, enough of them for the organizational pattern to be readily and easily adopted by all new organizations, public and private, in the growing economy.

Briefly, bureaucracy meant centralized control in one office manned by full-time professionals; a hierarchy that subdivided the increasingly complex work processes and established clear lines of authority and accountability; formalization of the hierarchy through job titles and formalization of all processes through rules and regulations, which can control without direct observation; formal training standards for all but the lowest positions; and finally, specialization of tasks and standardization of inputs, outputs and all related phenomena.

It was a magnificent social invention because formal rules and regulations generated less reaction than barking orders, and required less supervision. Standardization and specialization established control over the premises one used, and premise control is an unobtrusive and lasting control. Managers could easily direct an unskilled workforce of thousands in the mass production of cheap goods the growing society and world needed so badly. It also returned maximum profits to the owners and top managers. Enormous profits did not threaten legitimacy because bureaucracy delivered cheap goods to the workers and raised their standard of living.

In the world's history, no elites have had such a productive, economical and safe means of domination. As Max Weber put it at the time, all else is dilettantism, and he cited speed, precision, calculation, predictability, impersonality and accountability as its virtues.[16] Guaranteed a labor force through wage dependency, and able to ignore the externalities because of weak government, the economic elites found that the use of bureaucratic controls smoothed the radical cutting edges of democracy.

Naturally, bureaucracy quickly spread from factories to schools, hospitals, prisons, government bureaus, churches and voluntary organizations. All organizations realized its virtues, and all could grow to substantial sizes without losing all-important control.

Absorption in the Nineteenth Century

Without large organizations there could be no absorption of society by organizations, of course, and wage dependency, externalization and bureaucracy made the large organizations possible. But what was the absorption that I claim took place? Organizationally approved sex therapy and a department store branch at work were to come much later. In the nineteenth century the organization had fewer and far cruder concerns about the lives of its employees. Some worked hard to control drinking and used the religious revivals to advocate good Protestant life styles. Foremen were advised to go to church or lose their positions. Religious and other forms of discrimination were wide spread; indeed, the elements of discrimination against African Americans by organizations were virulent and in place in the northern cities well before and after the Civil War. But the new organizations were less notable for their concern about the employee's race or soul than for their lack of concern with the civil society around them. Indeed, it was their largely unwitting weakening of civil society in the nineteenth century that required organizations to do more absorbing in the twentieth.

Wage dependency destroyed varied work activity, broad if shallow skills, independent and multiple sources of sustenance, and the fusing of work and community, or economics and society, and their mutual enrichment. In the early nineteenth century work and social life were not very distinct, as one lived where one worked, or nearby, with children under foot and helping, there was less segregation of tasks by gender, and social ties with one's employees were stronger. (In the late twentieth century the line between work and society once again became blurred, as noted at the beginning of this essay, but this time social life was trimmed and packaged to fit the needs of the big organization, rather than the small employer adjusting to the social demands of work mates, customers, and family.)

With full dependency upon year-round wages from a large employer, the economy developed specialized, standardized and largely repetitive jobs that were as socially disembedded as possible. It also required enormous geographical mobility as areas prospered and declined, disrupting neighborhoods and dictating new residence patterns. Always a restless people, by necessity as the bountiful lands opened up to immigrants and the subsequent generations, the circulation sped up with the advance of industrialization and its large organizations. The victim was decentralized, localized, civil society with a stable membership.

The externalities gave birth to huge, for the time, government public works programs, pollution abatement, crowding, crime and disease. The externalities overwhelmed local government, and traditional sources of recourse such as local churches, neighborhood associations, charities and even the orphanages and workhouses. Village resources gave way to city and state organizations, with standardization, specialization, and cultural explanations for the social problems they dealt with that blamed the victims of layoffs and accidents. [17]

Bureaucracy extracted its toll on the civil society and the local, familial forms of socialization and community bonding. New "habits of the heart" had to be instilled in the immigrants and the huge population of child laborers. As Herbert Gutman notes, "In the 1880 manuscript census 49.3 percent of all Paterson boys and 52.1 percent of all girls aged 11–14 had occupations listed by their names." [18] Child labor rose as the prosperity of industry rose, until the technology made children inefficient. There were twice as many children under 12 working in Rhode Island in 1875 than there had been in 1851. [19] Punctuality, obedience, deference, impersonality, and narrow specialization was the lot of the workforce, eroding or rendering useless the traditional socialization patterns of the small firm, farm, village, kinship, ethnic and religious ties. Identity was transferred to the organization, away from the home, neighborhood, skill, and generation. You were someone who worked at the mill or the factory.

These were mainly destructions of the civil society; as yet the organizations provided little in return. Yes, the standard of living rose, but equality, resources, and civil society declined, unnecessarily so. The decline of civil society was, of course, resisted, and there is good evidence for family ties persisting in the work setting, for the work crews of the inside contractors being ethnically and religiously homogeneous, and for settlement patterns being homogeneous under the right conditions, and there was the progressive era.[20] New skills appeared and waves of immigrants at the bottom pushed the older settlers up into the middle class. Cultural activities increased, as did educational levels.

In every case, where you lived, the skills you owned, the value system you continually reconstructed, and the educational choices you had, were influenced by the employing organization as it extracted its loyalties and exerted its subtle or quite overt control. For example, in the case of high culture, the elites that established the museums and universities protected themselves from the masses and made their projects organizationally correct and standardized, welding high society and culture to the society of organizations.

By the time World War II was over, three large changes had modified the control of the organization over its employees. Starting feebly in the progressive era in the 1920s, government began to force organizations to internalize some social costs, first in the accident and unemployment areas, and then in health care. Next, technological change required more skills and less brute strength, increasing the investment in employees and improving their treatment. Third, labor organized the large mass production factories and extracted the first of the "fringe benefits," using, ironically, the employing organization as the basis for meeting the needs that the civil society it had weakened could no longer provide. But this gave the organizations control over the benefits and a strong say in what benefits there would be. The professions, interested in their own growth and dominance, cooperated with big business and big government, and became big enough to do their own absorbing of what remained of independent society.

By 1950 there seemed to be no counter trend, little resistance, and even little sense that what was happening was novel and far from past ideals. We identified our welfare with big organizations and the wages and salaries and benefits and services they increasingly provided. Since then, the process has sped up, falsely analyzed as the workings of a free market in social goods, when the market has all but disappeared into the employment contract. We now have the list of services and fringes I gave at the beginning, and a society with few spaces for small, independent groups and organizations of any consequence. Figure 2.1 suggests the change—the types of organizations, their density, and the unmanageable scale of complex interactions in a tightly coupled, high-powered system.[21] We keep trying, with self-help groups, entrepreneurship, small service firms and the like to provide some alternative. But these are either the trivial flotsam and jetsam of a declining economy, satellites of the big organizations, or desperate and doomed attempts to "organize," often bureaucratically, an independent society.

Finally, a brief word about other industrialized societies. We did not take the route of the U.S.S.R. and other command economies where the

32

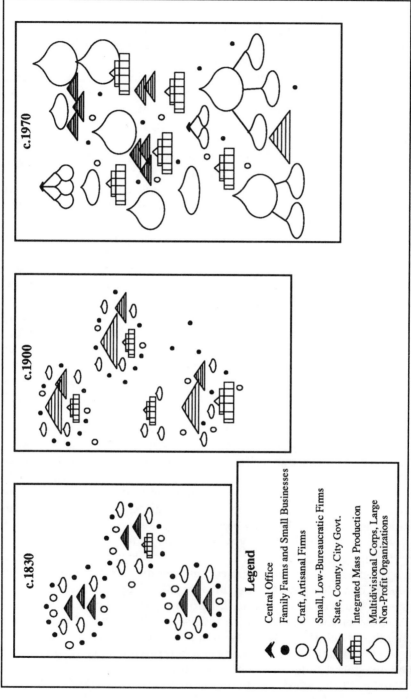

FIGURE 2.1 Organizational Change and Evolution in Society: 1830–1970

distinction between organizations and society was almost nonexistent—one big impossible inefficient organization controlling most of social life. But we also did not take the route of Europe, where the state gave people access to decisions about social services, and broke the close connection between a firm and a living. Education, retraining, relocation, and social services provided by elected governments have restrained the absorption there, though it is still marked. The most fascinating cases are those areas of Europe where networks of small firms out-compete the big firms, as in Northern Italy. Here local civil society is reemerging and is vibrant, with local government autonomy and a high degree of citizen participation.[22] But how much of our economic machine can be decentralized in this fashion is unclear, and it may be only a small faction. We find almost no small-firm networks revitalizing local government and communities in the U.S., which clings to the ideal of huge organizations and a market economy in all things economic and social. We are a population whose egalitarian and democratic culture is endangered.

Notes

1. Some of the historical material of this chapter is more fully examined in Charles Perrow, "A Society of Organizations," *Theory and Society*, Vol. 20, 1991, pp. 725–762.

2. *Handbook of Small Business Data*, U.S. Small Business Administration, The Office of Advocacy (Washington, D.C.: For sale by the Supt. of Docs., U.S. G.P.O., 1988), p. 203. The Handbook notes "almost every federal data source uses a different definition of 'business' when reporting data," p. 6.

3. Ibid., p. 217.

4. For all its rationality, the society may be given to dangerous outbursts that reflect continuing oppressions and racial and ethnic conflict, presumably in the search for some kind of community. But outbursts of civil violence is a topic which cannot, due to space constraints, be explored here.

5. Beth Enslow, "Up, Up and Away," *Across the Board*, July-August, 1991, pp. 18–25.

6. Most of these benefits are described in *Employee Benefit Plan Review* (Chicago: Charles D. Spencer and Associates) for the years 1990–1992; for the others, see the journals *Across the Board*, *Personnel Journal* and *Training and Development* for these years.

7. Jeffrey B. Williamson and Peter H. Lindert, *American Inequality: a Macro-Economic History* (New York: Academic Press, 1980).

8. For the classic works on the textile mill towns, see Thomas Dublin, *Women at Work* (New York: Columbia University Press, 1979); Hannah Josephson, *The Golden Threads* (New York: Duell, Sloan and Pearce, 1949); Carolyn F. Ware, *Early New England* (Cambridge: The Riverside Press, 1931). For a brief reference to the mills in established coastal towns, see John Coolidge, *Mill and Mansion: a Study of Architecture and Society in Lowell, Massachusetts, 1820–1865* (New York: Columbia

U. Press, 1942), p. 106. The railroads brought down the price of coal so steam mills could compete with the water-powered mills that characterized Lowell and the other mill towns. The steam mills were installed in vacant buildings of the declining northeastern port towns, such as New Bedford, with its "large supply of helpless and exploitable labor." A quote from 1903 indicates the shift from the somewhat paternalistic company town to indifference, though of course this happened in the 1830s and 1840s also: "The most satisfactory way in which to handle any class of labor is to have its sole connection with the mill one of work," p. 106. For company towns, see Stuart D. Brandes, *American Welfare Capitalism, 1880–1940* (Chicago: University of Chicago Press, 1970). Brandes does not emphasize that company towns grew in times of labor shortages, and were abandoned, except in the most remote locations, in times of labor excess.

9. See Sam Bass Warner, Jr., *The Private City; Philadelphia in Three Periods of Growth* (Philadelphia: University of Pennsylvania Press, 1968), for a useful picture of Philadelphia at three points in the nineteenth century and a lively description of the "walking city" at the end of the eighteenth century and still at mid-century.

10. See the description of the worker early in the century in Alexander Keyssar's excellent book, *Out of Work: The First Century of Unemployment in Massachusetts* (New York: Cambridge University Press, 1986).

11. Dan Clawson, *Bureaucracy and the Labor Process* (New York: Monthly Review Press, 1980), pp. 41–70. See also Sidney Pollard, *The Genesis of Modern Management* (London: Edward Arnold, 1965), p. 191, who notes that high wages in England by themselves would have been inadequate to attract a labor force to the factory, only external compulsion, poverty and the enclosure movement did.

12. Mass production with unskilled labor did not suddenly and quickly come to the society; most large plants were initially clusters of traditional crafts. Repetitive, unskilled work only gradually came to dominate the factories. Theodore Hershberg, ed., *Work, Space, Family, and Group Experience in the Nineteenth Century, Essays Toward an Interdisciplinary History of the City* (New York: Oxford University Press, 1981).

13. For textile mill blacklisting for insubordination or trying to raise wages, see Ware, op. cit., pp. 222, 267; for quitting without permission, see Dublin, op. cit., p. 59.

14. Barbara W. Tuckman, *A Distant Mirror: The Calamitous Fourteenth Century* (New York, Alfred A Knopf, 1978), pp. 120–121, 374–375.

15. Herbert G. Gutman, *Work, Culture and Society in Industrializing America: Essays in American Working-Class and Social History* (New York: Vintage Books, 1977), p. 30.

16. Max Weber, *Economy and Society: An Outline of Interpretive Sociology,* Guenther Roth and Claus Wittich, eds. (New York: Irvington Publications, Vol. 1, 1968), pp. 212–225. See also Randall Collins, *Weberian Sociological Theory* (Cambridge: Cambridge University Press, 1986), ch. 2.

17. Keyssan, op. cit., and for the social work profession blaming the victim, see Roy Lubove, *The Professional Altruist: The Emergence of Social Work as a Career, 1980–1930* (Cambridge: Harvard University Press, 1965).

18. Gutman, op. cit., p. 47.

19. Ware, op. cit., p. 76.

20. On the family in the work setting, see Tamara K. Hareven, "The History of the Family and the Complexity of Social Change," *American Historical Review*, Vol. 96, No. 1, February, 1991, p. 95. For work areas, Clawson, op. cit.

21. In brief, the argument is that "degrees of freedom" were wrung out of the system as units became larger and relied more and more on interactions with other large units; unexpected interactions following even small failures increased, and the tight coupling of large units prevented the quick recovery from failure and lead to a cascade of increasingly disastrous failures. This argument is developed, for high technology systems with catastrophic potential, such as nuclear power plants, in Charles Perrow, *Normal Accidents: Living with High-Risk Technologies* (New York: Basic Books, Inc., 1984). In my current research, I intend to apply it to U.S. society as a whole.

22. For an extended discussion, see Charles Perrow, "Small Firm Networks," in Nitin Nohria and Robert G. Eccles, *Networks and Organizations* (Harvard Business School Press: Boston, 1992), p. 445.

3

Social Security and the Construction of an Underclass in the United States

Linda Gordon

Exceptionally poor, stigmatized strata have long existed in a variety of societies, but a uniquely modern, and perhaps postmodern, discourse about an "underclass" has developed in the last 150 years. Whether or not one likes the term, it is a vivid marker of today's social anxiety and pessimism.

Indeed, it is not only a marker or a flare; it is also a force. One does not need to be a post-structuralist to see that talk about an "underclass" itself contributes to the stigmatizing of an impoverished and often desperate and hopeless stratum, one particularly evident in the U.S.

That discursive influence, of course, occurred in interaction with social, economic and political developments. But most scholars of social policy and its effects circumscribe their domain too narrowly.[1] I am arguing that such analyses should include cultural and ideological factors if they are to explain historical developments. This look at an alleged "underclass" is an attempt to provide one abbreviated example of the influence of culture and ideology in such an analysis.

I focus today on only one aspect of the construction of an "underclass," a paradoxical one. U.S. welfare programs, designed to alleviate poverty and even to mitigate inequality, ended by increasing inequality and creating an "underclass." With a bit of didactic exaggeration, this paper argues that the Social Security Act of 1935 helped create the "underclass." The claim is not simply that its inequities and exclusions left some people economically disadvantaged, but that the legislation contributed also to civil, political and social inequities, exclusions from "the edifice of citizenship,"[2] which made some of the poor appear as an "underclass."

Like everything about "underclass," this is a highly politicized argument, setting a political context which one cannot escape, so an introductory word about that may help. Blaming welfare for an "underclass" has been an argument made primarily by conservatives who want to abolish or reduce the welfare state. Liberals have mainly responded by denying these charges, defending welfare provisions. Both of these political perspectives ignore how the *meanings* of "underclass" were historically constructed and assume either that its meaning is self-evident or that it is simply a moralizing word which ought to be avoided. I see "underclass" a bit differently. There *is* a distinction, albeit not always easy to draw, between the poor in general and that portion of the poor driven into antisocial, destructive, and self-destructive behavior. "Underclass" is not only a middle-class concept used to beat up on the poor. Poor people above all have developed language that distinguishes and condemns this bad behavior. While some romantic outsiders and militant insiders have at times glorified criminal, daredevil, and violent behavior, these have usually been men, and only some men, while women, often the victims of "underclass" behavior as of poverty itself, have been more skeptical if not downright hostile. The problem for a critical observer is to distinguish what is antisocial, destructive and self-destructive from what is merely out of the "mainstream," to use the currently fashionable American word, and to cut through the moralism to analyze how an "underclass" was produced discursively and structurally.

This paper arose, in part, from my book, *Pitied but not Entitled: Single Mothers and the History of Welfare,* on the origins of what Americans call "welfare," a usage I will define below.[3] The paper springs also from a theoretical or metahistorical project, an attempt to integrate structural analysis of social problems with critique of how their meanings were constructed, including the role of social policy in creating these meanings.[4] Consider just one example of the variety of these meanings. Even though their daily experiences may be similar, there is a world of difference between a poor slum dweller honored as a gritty widow, surviving on a pension, identified as raising citizens for the next generation in the American republic, and a poor ghetto single mother, surviving on "welfare," identified as an idle dependent living off of workingmen's taxes, raising children who are assumed to become violent criminals (if male) and future single mothers (if female). The welfare system, I argue, determined not only the kind of financial help those two mothers can get but also this difference in meaning. So I want to approach this topic, first, by reviewing briefly the historical career of "underclass" talk, second, by examining a crucial piece example of the influence of social policy, that of the Social Security Act of 1935.

The Historical Career of "Underclass" Talk

"Underclass" talk leapt into popularity in the U.S. soon after Ken Auletta's 1981 *New Yorker* articles on the subject, published as a book in 1983.[5] If Auletta's usage hadn't grasped popularity, someone else's would have. The phrase attracts because it is so rich, encapsulating many escalating anxieties in the U.S.—about increasing unemployment, continuing racial inequality and growing opposition to affirmative action remedies, women's changing sexual and reproductive behavior and public participation, widespread use of hard drugs and dangerous weapons, highly visible homelessness, massive health problems and the near collapse of public health facilities, the actual collapse of several state and local governments' ability to provide minimal services which are legally required, and the hegemony of a conservative agenda cultivating animosity to taxes.

"Underclass," like many politicized and moralized words, has fuzzy and often contradictory meanings. While legions of social-science poverty experts have recently attempted to "operationalize" a definition, popular usage only tangentially incorporates their instructions. Indeed, it is precisely the fuzziness of "underclass" that gives the word its power. This particular word is one of a number of synonyms used widely in English for nearly a century and a half. Thus in the mid-nineteenth century we meet "dangerous classes," "outcast," "scum," "refuse," "residuum," "rough," "ragged," *"lumpen,"* "casual poor," "paupers," and many others. In the historical discussion that follows, comments about "underclass" refer to many of its synonyms as well.

Because the concept is rich, its meanings contain a number of paradoxes and subtexts. First, the concept arose from efforts to distinguish among the poor, to create a distinction slightly different from that between the deserving and undeserving: this new line was to separate the benign from the dangerous. Yet in practice the work of "underclass" and its synonyms has been to blur that line of demarcation by making a broad segment of the poor generally threatening. Second, "underclass" talk had a contradictory pity/revulsion/titillation effect. The earliest muckrakers, such as Henry Mayhew writing of the London poor beginning in 1849, often attempted to explain the bad conditions and behavior of his objects of study in such a way as to excuse them on account of their very difficult environment and lack of choice. But the writers' attraction to extremely sensationalist, even disgusting stories of depravity, suffering, and stench stimulated more revulsion than sympathy. At the same time, especially in relation to women of the alleged "underclass", the language contained strong pornographic undertones. Third, in this way as in others, "underclass" talk has always contained subtexts about gender and often about race. Men, women, and members of different racial/ethnic groups gain the "underclass" label in different ways, as we shall see. And fourth, in producing an "othering" affect towards the "underclass," making them appear alien in relation to readers, the rhetoric had the further effect of suggesting a fictive unity among the non-"underclass," among what in the 1990s U.S. is often called the "mainstream,"[6] as if there were no heterogeneity, immorality, and irresponsibility among the "us."

"Underclass" talk bears the marks of the specific historical context of its origin. The discourse arose with the growth of enormous commercial and industrial *cities*. "Underclass" is an urban concept.[7] Poverty and behavior reprehensible to the hegemonic culture was of course widespread in the countryside. But an "underclass" was discovered only when great cities, such as London and Paris put the very poor and the privileged side by side; and only when these crowded cities transformed certain practices which had been typical and unremarkable in the countryside—such as disposing of garbage by throwing it into heaps— into life-threatening perils. "The very *condensing* of their number within a small space, seems to stimulate their bad tendencies."[8] "Underclass" arose from a widespread but inadequately recognized historical phenomenon: the tendency of cities to attract more in-migrants than could be supplied with jobs.[9] These structural conditions were then partly explained in terms of cultural or psychological attributes of victims.

"Underclass" talk was equally tied to the expansion of *states*. It appeared from groups interested in government reform action. The British "discovery" of an underclass arose from state reform initiative and from journalistic sensationalism aimed at provoking state action. Chadwick wrote both of his influential reports (1834 and 1842) for parliamentary inquiries. Mayhew intended his "yellow" series of letters to a daily paper in 1849–1850 to encourage public health and welfare provision.

The journalists, reformers, and government experts who initiated an "underclass" alarm began their investigations to reveal the conditions of the entire working class, but ended, consciously or not, emphasizing only the most wretched. They hoped thus to shock the powerful into action. In this they had some success, but not only in reformist directions. Their stories were so horrifying that they diverted attention from more average proletarian conditions. The mental and behavioral depravity they found among the "underclass" were so threatening that the perhaps more common balance between decency and nastiness that characterized the proletariat, as the middle class, went unnoticed. The rhetoric of horror was much louder than that of sympathy, the condemnation of immoral behavior much more vivid than the analysis of structural causes.[10]

For example, the discussion of the Victorian "underclass" often prioritized smell over the other senses.[11] (This consciousness of smell was, of course, equally important in constructing "refinement" or "gentility.") Several commentators wrote of the "miasma" which emanated from the poor neighborhoods, of "putrefaction," "vapors ... that blind and suffocate."[12] The smells came from open cesspools, garbage and dead rats in the streets, the filth in the river and the "sewage that passed as drinking water," not from an "underclass" itself.[13] But the people who lived in such conditions became themselves polluted, literally and figuratively, with the stench. And they became contagious: in mid-nineteenth century medicine, bad air was itself considered to be the source of infection. American warrior against the "underclass" Charles Loring Brace described his Children's Aid Society as "a moral and physical disinfectant."[14] The largest impact of these exposés of a mid-nineteenth-century "underclass" was to frighten and horrify, to make the objects of these writings appear dangerous, disgusting, and very likely irredeemable.[15]

The rhetoric about "underclass" was above all moral, and structural explanations appeared as lame excuses. As Gareth Stedman Jones wrote about "outcast London," in the "residuum the ... psychological defects of individuals bulked even larger than before. ... The problem was not [perceived as] structural but moral, ... not poverty but pauperism ... with its attendant vices, drunkenness, improvidence, mendicancy, bad language, filthy habits, gambling, low amusements, and ignorance."[16] We can see, in fact, a tendency of words originating in a variety of descriptive intents to converge in a moral register. For example, the "miasma" caused by the waste-disposal practices of city dwellers—the practices of the privileged classes were no better at this time, except that they had more space—soon became a personal characteristic of "underclass" people, associated with their lack of individual hygiene. Or consider the term "ragged," which was first used literally to describe the clothing of the poor. Its usage became more and more metaphorical, and by the early nineteenth century one had "ragged homes," "ragged Radicals," and "ragged schools" for the poor.[17]

Other words moved in a different, although not exactly opposite, direction. They began as condemnations of specific behavior, but migrated to refer generically to entire groups whether or not all members of these groups exhibited such bad behavior. Words such as "dangerous classes," "disreputable," "underworld," "reckless," and "promiscuous" behaved this way.[18] Supporting this expansion of terms to encompass large groups was the biologistic language of the nineteenth century. Victorians, both in England and in the U.S., used "race" in many absolutely vague senses: it could refer to a bewildering variety of ethnic groups, nations, religions. But it always had physicality in it, and was thus a group in which membership was inescapable, not chosen. In England, the "underclass" "race" was further primitivized by being frequently called a "tribe." Thus the "underclass" became in this rhetoric pre-civilized, at a lower level of human development.[19] An 1883 British journalistic series spoke of "natural curiosities" akin to "the Zenanas, the Aborigines, and the South Sea Islanders."[20] These "outcasts" were a "residuum" "left behind by the mid-Victorian march of moral and material progress."[21] Intermixed with this popular anthropology of the primitive was a discourse of exoticism, in which the titillation of fear and revulsion combined with that of sexual attraction. The depravity of the "underclass" was formed of licentiousness, permissiveness, and lack of personal modesty. And of course wherever there was a sexual discourse there was a double standard and the complex mixed feelings so often directed by the elites towards the women of subordinated classes: attraction, hatred, and disregard.

"Underclass" depends for its meanings on a contrast with the respectable. All "othering," in fact, is produced by comparative, usually binary, assumptions and speech. The structure, membership, and values of the respectable were constructed by the contraposition. What is now in the U.S. called the "mainstream" (subsuming, as Christopher Jencks points out, both middle and working class) saw itself in the negative of the "underclass." This respectable majority became thus represented as homogeneous. This fiction was both self-fulfilling, as it pressured those who wanted to be "mainstream" towards conformity, and also productive of hypocrisy, since it encouraged dissembling not only about behavior but about wealth. In other words, the tendency to define an "underclass" as an "outcast" group in itself supervises the behavior of those who would be accepted as respectable; and then the spread of the term to take in more of the poor in general makes poverty itself disreputable and compels those who want to defend their respectability to separate themselves, both in public and in private consciousness, from the poor.

Separating the respectable from the disreputable is a highly gendered exercise. Men and women of the "dangerous classes" were threatening in different ways. The emphasis on tramps and bums, refusal to work, criminality and violence apparently directed attention to men, as did working-class hostility to scabs. Anxieties about sexual promiscuity, prostitution, and reproduction focused on women. Women of "loose" sexual behavior were regularly labeled as "underclass" and, conversely, "underclass" women were expected to behave immorally and thus to have no claim to protection or sympathy if they were assaulted. Women were dangerous reproducers in several meanings of that term: biologically, because they brought unwanted, delinquent children into the world; socially, because as mothers they passed on a defective culture to the next generation. Moreover in the Victorian gender system, "underclass" women were in some senses responsible for men's sins, because they failed at their prescribed task of domesticating men and disciplining them to work.[22]

"Underclass" was also a racial term in the U.S. It soon became illustrated in the popular imagination by the immigrants who crowded the eastern cities after about 1880. Their otherness was in part religious, as antiCatholicism and antiSemitism characterized professional and upper-class Anglo-Saxon elites. The strange ways of the new immigrants, especially those from southern and eastern Europe and Asia Minor— their cuisines, drinks, dress, methods of child care and housekeeping— combined with their darker complexions to make them seem racially other. At the turn of the century fear of these poor strangers threatened to spread to the entire working class, now mainly immigrant, the disdain and revulsion usually reserved for the uniquely disreputable.

Starting in the mid-nineteenth century there was also a counter-discourse about an "underclass" that sought to defend the working poor. Marxist hostility to a *lumpenproletariat* expressed a common working-class perspective. "Lumpen" means ragged too, but Marx and Engels hedged in their term with a more precise definition that did not spill over to stigmatize the poor in general. To the contrary, the heart of the lumpenproletariat in the Marxist view was its propensity to attack the working class, the laboring poor, by prostituting itself to a threatened capitalist class. I use a prostitution metaphor deliberately, for the nineteenth-century Marxists shared with liberals a sense of the importance of sexual respectability to the proletariat and to a viable working-class consciousness. If there were aspects of "underclass" behavior that might be defended as Bohemian, anti-authoritarian, or pleasure-loving, Marx would have none of them.[23] His revolutionary followers were just as moralistic: Bukharin, for example, referred to the lumpenproletariat's "shiftlessness, lack of discipline, hatred of the old, but impotence to construct or organize anything new, an individualistic declassed 'personality,' whose actions are based only on foolish caprices."[24] His concept of the vices of the "underclass" shared with that of liberals and conservatives a vision of a slippery slope to hell, with the first skid being decline in the work ethic; his greatest fear was that the slide led to loss of class solidarity, which liberals and conservatives were, of course, happy to dispense with. Not only Marxists but most unionists saw the "underclass" as a breeding ground for scabs and, worse, mercenary thugs, goons, infiltrators and provocateurs used by bosses and the state against strikers, demonstrators, and revolutionaries. This was, to them, the rabble, the masses as opposed to the classes, and, later, along with the *petite bourgeoisie,* the storm troopers.

The New Left produced an alternative analysis which led to a marginal defense of an "underclass." In criticizing institutions of "social control," such as prisons, schools, and asylums, New Leftists often suggested that norms of respectability were imposed on the poor by the upper and/or middle classes.[25] Respectability was sometimes labeled "bourgeois" by the New Left. In fact, there was a strong set of working-class norms of respectability which included hard work, cleanliness, religion or church attendance, and community or class solidarity, and a disapproval of disreputable behavior which did not come from "above." Recognizing this is not incompatible with recognizing that middle class social control often functioned to change these norms and to divide poor communities by inducing intolerance.[26] But failure to recognize it has led to an opposite, often distinctly male, tendency to romanticize "underclass" behavior as rebellious, the opposite of "up tight." The attraction to vagabondage, irresponsibility, the street life, violence, was and remains highly gendered.

Considering the Marxist notion of an "underclass" raises the question, is this really a class? Marxists tried to integrate the concept into a class analysis by emphasizing its role in supplying a reserve army of labor. But this is not precise enough, for women have also functioned, Marxists argued, as a reserve army of labor without demonstrating the "underclass" lifestyle that offended observers. Clearly "underclass"-ness always included lifestyle attributes, but for Marxists these were epiphenomena of structural locations. Moreover, a social class, as distinct from a stratum, is a relational concept; classes mutually produce each other through relations of production. By contrast in the common "underclass" talk of the past or present, the group was defined in contrast to certain respectable classes, to be sure, but without suggestion that the respectable ones have produced the "underclass" in the way that workers produce capitalists and vice versa.

Throughout the nineteenth century there was one dimension in which the "underclass" appeared to arise from social-structural relations rather than individual character: This is the notion that public provision created an "underclass." Just as today's "underclass" discussion focuses in part on the role of the welfare system, so did that of the nineteenth century U.S., using above all the concept of pauperism. In the sixteenth century, the term "pauper" had meant simply a poor person. By the late nineteenth century, it took on a more restricted definition, denoting a new class of persons who chronically subsisted on poor relief, had lost commitment to the work ethic and personal independence; the concept became increasingly derogatory.

In the late nineteenth-century U.S., the newly professionalizing field of social work developed a theory of "scientific charity" to which "pauperism" was central. Foreshadowing the concern of today's conservatives, these early social workers criticized earlier charity and public provision for encouraging "dependence" and discouraging "independence" by indiscriminate giving. Not only were some of the poor undeserving of help, but careless help could *create* pauperism. As geographer David Ward described the hegemonic attitude towards the early twentieth-century slums, "in order to limit the presumably damaging effects of relief on able-bodied workers, much attention was given to the size of a morally delinquent residuum."[27] Thus pauperism was sharply distinguished from poverty. Theoretically one could be poor without being a pauper, if one was hard-working and hopeful; indeed, in theory one could be a pauper without being poor, if one related to society as a sponger, although in practice, such a usage of "pauper"—which would have stigmatized many in the upper class—never caught on. Rather what happened, as with the language of "dangerous classes," is that the stigma of pauperism spread to include more and more of the poor, making the possibility of an honorable poverty disappear. Perhaps nothing expressed the horrifying stigma of pauperism as much as the possibility of being without a proper burial and ending up in a pauper's grave.

Politically, "pauperism" became in the U.S. not only an argument against generosity towards the poor but also an early "culture of poverty" analysis. Help could create pauperism not only in individuals but in groups and for generations. Charity leaders and social workers feared that social provision could accustom the poor to getting handouts without working and thus create a culture of pauperism which, once developed, could become self-perpetuating. This fear was not exclusive to one side of the political continuum. Although conservatives usually expressed themselves with more animus towards the poor in their characterizations of "underclass" behavior, socialists condemned the same behaviors. The nineteenth-century working-class mutual benefit societies that proliferated among virtually all ethnic groups in the cities also distinguished between the deserving/undeserving poor and carefully reviewed claimants of benefits to make sure that they were honest and upright.[28] Right through the Progressive Era in the U.S., social workers and activists continued to express anxiety that a too-good welfare system could pauperize unless accompanied by moral reform of the poor.[29]

But the nineteenth and early-twentieth-century discourse about pauperism did not create an "underclass" alarum in the U.S. The poverty, crime, and deviance that reformers saw in the immigrant ghettos of the early-twentieth-century U.S. cities was integrated into a context of general optimism about these poor newcomers' possibilities of upward mobility. Not even the African-American ghettos resulting from the Great Migration into eastern and midwestern cities produced an "underclass" discourse because these migrants, too, appeared to be on their way up.

"Underclass" warnings began to appear sporadically in the U.S. between 1930 and 1970, mainly from the political Left.[30] The Depression, of course, did not tend to provoke these fears because poverty was so widespread that its stigma decreased. Nevertheless, some observers began to observe long-term changes within the emergency. Rexford Tugwell, for example, Franklin Roosevelt's Secretary of Agriculture, aware of the large-scale evictions of sharecroppers (induced by New Deal policies), predicted the development of an "underclass" in 1934. Revealingly, it was in the officially prosperous 1950s and 1960s that close observers of economic trends became aware of the problems identified by the label "underclass" today. In an essay published in 1947 sociologist August Hollingshead discussed "scum of the city."[31] By 1966 sociologist David Matza wrote about the "disreputable poor," astutely concluding that the future development of this stratum depended on the outcome of the "Negro mobilization," i.e., the civil rights movement.[32] Socialists Michael Harrington and Stanley Aronowitz raised the specter of a hereditary "underclass" in 1963.[33] The Department of Labor began to report on "Men in Poverty Neighborhoods" affected by residential segregation, unemployment, low pay, and high rates of marital breakup, although it used no synonym of "underclass."[34] The most important of these predecessors of the contemporary debate was, of course, the "Moynihan Report" of 1965, to be discussed below. The term may have been slow to become common in the U.S. because of lingering notions that it was a classless society; a 1977 *Time* article attributed the concept to "class-ridden Europe."[35] Examining this semantic history, we see that it was not until after several decades of increasing immiseration and its attendant demoralization that the concept of "underclass" reached popular usage.

Welfare Constructs an "Underclass"

The Depression and New Deal not only lessened the stigma on poverty and unemployment, but also created the first federal government programs against poverty since Reconstruction and the Freedmen's Bureau. Nevertheless, the "underclass" that was harvested in the 1980s had been fertilized in the New Deal.

In 1934 and 1935 when the Social Security Act was debated, there was no fear of labor redundancy or overpopulation. No one considered the massive unemployment rates of the Depression to be permanent. Just a few years previously, southern landowners had been struggling to insulate their sharecroppers from the call of northern industrial jobs. FDR's social policy-makers were focused not on an "underclass" but on mass unemployment affecting even the previously stable and prosperous working class and lower middle class. Influenced by some Keynesian ideas, Roosevelt wanted relief for the unemployed (particularly those who were Democratic voters), the economy primed with new consumer spending power, and some long-term barriers against another such a terrible collapse.

When Roosevelt established a Committee on Economic Security to draft a welfare bill for him in 1934, he opened the door to a small but passionate stream of welfare thought that had been growing in the U.S. since at least 1890. This stream had two tributaries, about which I have written at length elsewhere, but which must be reviewed here.[36] One was identified with the notion of "social insurance," had been much influenced by European, particularly German, proposals, and focused on programs to replace wages lost through unemployment, disability, or death. An earlier enthusiasm for health insurance had by now provoked such opposition from the AMA that social-insurance proponents had subordinated it to proposals more likely to succeed. A second branch of welfare thought had grown from the charity and then social work tradition. It focused on helping the most needy, notably women, children, and the infirm. This group of social workers were keenly aware that the injuries of poverty were not only economic, and that the poor needed not only money but also other kinds of help, including medical care, education, and counseling, for example.

The class and race standpoint from which these two approaches arose were similar—virtually all the influential welfare proponents were white, Protestant, and from privileged families. But they differed sharply by sex. The social-insurance group was almost exclusively male and its perspective showed this. At the turn of the century, women alone with children were disproportionately impoverished, but social-insurance writings almost never mentioned the needs of women or children. Social insurance was designed in part to regulate the labor market and in part to maintain male breadwinners as heads of families and households. The recipient of social-insurance aid was envisaged as a male head of household and a prominent part of this vision was to provide payments in ways that did not reduce his dignity and authority. Thus the social-insurance planners designed programs in which the receipt of help would be an entitlement, ensuing automatically from a contractual position. In the two major programs they created in the Social Security Act, they devised special, earmarked forms of taxation so that unemployment and old-age insurance would appear to be independent of traditional government relief.

Meanwhile, by the turn of the century the strong U.S. women's movement, through the many women active in charity, social work, and social reform had given rise to a distinctly female approach to welfare. (A divide between women primarily oriented towards social work and those committed to societal reform did not materialize in the U.S. as it had in England.) The social work profession and social reform network were predominantly feminized, imbued with the maternalist-feminist views of several generations of social reformers. The greatest lasting victory of this group was in the mothers'-aid laws, programs passed by most states in the U.S. between 1910 and 1930 providing public aid to some needy single mothers with children, usually widows but sometimes also including deserted wives and unmarried mothers. Indeed, it is a measure of the strength of this women's welfare network that these mothers'-aid laws were the only area of welfare state development in which the U.S. did not lag behind European countries. The design of these programs, which came to be called, generically, public assistance, was one to which this female-influenced social-work network was committed, and it was considerably different than the social-insurance model. Let me enumerate some of these contrasts.

1. While social-insurance coverage was to be universal and automatic according to pre-specified criteria of eligibility—e.g., employment by employers of a certain size, steady employment for a certain length of time—public assistance was to be exclusively for the very needy. It was to be means-tested so as prevent those not in need from collecting, and those with any substantial personal resources, such as home-ownership, were to be excluded. In practice, public assistance recipients were often required to divest themselves of resources, such as a house, in order to receive aid.

2. While social-insurance benefits were to be paid in such a way as to preserve a claimant's privacy, public assistance benefits were to include supervision by trained social workers. A man receiving unemployment compensation or old-age insurance (that which is today called Social Security in the U.S.) could spend his entire benefit on opium, liquor, or gambling and live in a pigsty, with the clerk who administered his payment being none the wiser. A man or, more likely, a woman receiving public assistance would be supervised in a variety of ways. She would, ideally, be assigned an individual caseworker who would require her to prepare a weekly or monthly budget to make sure that the stipend was being properly used; she would receive home "visits" by caseworkers to evaluate her standards of housekeeping, child-care, and domestic

morality. To receive benefits, the public-assistance applicant had to position herself as a supplicant requesting help, one who might be refused, while the social-insurance recipient merely claimed his rights.

3. Social insurance went to the covered person as an individual. Although the justification for these programs sometimes dwelt on the plight of the worker's dependents should he fail to bring home wages, in collecting his benefit his entitlement was as an individual. He received the same amount regardless of his number of dependents, and they could leave or he could cut them off without losing his benefit. Public assistance by contrast was doled out in differential amounts according to need. The dominant model, state mothers' aid which then became federal ADC, was officially not a payment to an adult individual at all but to the support of children in the care of their mother. Since the mother had no individual entitlement, her receipt of a stipend was dependent on her proving that she was spending it on her children and not on herself.

4. Social insurance payments were designed to be big enough that a recipient and possibly even his small family might live on them, and often they were adequate for this. Public assistance was never sufficient to support a family, rarely even an individual.

5. Social insurance was designed to prevent poverty with money. Its assumptions were that this was what men needed to retain their health, dignity, citizenship, and family authority, and it self-consciously broke with the charity legacy of suspicion that the poor lacked character. Public assistance, by contrast, denied that money alone could solve the problems; it rested on the conviction that the poor also needed counseling, rehabilitation, guidance.

6. Social insurance was based on the workplace—eligibility was defined in terms of certain standards of employment, and some of the money was collected as an employment tax. This was deemed essential by its designers, not technically, but politically. Social insurance could have been as easily paid for from taxes and entitlements attached to citizenship; in practice, for example, old-age insurance funds were used by the U.S. government for other expenditures, and the stipends were not in fact directly connected to employees' contributions. The creation of apparently separate contributions was designed to make social insurance *appear* an entitlement which could not be abrogated and thus to separate it from poor relief. Public assistance, by contrast, appeared as charity, paid for by others, unconnected to work or any other kind of contribution to society made by its recipient.

All these differences were fundamentally, deeply gendered. The counseling or casework inherent in the public-assistance model assumed a subordination of the client that was culturally acceptable for women. Although there are today welfare programs that provide counseling for men, such as drug addicts or the homeless, these have developed in the context of several decades of the legitimation of psychotherapy and psychological modes of thought. In the 1930s prescribing counseling for poor men would have been perceived as undercutting their manliness and politically unacceptable. The smaller stipends of public assistance were understood as appropriate because their recipients—most visibly, single mothers—were not "real" heads of households but only temporary caretakers during men's absence. Gender norms of the time did not include imagining women as supporting families. Even women alone were conceived to need less to live on than single men.[37] Citizenship and its entitlements were still conceived primarily as male. After all, most of the mothers'-aid laws on which ADC was based were passed before women could vote, and woman suffrage was still a new innovation in the 1930s. Men had rights, women had needs. And men particularly had a right to personal privacy, while it was acceptable for women to plead for help and to be supervised. All these distinctions were naturalized by the association of social insurance with the workplace, which remained a predominantly male sphere.

These distinctions were carried over into the Social Security Act. Two major social-insurance programs were created, unemployment compensation and old-age insurance, and these titles of the Act were written by social-insurance men. Several public assistance programs— Aid to Dependent Children, Aid to the Blind, Old Age Assistance (for the elderly who did not qualify for old-age insurance)—were designed by leaders of the female-dominated social-work network. These different designs created a massive disparity, two tracks, in the government help various groups received.

The agreement to include two kinds of programs was in part a political compromise, giving two groups each a plum. But more deeply it was a compromise based on a mutually accepted division of labor, between male-style and female-style programs, and that division in turn was acceptable because it rested on considerable agreement. Both groups considered social insurance the master plan. It was a set of programs designed to rescue male family heads from undeserved destitution, and to support these men's dependents indirectly. Both groups understood that there were likely to remain some individuals not covered by a family head's entitlement, such as unmarried mothers, but both expected these groups to be small. One figure may provide a vivid example: the first appropriation asked for by the women who designed ADC, reflecting their sense of the size of the problem, was $25 million, to provide for an expected 288,000 families. Moreover, they expected the need to *decline* over time as more and more women and children could collect benefits as the dependents of social-insurance beneficiaries. They could hardly have been more wrong. In FY 1991 the total spent on ADC was $20.3 billion, serving 4,362,400 families.

In fact both male and female welfare streams rested on the same assumptions. Their joint premise was the family wage, the belief that men should be the sole breadwinners for families. This premise was also the source of the ADC authors' gross mistake in estimating the need for ADC. So strong was their belief in the family-wage *norm* that it blinded many experts to the *reality* that most working-class families could not survive on a man's single wage. So strong was this family-wage rule that many welfare advocates were reluctant to subvert it by making it too easy for single mothers to maintain themselves as heads of families. Too often these norms are described or assumed to be standards imposed by men on women. On the contrary, the fundamental determinants of the gender/family system were widely, almost universally supported by both men and women. It was not until the 1960s that most feminists began to question the necessity of male-headed families.

Moreover it was significant that Social Security was written during a relative lull in the women's-rights movement. The mothers'-aid model, which was relatively progressive in 1910, was rather conservative by 1935, given how much had changed for so many women. Still, the social-work network of the 1930s did retain some of their maternalist-feminist heritage in their commitment to helping those women and children left out of family-wage support. Their program expressed both their residual feminism and their own agenda for power in an expanded federal government. Like British women reformers of the early twentieth century, they were concerned to get some help directly to women as mothers, and thereby to protect their custody rights and their authority as mothers. By working in a public-assistance framework they resisted making the workplace the only source of welfare entitlements (as unemployment compensation and old-age insurance did). At the same time the public-assistance framework provided, they hoped, an institutional need for trained welfare caseworkers. By focusing on single mothers they kept alive the awareness that not all women and children were supported by men. And by focusing on single mothers rather than a universal children's allowance they could do so without challenging male economic dominance.

Thus the first reason for the two-track welfare system was the intersection of economic need with the gender system. However, the system was soon intersected even more powerfully by the racial system. A brief reminder is necessary here about the racial construction of citizenship in the U.S. in the 1930s. Blacks remained mainly in the South where they were almost entirely disfranchised and deprived of most rights pertaining to citizenship; white southerners and many northerners simply did not perceive Blacks as citizens. The South was a one-party Democratic region and it was an essential part of FDR's electoral coalition. Because southern politicians were uncontested in elections, they acquired seniority in the Congress and seniority within the majority party was at the time the only principle determining Congressional leadership. Southern Democrats thus controlled powerful Congressional committees which had to approve legislation before it could reach the floor. The powerful white constituents feared that a federal government welfare program would loosen the stranglehold that southern landowners maintained on their low-wage agricultural labor force, notably sharecroppers but also urban workers and domestic servants.

So key Southern Congressmen and Senators insisted on crucial amendments to the Social Security Act. First, they eliminated agricultural and domestic workers—virtually all African and Hispanic Americans—from the social insurance programs. Workers with female employment patterns—working for small businesses, dropping in and out of the labor force—were also excluded. Second, amendments to the public-assistance programs, which were operated on the basis of joint federal-state funding, eliminated federal standards which might have prevented southern states from discriminating. State and local authorities were thus left free to determine eligibility for public assistance and minorities were largely excluded.

The result was a program of economic security that increased economic inequality. The groups left out—Blacks and other poor minorities such as American Indians, white women, single mothers especially—are precisely the core of the "underclass" today.

But the result was not just a simple stratification in which certain groups were excluded from good-quality programs. It was also that the meanings of these programs solidified a distinction already present embryonically—that some government provision is an entitlement while some is charity; that some is earned and deserved, while some is not. We see this in American usage today: the good programs are called by specific names—Social Security or Unemployment Compensation; the second-class programs are called "welfare," a last resort and mark of shame. The nature of the second-class programs is such that the economic help they provide comes with high costs: the supervision is costly to taxpayers, the means-testing keeps alive a fear that recipients are cheating, the morals-testing stimulates a sense of widespread immorality at government expense, the recipients hate the program as much as do wealthier taxpayers. While recipients of Social Security old age insurance feel as entitled as veterans, accepting their payments almost as a symbol of citizenship, ADC recipients are likely to experience their payments virtually as proof of non-citizenship. They receive so many messages in which they are described as parasitical, dependent, disreputable, immoral, and greedy that it is a wonder that any are able to value themselves and their parenting work. It is not surprising that so many studies show that the poor share some of the same hostility to "welfare" that the middle class do.

Contemporary "Underclass" Talk

"Underclass" rhetoric in the U.S. today is at times quite as inflammatory as that of Victorian England. A liberal child-welfare scholar refers to a "new class of 'untouchables' ... emerging in our inner cities ... young people who are functionally illiterate, disconnected from school, depressed, prone to drug abuse and early criminal activity, and eventually, parents of unplanned and unwanted babies."[38] A lawyer in a 1982 Saul Bellow novel, well-meaning but despairing, explains: "Your defendant belongs to that black underclass everybody is openly talking about, ... economically 'redundant,'... falling farther and farther behind the rest of society, locked into a culture of despair and crime—I wouldn't say a culture, that's a specialist's word. There is no culture there, it's only a wilderness, and damn monstrous, too ... a people denuded. And what's the effect of denudation, atomization? ... just a lumpen population ... nothing but death before it. ... They kill some of us. Mostly they kill themselves."[39] Metaphors of primitivism, ugliness, a residuum, and sexual license proliferate. As in the last century, the word attempts to distinguish the respectable from the disreputable poor but contributes to stigmatizing both groups of the urban and especially the minority poor. A brief scrutiny of print, broadcast, and movie exposés of ghetto life, drugs, and drive-by shootings reveals a combination of pity/revulsion/titillation similar to that of the nineteenth century.

Many of the old patterns in "underclass" talk remain. The discourse is almost entirely urban and state-centered, dwelling as it does on state responsibility in the past or future. The concept remains fundamentally moral despite the continued attempts of experts to define it objectively. Indeed, the "underclass" concept has been used by the poor to place themselves in the "mainstream" by distinguishing themselves from the disreputable. And the "underclass"/"mainstream" dichotomy offers a binary taxonomy of "class" which substitutes for a more complex analysis of economic and social power.

The gender and racial meanings are abundantly clear, in the professional as in the popular discourse. Today in the U.S., the dominant scholarly definition of "underclass" employs four indicators: chronic joblessness or "weak labor-force attachment," welfare "dependence," social isolation in ghettos, and several kinds of social deviance. Experts argue that these are objective and sex- and race-neutral. Let us consider these claims. For example, what does chronic joblessness, or "weak labor-force attachment" as it is often called, mean for women? "Weak attachment" was the preferred normative behavior for the majority of U.S. women for centuries. Defining "underclass" in terms of welfare "dependence" is equally problematic. Women's responsibility for raising children makes them far more likely to collect welfare than men. Moreover, "dependence," too, has been part of the female norm; what is different, in terms of "dependence," between a woman raising small children on a husband's allowance and a woman raising small children on a government allowance?[40] Behavioral definitions are equally problematic in the absence of gender analysis. Women are less often active in crime and drug-selling, and when they are they are often tools, frequently involuntary, of men. Many women could be said to become "underclass" because of their dependence on "underclass" men, just as many women enter the middle class because of their dependence on men. A central "deviance" which defines the "underclass" today is by definition female—teenage pregnancy and out-of-wedlock childbirth. Often this discussion proceeds as if the conceptions were immaculate. Thus we read that "women who start their families before marriage and before the end of adolescence [are] the main engine propelling the underclass disaster."[41] Out-of-wedlock fatherhood is out of sight. So is inadequate parenting an exclusively female deviance; fathers are virtually never charged with child neglect.[42]

Racial structures, equally, underlie "underclass" talk. What does "weak labor-force attachment" mean for minorities? Long-term discrimination has created disproportionate levels of long-term unemployment among them. As late entrants into the industrial economy many migrated from the agricultural South or Southwest, or into the U.S. from Mexico, just as the long expansionist phase of U.S. industrial production ended. In shop closings, labor-force reductions and other manifestations of de-industrialization, minorities were often the last hired and thus the first fired. Forced onto reservations, American Indians were often far from available jobs. Measuring weak or strong labor-force attachment does not make useful distinctions between the ordinary and the "underclass" poor among young minorities who are chronically jobless. Nor is "social isolation in ghettos" a sharp discriminating measure given patterns of residential segregation which force many employed and even middle-class as well as poor Blacks to live in ghettos. Out-of-wedlock childbearing has considerably different meanings for poor Blacks and middle-class whites. Not only is disapproval of out-of-wedlock childbirth and female-headed households less in African-American than in European-American family culture. In addition, Black female-headed households are often extended, taking in non-nuclear family members and nonkin as an antipoverty strategy. (From the 1940s through 1980, female-headed households were twice as likely to be extended as male-headed households.)

High rates of welfare "dependence" among minorities also have different meanings. We have seen that racial minorities were excluded from most programs of government provision. In the 1950s and 1960s many minorities, stimulated by the civil rights movement, demanded and won access to welfare provision, and fought for reforms which made it harder for them to be arbitrarily excluded or cut off. Seen thus historically, rising welfare claims were in some ways a sign of increasing resourcefulness and self-esteem among poor and especially minority single mothers, even a step ahead in citizenship, and not necessarily a sign of impoverishment or character flaw. Moreover, claiming welfare was, as Kathryn Neckerman has shown, a family economic strategy developed in adaptation to a severely discriminatory labor market; using it as a criterion for "underclass" membership ignores the ways in which it was part of an effort not to be "underclass."[43]

"Underclass" definitions tailored, albeit perhaps unconsciously, to describe Black poverty may not fit other racial minorities. A recent study of poor Mexican Americans in California is instructive. High proportions are indeed extremely poor, educationally deprived, and their young men display some of the gang and criminal behavior associated with an "underclass." But these Latinos have fewer health problems than the Black *or Anglo* poor, are nearly twice as likely to live in two-parent nuclear families, and are less likely to collect welfare. California Latinos have higher life expectancies and lower infant mortality rates than Blacks or Anglos; Latina women are less likely to be smokers or alcohol and other drug abusers. That so many of them remain extremely poor suggests what is wrong with behavioral theories of the "underclass;" as one scholar put it, they do everything "right" but remain poor.[44]

The fact that these definitions are not sex- or race-neutral is not marginal but central to the problem, because minority men and women and white women are so disproportionately represented in the "underclass." A leading attempt to quantify the "underclass" found it 59 percent Black and 10 percent Hispanic. Sixty percent of "underclass" families are headed by single mothers.[45] These groups are prominent among those excluded from the better Social Security programs.

Moreover, we need to understand the effects of Social Security from two sides—how it affected the poor and the non-poor. During the Depression, emergency government relief and public works had a bigger impact than long-term welfare programs. New poor and old poor often collected from the same programs. But after World War II brought back prosperity, the differential effects of the Social Security Act were felt keenly. Its benefits to middle-class and upper-working-class men and their dependents were substantial and greater, absolutely and proportionately, than its contributions to the poor. In the 1980s, it has been estimated that 80 percent of the U.S. social welfare budget goes to the non-poor.[46] Moreover, these welfare benefits accounted for a larger share of economic improvement than income. That is, more employed people would have been poor had it not been for government provision. Even the War on Poverty contributed more to the non-poor than to the poor.[47] In the last fifty years, the "good" Social Security programs got steadily better. Old Age Insurance benefits were increased, protected against inflation, and extended to more beneficiaries, especially dependents. By contrast, the real value of AFDC and other public assistance programs fell and through 1970s eligibility criteria began to exclude more of the poor.[48] Moreover, welfare regulations frequently provided disincentives to upward mobility: for example, extended family strategies, so common among the poor and especially the Black poor, conflicted with welfare requirements and often led to suspension of benefits.

These non-redistributive dynamics cannot be understood, I am arguing, without examining the social and cultural meanings constructed around Social Security's tracking system. These fifty years of Social Security's history and change did not happen inevitably or in a political vacuum. The dynamic in which the well-off got more and the poor got less from welfare was itself influenced by the Social Security system, which identifies some claimants as entitled, collecting something as much theirs as wages, other claimants as parasites, dependents. For example, the fact that recipients of old-age insurance were labeled as entitled by Social Security strengthened their lobbying power, which in turn strengthened their identity as entitled still further. Public assistance claimants, meanwhile, grew steadily more poor and more stigmatized which in turn undercut their ability to organize to create political pressure, and their lack of organizational strength further weakened the respect they could evoke. Nothing illustrates this better than the substantial gains welfare claimants made during the period in which they built the National Welfare Rights Organization, and their losses since the decline of that organization in the 1970s.

As a result, even during periods defined as prosperous, the 1950s and 1960s, relative indicators for stigmatized groups moved downward. For example, even while Black employment and income was growing, Blacks' *share* of unemployment steadily increased. And the numbers of the poor who were marginally employed also increased, notably those who could not get into full-time major industry jobs but depended on service-sector, seasonal, temporary employment.

Some qualifications must be reemphasized: Of course the Social

Security Act was not the only social policy that contributed to creating an "underclass."[49] Nor were Social Security's influence all in the direction of inequality. But opposite trends were developing even in these decades usually labeled prosperous. For these the state must share responsibility with the society.

While this paper has focused on the cultural/ideological construction of "underclass," we need at least three levels of analysis, complexly interconnecting to create a full explanation of this rhetoric. We need structural analysis of the processes of capitalist industrial development, especially in creating and reproducing international, ethnic/racial, and gender divisions in the working class and in maintaining irregular, seasonal employment for many. Second, we need policy analysis of how private and public relief functioned to maintain and deepen divisions between the deserving and the undeserving poor, in part because of autonomous dynamics among bureaucrats and professionals, in part because relief systems have been constrained by pressures from employers and the segmentation of the working class. But we also need a cultural and ideological analysis of how these social divisions acquired— and not only from the top down—strong moral and emotional meanings, which were of course manipulated and resisted in different ways at different historical moments. Into such a complex force field came the Social Security Act, which, under pressure from an emergency, wound a way through and past contemporary constraints. We need to recognize that it created not only a system of provision, but also a set of social values that represent today a major force in policy options.

Notes

1. Linda Gordon and Theda Skocpol, debate, *Contention*, Vol. 2, No. 3, Spring 1993.

2. Ralf Dahrendorf, *Law and Order* (London: Stevens & Sons, 1985), p. 98.

3. *Pitied but not Entitled: Single Mothers and the History of Welfare 1890–1935* (New York: Free Press, 1994).

4. Section one of this paper was influenced greatly by Nancy Fraser, and I am indebted to her for helping me develop my thinking about the importance of language.

5. Ken Auletta, *The Underclass* (New York: Vintage, 1983).

6. E.g., Erol R. Ricketts and Isabel V. Sawhill, "Defining and Measuring the Underclass," *Journal of Policy Analysis and Management*, Vol. 7, No. 2, 1988, pp. 316–325; Barbara Schmitter Heisler, "A Comparative Perspective on the Underclass: Questions of Urban Poverty, Race, and Citizenship," *Theory and Society*, Vol. 20, 1991, pp. 455–483; "Defining Help for the Underclass," *America*, Vol. 155, October 11, 1986, pp. 177–178; IRP Reprint Series #535: William Julius Wilson, "Cycles of Deprivation and the Underclass Debate," *Social Service Review*, Vol. 59, No. 4, December, 1985, pp. 541–559.

7. L. Chevalier, *Classes Laborieuse et Classes Dangereuses a Paris, Pendant la Premiere Moitie du XIX Siècle* (Paris, 1978).

8. Children's Aid Society, *2nd Annual Report* (New York, 1855), p. 3.

9. Stanley Aronowitz, *False Promises: The Shaping of American Working Class Consciousness* (New York: McGraw Hill, 1973), considers the underclass a "result of the disparity between the historical tendency of capitalist production to require less labor for the production of commodities and the urbanization of the whole population," p. 11.

10. Gertrude Himmelfarb, *The Idea of Poverty: England in the Early Industrial Age* (New York: Knopf, 1984), pp. 328–329; Gertrude Himmelfarb, *Poverty and Compassion: The Moral Imagination of the Late Victorians* (New York: Knopf 1991), p. 11.

11. E.g., Ladies of the Mission, *The Old Brewery and the New Mission House at the Five Points* (New York: Stringer & Townsend, 1854). There is a brilliant description of the stench of the cities in Patrick Suskind's novel *Perfume: The Story of a Murderer*, trans. John E. Woods (New York: Pocket Books, 1987).

12. Ladies of the Mission, Ibid., p. 20; Children's Aid Society, op. cit., p. 5.

13. Himmelfarb, *The Idea of Poverty*, op. cit., pp. 356–57.

14. Quoted in Robert H. Bremner, *American Philanthropy* (Chicago: University of Chicago, 1960), p. 60.

15. I do not mean to imply that sensationalist writing inevitably produces such moralistic responses. Some socialist writers, such as Upton Sinclair, sensationalized the depravities of the capitalist class, thus positioning poor workers as victims.

16. Gareth Stedman Jones, *Outcast London: A Study of the Relationship Between Classes in Victorian Society* (Oxford: Oxford University Press, 1971), p. 11.

17. Ibid., 371–372.

18. Jennifer Davis, "Jennings' Buildings and the Royal Borough: The Construction of the Underclass in Mid–Victorian England," in *Metropolis–London: Histories and Representations Since 1800,* David Feldman and Gareth Stedman Jones, eds. (London and New York: Routledge, 1989).

19. Linda Gordon, *Woman's Body, Woman's Right: Birth Control in America* (New York: Viking/Penguin, 2nd. ed., 1990); Himmelfarb, *The Idea of Poverty*, op. cit., p. 324.

20. George Sims quoted in Himmelfarb, *Poverty and Compassion*, op. cit., p. 58.

21. Davis, op. cit., p. 11.

22. Thanks to John Clarke for explaining this important point.

23. Indeed, Marx did contest with a more positive and romantic view of the underclass, that enunciated by Max Stirner in the 1840s, against which Marx and Engels wrote their *German Ideology.*

24. Nikolai Bukharin, *Historical Materialism* (New York: International Publishers, 1925), pp. 284, 290; quoted in David Matza, "The Disreputable Poor," in Reinhard Bendix and Seymour Martin Lipset, eds., *Class, Status, and Power: Social Stratification in Comparative Perspective* (New York: Free Press, 1966), p. 291.

25. See my introduction to *Women, the State, and Welfare,* Linda Gordon, ed. (Madison: University of Wisconsin, 1990).

26. E.g., Judith Walkowitz, *Prostitution and Victorian Society: Women, Class, and the State* (New York: Cambridge University Press, 1980).

27. David Ward, *Poverty, Ethnicity, and the American City, 1840–1925: Changing Conceptions of the Slum and the Ghetto* (Cambridge: Cambridge University Press, 1989), p. 97.

28. David T. Beito, "Mutual Aid, State Welfare, and Organized Charity: Fraternal Societies and the 'Deserving' and 'Undeserving' Poor, 1890–1930," *Journal of Policy History,* Vol. 5, No. 4, 1993, pp. 419–434.

29. Linda Gordon, "Social Insurance and Public Assistance: The Influence of Gender in Welfare Thought in the United States, 1890–1935," *American Historical Review,* Vol. 97, No. 1, February, 1992; David Matza, op. cit., speaks mistakenly of fear of pauperization as exclusive to conservatives, p. 296.

30. June Axinn and Mark J. Stern, *Dependency and Poverty: Old Problems in a New World* (Lexington: Lexington Books, 1988), pp. 97–99.

31. August B. Hollingshead, "Selected Characteristics of Classes in a Middle Western Community," *American Sociological Review,* Vol. 12, 1947, pp. 385–95, reprinted in Bendix and Seymour Lipset, eds., *Class, Status, and Power: A Reader in Social Stratification* (Glencoe, Illinois.: Free Press, 1957), p. 222.

32. Matza, op. cit., p. 302.

33. Michael Harrington, *The Other America: Poverty in the United States* (New York: Macmillan, 1963); Aronowitz, op. cit., p. 11. Aronowitz discussed the development of "a substantial underclass ... [unlike] a reserve army of labor since it is characteristically not employed in the expansion of capital but enters the labor market only in the most marginal service occupations or as seasonal agricultural laborers."

34. Hazel M. Willacy, "Men in Poverty Neighborhoods: A Status Report," *Monthly Labor Review,* February, 1969, pp. 23–27.

35. "The American Underclass," *Time,* August 29, 1977, pp. 14–27, this usage from William J. Wilson, "Introduction to the Wesleyan Edition" in Kenneth B. Clark, *Dark Ghetto* (New York: Harper and Row, 1965).

36. Gordon, *Pitied but not Entitled,* op. cit.

37. Alice Kessler-Harris, *A Woman's Wage: Historical Meanings and Social Consequences* (Lexington, Kentucky: University Press of Kentucky, 1990).

38. Joy Dryfoos, *Adolescents At Risk: Prevalence and Prevention* (New York: Oxford University Press, 1990), p. 3.

39. Quoted by Michael Katz in his introduction to *The "Underclass" Debate* (Princeton: Princeton University Press, 1992), p. 3.

40. Nancy Fraser and Linda Gordon, "A Genealogy of 'Dependency': A Keyword of the U.S. Welfare State," *Signs,* Vol. 19, No. 2, Winter 1994, pp. 309–336.

41. John Leo, "The High Cost of Playing Victim," *U.S. News and World Report,* October 1, 1990, p. 23.

42. Linda Gordon, *Heroes of Their Own Lives: The Politics and History of Family Violence* (New York: Viking/Penguin, 1988).

43. Kathryn M. Neckerman, "The Emergence of 'Underclass' Family Patterns, 1900–1940," in Katz, op. cit., pp. 194–219.

44. Karen J. Winkler, "Researcher's Examination of California's Poor Latino Population Prompts Debate Over the Traditional Definitions of the Underclass," *Chronicle of Higher Education,* October 10, 1990, pp. A5–A8.

45. Ricketts and Sawhill, op. cit., p. 322.

46. James T. Patterson, *America's Struggle Against Poverty* (Cambridge: Harvard University Press, 1981), pp. 76, 92–94; Sheldon Danziger, Robert Haveman and Plotnick, "Antipoverty Policy: Effects on the Poor and the Nonpoor," in Sheldon H. Danziger and Daniel H. Weinberg, eds., *Fighting Poverty: What Works and What Doesn't* (Cambridge: Harvard University Press, 1986), pp. 66–67.

47. Thomas F. Jackson, "The State, the Movement, and the Urban Poor: The War on Poverty and Political Mobilization in the 1960s," in Katz, op. cit., pp. 403–439.

48. Michael R. Sosin, "Legal Rights and Welfare Change," in Danziger and Weinberg, eds., op. cit., p. 276.

49. For example, housing policy, public and private, raised walls around ghettos which concentrated the minority poor. Transportation policy, public and private, increased the difficulty the poor faced in commuting to jobs. Police policy, from discriminatory harassment to gross brutality, added to the despair and bitterness of racial minorities. Education policy, public and private, deepened existing inequality. Economic policy which made capital flight easier contributed.

4

Poverty and Public Policy
in the 1990s

Rebecca M. Blank

Poverty is one of those issues that rubs uncomfortably against our social conscience. We don't want homeless people living on the streets of our cities. We don't want children growing up in neighborhoods controlled by gangs, and where gunfire is taken for granted. We don't want mothers to worry at the end of every month about food and rent payments. Yet, as much as we ardently wish that nobody in America was poor, we are deeply ambivalent about anti-poverty policies. In a country of immigrants, where many of us came from families that had virtually nothing, there lingers suspicion about the poor: How much should we help them? Will they misuse our assistance? What has kept them from "making it" when so many our of immigrant ancestors were able to escape poverty?

I want to discuss poverty in the 1990s, which is very different from poverty even thirty years ago when Lyndon Johnson launched his now famous War on Poverty. As the nature and causes of poverty have changed, so also have the proposed anti-poverty policies changed over the past decade. I will talk about what I consider to be the most promising "new ideas" for anti-poverty initiatives. To preview my conclusions, I think the prognosis for effective anti-poverty policy is currently quite mixed: On the one hand, a useful consensus has emerged over the past decade about the direction which policy should take—a direction with which I strongly agree. On the other hand, some of the problems faced by the poor in the 1990s are less readily "solvable" by public policy, so that the promised results of these new policy directions are necessarily somewhat limited. But I get ahead of myself.

Who Are the Poor?

I'm an economist, so I'll start with some statistics. Currently, over 35 million people—14.2 percent of the population—are poor, meaning that their total household income is below the officially defined U.S. poverty line.[1] For a married couple with two children, this means their annual income is below $14,000. For a single mother with two children, it means that she is making ends meet on less than $11,000. There is an ongoing argument about the appropriate definition of poverty and whether our current measures are really the right ones. This is a topic for an entirely separate investigation; suffice it to say that these numbers would be somewhat larger or somewhat smaller with alternative definitions.

In general, there's both good news and bad news about poverty in the United States. The good news is that poverty is not a widespread phenomenon in this country. Compared to the years before World War II, the enormous economic expansion that this country experienced between 1945 and 1973, brought poverty down to all-time lows. Figure 4.1 graphs the changes in the official rate of poverty since 1960 in this country. The poverty rate fell steadily through the 1960s, reaching a low of 11.1 percent in 1973, but rose again to a peak of 15.2 percent during the recession of the early 1980s. By 1989, the poverty rate was down to 12.8 percent. Since then it has risen to 14.2 percent, with the economic recession and stagnation of the past two years. Since the mid 1960s, poverty has hovered at around 11 to 15 percent of the population. This means poverty is a relatively rare occurrence in this country; it makes the anti-poverty efforts of our nation very different from those of a country like Bangladesh.

The bad news, of course, is also visible on Figure 4.1. Poverty rates did not fall over the last two decades and in fact, after the last two years of economic stagnation, poverty rates are higher now than they were throughout the 1970s. This "stickiness" in poverty was particularly visible over the 1980s. Between 1983 and 1990, this country experienced the second longest economic expansion in our history. Yet, poverty fell by only a few percentage points. This is in sharp contrast to the 1960s, when a sustained economic expansion brought poverty down by 10 percentage points.

Of course, poverty is not spread equally across the population. Poverty rates among African Americans are three times those among whites, with 1/3 of black Americans living below the poverty line. Hispanics have poverty rates slightly below blacks.

Poverty among children has been particularly high over the past decade. Currently over one fifth of all children live in families whose income is below the poverty line, the highest share since the early 1960s. This is in sharp contrast to poverty among the elderly, who are

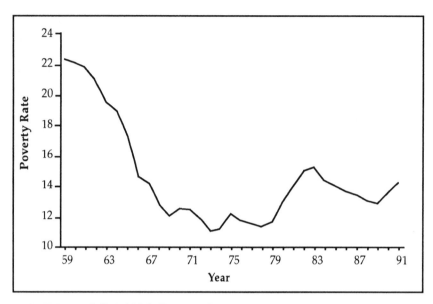

FIGURE 4.1 Official U.S. Poverty Rates: 1959–1991

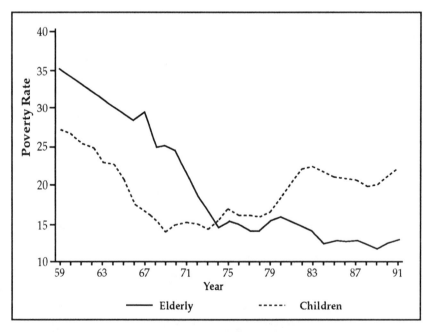

FIGURE 4.2 Children vs. Elderly Poverty Rates: 1959–1991

experiencing historic lows in poverty rates. If you are elderly in America, your chance of being poor is below that of a non-elderly individual. The elderly benefitted the most from the expansion of social programs in the late 1960s. Expansions in social security and other income assistance programs, as well as steady improvements in private pension plans, have continued to decrease poverty among the aged. Figure 4.2 plots the dramatic change in the well-being of elderly versus children in this country over the past three decades. This is a chart that is well known in Washington, D.C. In a time of tight budgets, the question arises whether increased funding for families with children should come at the expense of decreased funding for the middle-income elderly. Such policies as taxing social security or targeting its benefits more closely on the elderly poor are frequently discussed. Of course such reallocation of funds may not be politically possible, given the well-organized political clout of the elderly, which children lack entirely.

The primary reason that children's poverty rates are so high is because of the trend toward increases in the number of single-parent families. Single-parent families, which almost always means female-headed families, are the poorest group in this country. Currently, over half of all children will spend some time during their childhood in a family headed only by their mother. This has serious economic implications. Almost half of all female-headed families with children—47 percent—are poor. Among black and Hispanic mothers who head their own household, the number is close to two-thirds. These are appallingly high numbers. If you believe that the investments we make in children are important, these numbers are frightening. Poor families are much more likely to face problems of inadequate health care, low-cost housing in unsafe neighborhoods and, in the worst situations, regular times at the end of every month when there's just not enough money to quite cover the food budget.

Poverty in the U.S. is not equally distributed today. It is a problem precisely because there are some groups who are much more likely to become poor and to stay poor. In fact, there are certain groups of short-term poor that we simply don't worry about at all. Most notably, somewhere under 5 percent of all poor are students—undergraduates or graduate students. For better or worse, no one worries about this group. Their poverty is short-term; in some sense it is "self-chosen." Many of these students receive substantial assistance from families and their current poverty is not taken as a sign that future poverty is likely. Quite the opposite. In economic terms, these students have chosen to forego current consumption in order to invest in education, so that they will have higher incomes in the future. But those who are caught in poverty—who are poor today, were poor yesterday, and are likely to be poor tomorrow, are the group that we worry most about.

The Current Problems of Poverty

The public conversation about poverty has focused on three issues since the mid 1980s. I want to review those issues and then see what implications they have for the current policy agenda.

The Feminization of Poverty and Its Relationship to Changing Demographic Characteristics

I've already talked about the enormous problems of poverty among single women who head families. Female-headed families have always faced a somewhat different set of problems than two-parent families or single individuals. By shouldering the roles of both sole parent and sole income-earner, these women may be less able to take advantage of expanded employment opportunities because of their need to find acceptable child care. Many of these women also face problems of low wages and limited career advancement options, typical of the job opportunities in those feminized occupations most readily available to women with limited skills.

Over the past ten years there has been increasing attention to the problems of single mothers, which has led to two major new directions for policy.

Reform of the Welfare System. Single parents are the primary group for whom public assistance or welfare is available. A mother with two children and no other sources of income can, on average, receive $370 per month in support from AFDC (Aid to Families with Dependent Children, the primary public assistance program) and another $275 per month from Food Stamps, which will provide her with a total annual income just over $7,400 per year, about 72 percent of the poverty line for her family.[2] This amount differs substantially however across states. In New Hampshire, a woman on public assistance is at 83 percent of the poverty line, while in Arkansas she is at 55 percent.

AFDC, established as part of the Social Security Act in 1935, was explicitly designed to allow mothers to stay home with their children. But the world changed and today the majority of women—even mothers of pre-school children—are working at least part time. As a result, the AFDC program has increasingly focused on providing job assistance to help women enter the labor market. Since 1990, all states are required to run a JOBS program—a program designed to provide job training and job search assistance to eligible women on public assistance. These programs also help women find adequate and affordable child care.

These efforts at linking welfare and work have been extensively evaluated over the past decade and the news is both good and bad. On the one hand, linked work/welfare programs appear to increase the labor-market involvement of women, increase their earned income, and decrease welfare payments. All of the evidence says that the benefits from these programs are greater than the costs involved. But on the other hand, the impact of these programs, while positive, is relatively small. Most women experience earnings increases of about $500–$800/year. These women work more, are more connected with the labor market, and use less welfare. But almost none of them escape poverty. They are somewhat less poor, but they are still poor. If you believe that increasing women's economic self-sufficiency is important—and I do believe that— then you support expanding and encouraging these efforts. But by themselves, they are hardly a solution to poverty among women.

Increasing Support from Absent Fathers. Increasing attention over the past decade has been paid to the missing member of the family in female-headed families, namely, the father. The statistics on child support payments are shockingly low. Only about 30 percent of poor women with minor children receive child support; of those who do, the average amount received is less than $2,000/year for all children.[3]

The Family Support Act of 1988, which also created the JOBS program, has made it easier for states to track absent fathers and collect child support payments. Most of the efforts have so far focused on trying to increase child support payments to women on welfare and decrease state welfare payments. But of course, any move in the direction of increasing the level and enforcement of child support will also help those millions of low- and middle-income women who are also raising children on their own.

Concern for the Poor Living in Areas of Concentrated Urban Poverty

Increasing attention in recent years has focused on the so-called "underclass debate," a discussion of the nature of urban poverty in neighborhoods with high overall levels of poverty, crime, welfare use, and unemployment. The L.A. riots have been the most recent event reinforcing this concern. The problem is that persons caught in these areas face not only income poverty, but a whole host of neighborhood social problems, including high crime, limited nearby job opportunities, poor schools, deteriorating housing, gang violence, and so forth. These problems are particularly acute in poor African-American neighborhoods, where the problems of poverty are overlaid with a long history of housing segregation and economic and social discrimination.

Unfortunately, data on areas of concentrated poverty are only available from the decennial census and our most recent evidence is from 1980. In that year, according to Mary Jo Bane and Paul Jargowsky, 9 percent of the poor (2.4 million people) lived in an urban area where over 40 percent of the residents were also poor.[4] Minority groups were most likely to be in these concentrated poverty areas. Among the black poor, 21 percent lived in concentrated poverty areas and 16 percent of Hispanic poor were in such areas. The number in these concentrated poverty areas grew between 1970 and 1980 by 30 percent. Whether these numbers continued to increase between 1980 and 1990 is still unknown. Certainly the fact that the overall poverty rate is higher now than ten years ago strongly implies that concentrated poverty is unlikely to have declined over the past decade.

On the one hand, these numbers indicate that only a small percentage of the poor face the problems of living in ghetto poverty areas. On the other hand, there is a perception that the level of social problems in these areas is extremely high and costly for the rest of society. This growth in concentrated urban poverty is less disturbing from an income poverty perspective than it is from a broader social perspective. Sociologist William Wilson has discussed the potential problems of areas that are heavily populated by persons who do not participate in the mainstream economy.[5] Poverty may be more persistent and may be more closely linked to problems of illiteracy, drugs, and crime in such areas. The growing concern with the nature of poverty in these urban areas is related to the emerging discussion on the failure of public institutions in such areas, including serious problems in public schools and in effective law enforcement. Reducing poverty and its related problems in these areas might result in a greater social benefit than reducing poverty among other groups.

The policy response to the "underclass discussion," as it has come to be called, has been to emphasize the inter-relatedness of policy changes. In communities where individuals face multiple barriers to economic escape—few jobs, poor schooling, inadequate public transportation, lack of job contacts, etc.—working on single policy changes will probably be inadequate. Attempts merely at welfare reform, or at school reform, or at changes in the criminal justice system, are likely to be inadequate by themselves. There is increasing discussion of the need for coordinated and multiple changes. I'll address this topic later.

Growing Wage Inequality and Limited Earnings Opportunities for Less-Skilled Workers

When Ronald Reagan claimed in 1980 that economic growth would help the poor, few poverty analysts could have argued with him; earlier periods of economic growth in this country were clearly associated with declining poverty rates, most notably the sustained economic expansion of the 1960s. Unfortunately, poverty rates fell only moderately during eight years of sustained economic growth between 1982 and 1990.

The primary reason behind the sluggish response of poverty rates to economic growth over the 1980s was the declining level of real wages for low-skilled jobs. Since 1979, real wage levels for many low-skilled workers have fallen dramatically. Among men with less than a high school education, inflation-adjusted weekly wages fell 13 percent between 1979 and 1989; among high school graduates, weekly wages fell 4 percent. In contrast, among men with a college education, they rose by 11 percent over this same time period.[6] These wage declines for less-skilled workers occurred not just over the recession of the early 1980s, but continued even in the strong economic recovery of the latter 1980s. After the steep recession of 1982–1983, the average number of weeks worked per year increased among low-income workers. But declining real wages offset this increase in labor market effort. Thus, the employment expansion that occurred during the economic growth of the mid 1980s did not lead to substantial increases in household income among low-wage earners, because of declining real wages.

The causes of this ongoing wage decline are a subject of extensive research and debate. Among the reasons are changes in technology, changes in international markets that have produced changes in the skill mix of labor demand, and changes in the relative supply of more- and less-skilled workers relative to the rapidly growing demand for more-skilled workers by employers. Regardless of the cause, however, these wage changes have steadily reduced the incentives for mainstream employment among low-skilled workers and limited the income growth of low-income households.

The result of these changes is that "employment strategies" designed to help poor families escape poverty through increased earnings and work are more difficult to implement now than they have been at any time over the past three decades. Not only are the earnings opportunities more limited for low-skilled workers, but, as noted, an increasing number of the poor are single parents, which often places other constraints on the location and hours of any jobs that they can find.

The big policy question is "What can we do about this?" It was striking how little the Democrats emphasized the problem of declining real wages among low-skilled workers during this past presidential election. Given the overall concern with economic issues, you might expect that this would be a major weapon in their attacks on George Bush. But the only problems that get talked about in the political arena are those for which there are possible solutions. Given there are no easy solutions to these wage shifts, it was dangerous to talk about them because Bill Clinton couldn't promise to fix this problem.

I think it's clear to most economists that this problem isn't likely to disappear on its own. The forces that have led to a widening wage/skill distribution are, if anything, going to continue over the next decade. The international share of the U.S. economy will continue to grow, meaning further competition for U.S. labor from abroad. To the extent that technological changes are a cause of these wage changes, these are also likely to be permanent. This means that many people—particularly people in their 20s and 30s whose training is limited to a high school degree or less—are facing long-term permanently lower incomes than their parents.

If wages are lower, work is a less attractive option. If we want to emphasize employment as a way out of poverty, we need to assure that work pays—that an individual who works full time can support his or her family. One major policy change over the past decade that is receiving increasing attention is the Earned Income Tax Credit or EITC. This is a refundable tax credit for low-income workers with children, meaning that parents whose total earnings fall below a certain level actually get a check back from the government, supplementing their wages. Very large expansions in the EITC have been enacted in the past few years, so that this year a full-time worker at the minimum wage, who heads a family with children, will earn not just the $8,500 paid by full-time minimum wage employment, but will receive another $1,300 as a tax credit from the government.

In some ways the EITC is one of the best-kept secrets in the United States—very few persons have heard about it, yet in the years ahead it is likely to provide more income assistance to low-income working families than the AFDC program. As the EITC becomes more widely known, this may create political problems. The EITC provides a long-term permanent subsidy to workers who are unable to find higher-wage jobs. That's exactly what some workers will need to support their families. But long-term permanent income subsidies are not very politically attractive in a nation that worries ceaselessly about "welfare dependence."

I should note that these wage trends underscore another major area of policy concern that I've mentioned only in passing. The only way to mitigate the effects of declining wages for low-skilled work in the long run is to assure that today's children and teenagers receive the skills and education that will assure them of adequate wages. Educational reform—particularly in those urban schools which are social and educational disasters—should be at the top of everybody's list. One thing we particularly have to do better, is to assist the non-college bound before they leave high school, providing assistance and information on post-high school training, linking high school students with employers in apprenticeship programs, and finding ways to communicate to today's elementary school students that education *will* matter.

The New Ideas of the Past Decade:
Melding the Liberal and Conservative Agendas

The problems facing us in terms of poverty are enormous, in part because the target keeps changing. If the world had stayed the way it was in 1960, the war on poverty would have been quite successful. But changes in family demographics and in economic opportunities have created new poverty problems. This has led to a change in the policy discussion—much of it very promising. I've been talking about specific new policy initiatives. Let me shift the conversation slightly, and talk about the theoretical concepts underlying these policies.

The conceptualization about how to fight poverty has changed over the past decade, as our understanding of the nature of poverty has changed. One of the most striking aspects of the new conversations about anti-poverty policy is that they merge the best of both the traditional conservative and liberal approaches to these issues. Let me indicate three ways in which the conversation about anti-poverty policy has changed in recent years.

An Emphasis on Mutual Obligations

The phrase "mutual obligations" came into currency in the debate over how to structure effective work/welfare programs for AFDC recipients in the 1980s. It has since acquired a broader meaning in the social policy arena. Mutual obligations is a statement that individuals can be held to certain responsibilities by public institutions, linked with a demand that those institutions operate effectively. On the one hand, there is the claim that individuals have responsibilities to society. Students are validly required to meet attendance and performance requirements in the schools and to adopt behavior that allows others to learn. Parents are validly required to support their children, even if they no longer live in the same household. Welfare recipients are validly required to acquire the skills and participate in the programs that will help them move off welfare and onto employment.

But "mutual obligations" is more than the traditional claim that individuals have a duty to their society. Society also has a duty to these individuals. In particular, the public institutions must also meet their obligations. Public schools must provide effective learning environments. Criminal justice systems must provide effective law enforcement. Employment programs must provide training that is truly useful in finding and holding a job. If these institutional responsibilities are not met, it is difficult to enforce or require the reciprocal individual responsibilities.

The rhetoric of mutual obligations reflects a blending of traditional conservative and liberal agendas, where the conservatives have historically focused more on individual responsibility and the liberals have focused more on institutional responsibility. In contrast, mutual obligations recognizes the importance of both. Permanent escape from poverty can only occur when individuals accept responsibility for schooling, work, and families. But these obligations can only be enforced when public institutions operate effectively.

Recognition of the Need for Public/Private Partnerships

The rising call for "public/private partnerships" recognizes that public policy need not be the exclusive province of government agencies. In its broadest sense, the "private" part of public/private partnerships implies programmatic involvement in public efforts by both the private for-profit sector and the non-profit and volunteer sector.

The traditional liberal agenda for social policy has been to design Federally funded and run programs. The traditional conservative agenda has been to leave social choice to the private sector; to let non-profit or for-profit agencies run programs because it is presumed that they are more efficient. Certainly, one of the lessons that we have learned over the past several decades is how ineffective the Federal government can be at certain things. It does an excellent job of writing checks and distributing funding. But it's much less effective at implementing effective local programs. There are differences in local circumstances, local politics, and local history that validly demand flexibility. Programs designed with uniform federal regulations often face problems with seemingly arbitrary rules that fail to recognize valid situational differences.

Yet, one of the other lessons that we've also learned is just how ready the private sector is to take money from social programs without providing very good services. The major scandals in public housing and in medicaid and other public health care programs did not occur because recipients misused funds, but because private sector contractors used these programs as a way to get rich while delivering shoddy services.

Out of this history has emerged a growing recognition that both the public and private sectors have certain comparative advantages in social programs, and that joint partnership efforts may be the best way to proceed for some programs. Such shared partnerships, it is claimed, should utilize the most effective part of each economic sector. The government, with broad redistributive tax powers, can provide the necessary funds to assure the ongoing operation of social programs. Government agencies may be best at coordinating and evaluating these programs. But the for-profit private sector may operate programs with greater efficiency, while the non-profit sector may provide more personalized, lower cost, or less bureaucratic services.

Thus, the actual training slots for job training programs may best occur in local firms, although the program is administered by state employment and labor departments. Non-profit community housing organizations may subcontract with public housing authorities to renovate and restore low-income housing. Similarly, in many cities, homelessness services are operated by non-profit organizations, but funded with Federal and state money. The emphasis on shared internship programs and school-to-work programs, where local businesses and local high schools work together, is another example of this approach.

Recognition of the Need for More Coordinated Programs

Increasingly, policy discussions are focussing on the need to think about packages of reforms and to understand their overlapping effects. This approach emphasizes coordinated community reform efforts, designed within each local area. Historically, discussions of educational reform, welfare reform, criminal justice, or job training programs have frequently been conducted in separate rooms with separate audiences. A coordinated strategy emphasizes the importance of linkages between institutions and between problems. Welfare reform may be ineffective if schools are inadequate. School reform may accomplish little if gang activity remains high. Efforts to reduce crime may fail if employment opportunities are low. The linkages between these programs are important.

The work/welfare programs of the 1980s led to the recognition that welfare reform must be linked with job training, which in turn requires attention to child care, transportation, and health insurance. Coordination, however, need not mean just coordination across service areas. The school reform efforts pioneered by James Comer, provide another example.[7] Comer doesn't have a specific reform plan; he has a *process*, which requires that everyone—including students, parents, teachers, administrators, maintenance staff, etc.—in the school sit down together around a table. Through a facilitated process, these groups talk about their specific concerns, and try to find common ground. Each group is often willing to make changes (and perhaps face risks) as long as they feel that other groups are also making changes and accepting comparable risks. The early evidence indicates that schools which have gone through this facilitated process show substantial improvements in the academic achievement of their students.

Efforts within individual communities to work on coordinated reform strategies are mushrooming in urban areas around the country. Within Chicago, a wide variety of profit and non-profit agencies are trying to run community-wide programs, focusing on particular neighborhoods.

The model is one of coordination and cooperation—with multiple actors working together. For urban areas that face multiple social and economic problems, it is unclear that any more partial solution has much promise.

While there is more than a little utopian dreaming in the hope that coordinated community reform can involve local and state government officials, law enforcement personnel, welfare administrators, school official, parents, residents, and employers, it is not impossible to think that such efforts could make a difference in communities with concentrated poverty and multiple social problems. There are examples of similarly organized coordinated planning efforts, aimed at bringing all involved parties around the table together, that have been successful in regional development efforts or in environmental cleanup. The potential of such strategies to produce long-term change in poor urban areas is still unclear, given the obvious problems of implementing coordinated and mutually agreed-upon social change. What is clear, is that the incremental program-oriented reform that has dominated the policy agenda for the past two decades has been largely ineffective in improving our worst city neighborhoods.

What's the Agenda?

I find the discussion over the past decade extremely promising. There has been a merging of the agendas of traditional liberals and traditional conservatives. This provides an opportunity for change. One striking example of this was played out in the recent presidential campaign. *Both* Bill Clinton and George Bush talked about job training, economic empowerment, and educational reform. Whatever else he may be, Bill Clinton is not a big-spending 1960s liberal on anti-poverty issues. He has explicitly de-emphasized income-assistance programs and emphasized programs that move people into work. His rhetoric has emphasized personal responsibility, effective institutional behavior, and a role for public and private groups to work together. This is not a return to the 1960s, but the evolutionary outgrowth of the changing discussion about poverty of the past two decades.

Let me indicate briefly the agenda that I think is emerging:

1. Emphasize economic empowerment and employment strategies through strengthening and pursuing such things as work/welfare programs for women receiving public assistance, and job creation and training for targeted populations. But also recognize the problems on the demand side of the labor market that are working against employment strategies. Sustain and perhaps expand programs like the Earned Income Tax Credit.

2. Do everything possible to assist single parents. This means both helping them increase their earnings through employment, as well as enforcing responsibility on absent parents. This may also mean attention to items I haven't talked about very much, like child care and health insurance.
3. Do everything possible to help today's children avoid the problems of today's low-skilled adults. Place first priorities on improving those schools with inadequate resources, and where children are unsafe.
4. Establish effective communication between public and private agencies involved in this process. Where possible, coordinate activities among different groups. Encourage public/private partnerships in the schools, in housing rehabilitation, and in job creation and training programs.

Will this Agenda Reduce Poverty?

While this agenda is a good one, which I think can effectively reduce poverty in the long run in this country, there are a number of barriers to its effective implementation. I've already talked about the economic changes in the labor market that may limit the effectiveness of employment and training programs in the decade ahead. Let me also mention three other barriers that will create serious problems for this agenda.

First, the Federal budget problems are a major barrier to any effort at social policy reform. Until there is a decline in the deficit problems facing the federal government, there aren't going to be new federal dollars available for poverty. And the programs mentioned above, while they may not necessarily require large federal expenditures, will require some expanded funding. For instance, one of the real political problems with job training programs is that they cost a lot of money up front. If effectively run, that money is recovered through increased taxes, decreased welfare, and greater productivity. But these long-term rewards may not create the political impetus necessary to fund the program today.

Serious anti-poverty activists have to be good budgeters. For better or worse, in the next decade, expansions in social spending will require cuts elsewhere. This means we've got to face up to the difficult issues like the following. To what extent are we willing to make hard priority decisions between programs? Will anti-poverty efforts come out on top of a serious national debate about federal spending priorities? Or, if we don't want to substantially cut existing programs, are we willing to increase tax rates?

Finally, the hardest question all, to what extent can Bill Clinton or anyone else create the political will necessary for this to happen?

Second, the race problems in this country are a major reason why anti-poverty issues remain difficult and divisive. Over the past decade, the image of "poverty" presented by our national leaders and by the media has been "black urban poverty." And if "poverty" is equated with "black" in people's minds, then the rising level of racial distrust in this country will stymie any effort at anti-poverty policy. The intense public attention to the urban "underclass"—a word I intensely dislike—I interpret as a way to distance ourselves from the problem; to envision the poor as an extremely different and alien "underclass" whose behavior cannot be controlled or understood.

This is untrue and dangerous. Poverty is a diverse problem. Although blacks and Hispanics are disproportionately likely to be poor, the majority of the poor are white, as are the major of welfare recipients. And even among the black poor, as I've noted above, only about one fifth live in extremely poor urban ghetto neighborhoods. Most of the poor—black and white—are people we would all recognize: women trying to make it with their children, individuals with some employment handicaps, or low-skilled men who have difficulty finding jobs above the minimum wage. They live and work and shop in our communities.

One thing which I believe Bill Clinton has done very well so far—both in his words and in the media events his team has orchestrated—is to use images of America that envision it as an inclusive community. This sends a message that is vital if we are to pursue effective anti-poverty policy: We cannot think of the poor in our nation as "different," "deficient" or "hopeless." If we are going to be effective in creating the political will necessary to seriously address current poverty problems in this nation, we must recognize not what is different between ourselves and the poor, but what we hold in common: hope for our children, hope for our future, and a willingness to try to make those hopes come true.

Finally, the last barrier to effective anti-poverty policy is our tendency to oversell any solution. How many times in the past three decades have we been promised a new program to "solve poverty?" I am going to let you in on a secret that you'll never understand if you only listen to the political discussion about anti-poverty policy: There is no "solution" to poverty. There are multiple possible programs that address different aspects of the economic and social conditions that lead to poverty. What we should be looking for is not one "magic bullet" of a program which will eliminate all problems, but a set of programs which reinforce each other and which attack poverty from multiple angles.

No one program will ever be adequate. As I've noted, work/welfare programs have good effects, but increase women's earnings only modestly. The success of employment programs is limited by declining wages among less-skilled workers. Education reform efforts will be limited by other problems children face in their families and neighborhoods. Rather than searching for a single magical solution—which usually results in overblown rhetoric when a program is introduced, followed by an inevitable political letdown when it fails to live up to all of the promises—we should be looking for a mix of programs that have proven effectiveness, whose benefits are clearly greater than their costs, and that we know can be effectively implemented in a variety of situations. Our best hope is that a mix of programs, each producing small benefits in their own area, will reinforce each other and produce synergistic changes that result in greater combined effects than any one program by itself could ever accomplish. In short, we should think about packages of programs with combined and overlapping effects, and not try to find the one single all-effective "answer" to the poverty program.

The problems of poverty in the 1990s are not the same as they were in 1970 or even 1980. It is appropriate that our ideas and strategies have changed. I'm quite convinced that anti-poverty efforts are not limited by the lack of good ideas or new ideas or effective program models. We know how to produce clear reductions in the number of Americans living in poverty. The problem is not one of economic feasibility, but of political will. We as a nation must decide that anti-poverty efforts are at the top of our agenda and act accordingly. The first task of anyone wishing to pursue a strong anti-poverty agenda in this country in the years ahead will be to create the necessary social consensus that poverty is a problem we cannot ignore. Problems of political will and social consensus, however, lead me well outside the domain of economics and into the domain of political science and sociology. With typically disciplinary narrowness, I will stop at this point and hope that social scientists from other disciplines will be able to tell us how to create that social consensus.

Notes

1. All poverty figures cited are from U.S. Department of Commerce, "Poverty in the United States: 1991," *Current Population Reports*, Washington, D.C.: U.S. Government Printing Office, Series P-60, No. 181, August, 1992.

2. Data from U.S. House of Representatives, Committee on Ways and Means, *1992 Green Book*, Washington, D.C.: U.S. Government Printing Office, May, 1992, Table 9, p. 636.

3. Ibid., Table 5, p. 715.

4. Paul A. Jargowsky and Mary Jo Bane, "Ghetto Poverty in the United States, 1970–1980," in Christopher Jencks and Paul Peterson, eds., *The Urban Underclass* (Washington, D.C.: The Brookings Institute, 1991).

5. William J. Wilson, *The Truly Disadvantaged* (Chicago: University of Chicago Press, 1987).

6. Data from Rebecca Blank, "The Employment Strategy: Public Policies to Increase Work and Earnings," in S. Danziger, G. Sandefur, and D. Weinberg, eds., *Confirming Poverty: Prescription for Change* (Cambridge: Harvard University Press, 1994).

7. For a summary, see James P. Comer, "Education for Poor Minority Children," *Scientific American*, November, 1988.

5

Inside/Outside:
The Dialectics of Homelessness

Jennifer R. Wolch

A homeless woman in Los Angeles once shook her finger at me, and warned: Don't ever say that you ain't gonna be homeless. Don't ever say that you won't be living on the streets, because that's what I said. Look at me now. ... I don't care if you're rich, you're black, you're white, purple, green—don't ever let that come past your lips. You never know what the Man upstairs got planned for you.

My purpose in this chapter is to explore the consequences of ignoring this sober warning. For Americans have, in fact, failed to take heed. Although in the United States "homelessness is a growth industry," as one prominent shelter operator declared,[1] the vast majority of Americans believe that homelessness will never be part of their own future. Winding up on the streets is a fate that befalls only Other people with whom they have nothing in common.

This divide between the homed and the homeless, between those who stay "inside" and those who stay "outside," illustrates a bitter dialectic now being played out on the American urban landscape. Rather than simply being a place where human social activities occur, urban landscapes hold vital clues about the nature of social relations. According to Michael Sorkin, the "city has historically mapped social relations with profound clarity, imprinting in its shapes and places vast information about status and order."[2] As homelessness arrives and takes root in suburbia, the homed and homeless are increasingly forced to share urban space. The landscapes being created are replete with signs and symbols of the rift between the haves and the have-nots, between the homed and the homeless. Today, even in the far reaches of "exopolis"— the outer city—there are people waiting at freeway off-ramps holding signs requesting work, food, or money. There are also homeless women living in their cars, parked on manicured streets of residential subdivisions, hoping no one will notice. And there are homeless laborers, waiting patiently in front of the lumber yard, hoping to be picked up for $15 dollars in exchange for a day's hard work.

This spread of homelessness and a widening fear of the homeless have pitted people on the inside against those on the outside in battles for the control of public space and community resources. In the course of this chapter, I hope to articulate the dimensions of this conflict between homed and homeless people. My method is to consider first the everyday lives and survival strategies of the homeless to illustrate how survival of the homeless depends on sharing the urban landscape with the conventionally domiciled population. I will juxtapose the situation of the homeless with a description of how they are greeted by most urban residents and neighborhoods. Second, having framed the conflict between the homed and the homeless, I argue that this conflict has its basis in recent economic and political trends, and show how homelessness is just the tip of an iceberg of social polarization carved out of the economics and politics—both global and local—of the 1980s. Finally, I take the question of what is to be done. How can we move from knowledge to action in the pursuit of a new moral landscape of American cities that embraces rather than excludes the homeless?

In doing so, I draw on the work of many social scientists and critics, including geographers, anthropologists, economists, and city planners. By avoiding disciplinary parochialism, the story becomes more interesting and useful. I also use examples from Los Angeles. This is not only a matter of convenience, but also part of the chapter's message. Los Angeles—its polycentric geographies, its diverse racial groups and ethnic cultures, its profound economic, political and social dilemmas—is widely noted as a harbinger of what is in store for other cities across the country. To quote Joel Garreau, "every single American city that *is* growing, is growing in the fashion of Los Angeles."[3] As such, we can learn from Los Angeles.[4]

Outside

In order to understand the deep-seated conflicts between the homeless and homed, it is necessary to understand how homeless people cope with life on the streets, and how their survival strategies shape relations with homed communities.

Many people who are homeless adapt to the rigors of survival outside by joining together in loose-knit communities. *Homeless communities are substitutes for a home-base.* In fact, impressive efforts are made by many communities to simulate a traditional home environment. Elements of "home" can be seen in most auto-construction projects of the homeless, including a functional separation of internal and outdoor space for different daily activities, interior decorations or plants, photographs and posters, and even "landscaping" around the front door. Sleeping spots are accorded the status of home through everyday discourse; homeless people often refer to their sleeping location as "home," despite the yawning gap between their current sleeping spot and the home of traditional expectation.[5]

The everyday routines associated with home life are replicated in the rhythms of camp life, allowing the re-establishment of routines that bring order, predictability, and comfort into lives that are by definition lacking in permanence and stability. Through the creation of what geographers call time-space continuity, homeless people establish and maintain their social ties and access various sources of formal assistance such as soup kitchens, shelters, or thrift stores. They also use resources of the urban environment, like parks, libraries, or shopping malls, but also restaurants, grocery stores, and transit facilities. In so doing they replicate in some fashion the routines of a prior existence involving work, shopping, socialization, and recreation. In this, the homeless are just like everyone else.[6]

There are wide variations in types of homeless community.[7] Many involve a mix of men, women, even children, organized to enhance survival chances. Others are groups of families, where a traditional domestic division of labor means that the men look for work during the day, while the women guard possessions and mind children. Some are composed of gay men or Vietnam veterans or runaway teens. There are, however, also negative aspects to some communities. Especially negative are those communities constructed around shared drug habits or subsistence prostitution, where survival benefits may be partially or wholly offset by reinforcement of destructive and/or dangerous behaviors.

The most common spatial expression of homeless communities is the street encampment. These are typically small, fragile, and limited in duration, but in the absence of more traditional forms of social support (from, for example, family, neighbors, or work mates), encampment community ties are significant.[8] They may even be a matter of life and death. Homeless friends, relatives, and acquaintances help out in several ways. They provide much-needed security, as well as material assistance. They also offer informal counseling or advice, and commiserate with the suffering experienced on the streets. Sharing in this way is essential to *coping*, to avoid being overwhelmed emotionally or blaming only themselves. Conviviality and mutual emotional support serve to buoy spirits and help reduce anxiety and depression. As one homeless encampment resident responded when asked if she received any psychological support services, "Of course—I talk to my homeless neighbors when I'm down."

Homeless communities also provide material aid to their members. In fact, many communities arise out of what are essentially exchange relations: Trading involves material goods, such as food, clothes, money, as well as emotional support and vital information on, for instance, how to get public assistance, when and where to find work, or where to panhandle. Such relationships, driven by survival needs and predicated on scarce resources, may fluctuate quickly as needs change and resources are depleted. The initiation of an exchange without an expectation of—or need for—reciprocity also allows homeless people to express kindness and generosity, bolstering their typically meager self-esteem.

Inside

Homeless communities rely upon urban public spaces, urban resources and amenities. Survival thus depends on the tolerance of local governments, businesses, and homed residents who also use the cityscape. What has been the response of these dominant groups to the formation of homeless communities? Have they sought to make contact with such communities or provide assistance in the form of food, clothing, jobs or housing? Unfortunately, increasing numbers of jurisdictions are adopting local ordinances forbidding camping, panhandling, sleeping in parks, or outdoor meals programs, and many have zoning codes blocking the entry of homeless services.[9]

The basis for rejection of homeless people is typically that they are a breed apart, a notion continually reinforced by media images.[10] Ironically, this is despite the fact that homeless communities strive so hard to reconstruct every "normal" aspect of home life. Over the past decade, as the homelessness crisis intensified, a raft of social science studies of the homeless was conducted by psychiatrists, demographers, and social workers.[11] These studies focused on the characteristics of the homeless themselves. At the same time, economists, housing experts, and welfare policy analysts drew attention to their broader economic, housing, and social support circumstances.[12] Some of these studies portrayed the homeless as "just like you or me," and hence blameless victims of unfortunate circumstance. But an epidemiological model dominating much of the research, which focused on the etiology of homelessness as if it were a disease, told much about the types of personal vulnerabilities under which the homeless labor.[13] An unfortunate, albeit inadvertent, outcome of epidemiological research on the homeless was to medicalize and psychiatrize homelessness.

Reinforced by media reports, these studies created dominant images of the homeless as *different, diseased, or demented.*

Thus the homeless became what anthropologists term "the Other"—strangers with perceived differences in origin, appearance, or behavior so profound that they are impossible to integrate into a host society. Louisa Stark, for example, suggests that homeless people are today's urban nomads, moving from place to place, never able to settle, and hence always strangers.[14] Stefanie Golden assesses the similarities between the treatment of homeless women and that of witches in prior times.[15] Others portray the urban homeless as postmodern primitives, tribes of hunter-gatherers, foraging to secure their needs from the middens of the American metropolis.

As a result of this identification of the homeless as strangers, neighborhoods and cities have acted in case after case to expel homeless outsiders, vociferously defending local turf against incursions by the homeless. This spatial strategy of separation and exclusion can be witnessed anywhere from downtown to the distant suburbs. In Skid Row, Los Angeles for example, homeless sidewalk encampments and their members are forcibly removed on a routine basis. Street sweeps routinely involve police to roust sidewalk dwellers, a skip-loader to remove belongings and structures on the sidewalk, and the street sweeper itself. Equally subtle are the sprinklers attached to the walls of many businesses, which randomly shower the sidewalk with water to drive homeless people away. And in the suburbs, the exclusionary milieu is perfectly captured by the proliferation of privatized police and defended spaces.

Systematic land-use policy measures are also operative in excluding the homeless. For more than a decade, the Community Redevelopment Agency in Los Angeles promoted the redevelopment of the city's downtown through massive developer subsidies in exchange for high-rise "trophy" towers, each one more elaborate than the last. The Redevelopment Agency also maintained a policy of "homeless containment" to remove offending people and activities from the glittering phoenix rising out of the ashes of old Los Angeles. Containment has meant that homeless shelters and services were primarily relegated to a clearly defined area within Skid Row, at intolerably high densities.[16] In other cities, most notably Miami, this sort of strategy also entails the creation of a system dangerously close to apartheid. Homeless people are offered "safe zones" (or homelands?) but then forego rights to exist in any other part of the city's public realm.

As more upscale, suburban communities experience an influx of the homeless, their response is even more forceful. This is especially true in what Joel Garreau terms "edge cities" on the urban fringe.[17] Here, the intensity of rejection follows the contours of wealth.[18] Many cities jump on the bandwagon to criminalize the homeless. They re-write municipal codes to outlaw camping or sleeping in public parks and other public spaces. Some routinely remove encampments hidden under freeway overpasses, near railway tracks, or on utility easements. And more and more are circumventing the constitutionally guaranteed freedom to panhandle by defining something termed "aggressive" panhandling and making it a crime. [19]

Other cities exclude the homeless through passive-aggressive behavior. Many simply deny the existence of the homeless. When asked about homelessness in his city, one official responded, "We don't have any homeless people in our community. If there are a couple of homeless people, they are just passing through." Why just passing through? "Because this community doesn't have any shelter or other services to help them, so they're on their way to downtown Los Angeles." Such remarks are reflected in the fact that over half of the almost 90 cities in Los Angeles county—including cities with a population of almost half a million—spend no money whatsoever on services for the homeless. Among those that do spend, the amounts are almost always negligible.

In short, local policy can all too often be summed up as "Hear no homeless, see no homeless, do nothing for the homeless, and hope that the homeless will go elsewhere."

Homelessness and Social Polarization

The conflict between insiders and outsiders over urban space and city resources is often blamed on both parties: the homeless smell bad, are aggressive, are shiftless and lazy; homed neighbors are snobby, exclusionary, and treat the homeless unfairly. Defined in this way, it is tempting to reform the behavior of individual homeless people and localities. But although this solution seems neat and simple, it is also wrong. The inside/outside conflict is not rooted in individual behavior or local policy, but rather in the complex economic restructuring and deepening social cleavages of the 1980s.

Over the past decade, social relations in cities became globalized at the very same time that increasingly localized efforts sought to protect more intimate cultural spaces from global takeover. The urban landscapes of contemporary economic transformation are perhaps best expressed by the streets of skid row areas—where we see the most marginalized survival communities confined to an action space of a few city blocks, typically cheek by jowl with spreading, shining skyscrapers shielding the networks and control centers of global capital. [20]

Homelessness, spectacular affluence, and downward mobility of much of the middle classes are all linked to the dynamics of what Scott

Lash and John Urry call "disorganized capitalism,"[21] characterized by de-industrialization and the flight of capital to international locations, globalized markets and global competition, and the rise of flexible production systems.[22] Despite the fact that explosive service sector growth appeared to partially offset job losses in traditional manufacturing industries, the types of jobs created and the terms of employment were vastly different. A huge proportion were minimum wage jobs, with no benefits such as health insurance.[23] And increasingly, employers in both manufacturing and service industries sought what is now termed "contingent labor:" non-unionized, part-time, temporary, and contract workers who could accumulate no seniority, had no job security, and were ineligible for benefits.[24]

Global-to-local dynamics are also played out in an urban land-market dialectic. Described by Neil Smith, this dialectic is "a microcosm of a new global order etched by the rapacity of capital."[25] In this process, economically marginalized people are displaced from their homes and neighborhoods in order to make way for upscale "urban frontiers" tamed through gentrification. This process has been explicitly and implicitly promoted by city governments eager to garner the increased tax base associated with redevelopment, gentrification and rising property values.

In the face of widespread economic depredations, growing inequality, and a mounting housing crisis, public protection for families and individuals has dwindled and in some places disappeared.[26] The welfare state is in full retreat, as fiscal conservatism and fiscal crisis have led the federal government and state after state to slash benefits, tighten eligibility, and cut people from the public assistance rolls. Affordable housing supplies plummeted as the federal commitment to housing collapsed. Federal spending on subsidized housing fell from 7 percent of the domestic budget in 1980 to a mere 0.7 percent by the end of the Reagan era. But because the number of people who have become impoverished and request assistance has increased (1 in 7 people in Los Angeles County are on welfare),[27] the reaction in some quarters has been even more draconian. Michigan for example, eliminated even the last-resort, most penurious program—a program so minimal that it did not cover the cost of a flop-house hotel room, let alone food or medical care.[28] Other states are following suit.

In the incremental dismantling of social welfare programs, lies a triumph of individualist philosophy and an enduring privatism in American life. While the economically marginalized are increasingly deemed undeserving of safety net protections, the affluent argue that they deserve their bounty since they work so hard—never realizing that the rich have grown richer (with the number of millionaires and billionaires doubling over the 1980s),[29] precisely because the poor have grown poorer. Repeatedly, the well-to-do have put their individual rights above community obligations to assist those who are less well-off.

In any explanation of social polarization, demography matters too. The aging of the baby boom cohort, the rise of nontraditional household types, and changing patterns of marriage and childbirth influence (and are influenced by) individual economic opportunities; particular demographic groups, such as young minority males, face the most limited life chances.[30] Moreover, economic restructuring along with regional wars and geopolitical crises have spawned immigration waves unprecedented since the end of the nineteenth century. Cities like Los Angeles, but also many smaller cities now boast a most amazing cultural diversity. Right now, over 100 languages are spoken by kids in the Los Angeles Unified School District. But with such diversity has also come extreme fragmentation and a breakdown of earlier understandings between a dominant white or anglo culture and minority groups, and between the wide array of minority groups themselves.[31]

In Los Angeles, these forces have converged to create what Manuel Castells once termed a "wild city" characterized by a polarization of social relations and a breakdown of social control.[32] Another urban theorist, Mike Davis, calls out the elements of what he terms "a geography of fear."[33] His concentric zone model of the city, weirdly reminiscent of famous human ecology studies done by Chicago sociologists in the 1920s, portrays a starkly polarized city in which the have-nots are herded into the core while the haves control the periphery. It is a city preoccupied with security, in which a panopticon-like design facilitates surveillance by police, neighborhood watch groups, and gated communities. Squadrons of space police keep the criminal elements in line and make certain districts safe from drugs and child abuse. Rich neighborhoods are cordoned off from the urban chaos, epitomized by the homeless, who inhabit containment zones created to keep the Other, the stranger, safely at bay.

The Limits of Postmodern Urbanism

How can we solve the problem of homelessness? In approaching this question, it is vital to understand that the metropolitan context of homelessness is rapidly changing, as the city is shaped both by global forces and a growing fragmentation of personal subjectivities and meanings. In his book, *Soft City*, Jonathan Raban suggests that, "the city goes soft; it awaits the imprint of an identity. For better or worse, it invites you to remake it, to consolidate it into a shape you can live in."[34] We must decide who we are as individuals and as a society, and what we want to be, since our subjective identities will mold and remold the urban landscape. So we must embrace the question: Who do we want to be, and how might our answers serve to end homelessness and the polarization of the urban landscape that it symbolizes?

Any answers must face the fact that homelessness is deeply implicated in the structure of society. The globalization of the economy implies a weakening of local and even national autonomy. This means that the dynamics that produce homelessness, shape our everyday lives, or underlie the urban experience, are not fully under our control.

Answers are also constrained by a rapidly changing metropolitan context, what Michael Dear terms a postmodern urbanism.[35] Along with socio-economic polarization produced by global forces has come a proliferation of architectural styles and community designs which supposedly celebrate diversity but obscure deep-seated tensions, conflicts, and struggles. The postmodern urban landscape is characterized by a pastiche of styles, by a sense of collage and ephemerality, discontinuity and above all, a *fragmentation of experience.* Lacking any over-arching physical or social vision, postmodern cities like Los Angeles have "come to resemble more than ever a significant agglomeration of theme parks, a life space comprised of Disney Worlds."[36] Los Angeles, for instance, is a city of consumption spectacles, where shopping malls and theme parks serve as leitmotif of a Tomorrowland of edge cities. It is a city where authenticity and history are commodified, packaged, and merchandised in the form of themed communities—Tudor Townhomes, Mediterranean Villas, Victoriana Place. It is a city of high-security, where gated communities insure a minimum of shared experience, especially shared insulation from pain. And it is a carceral city, where those left behind during the go-go 1980s are contained behind graffiti-smeared walls of deprivation and poverty.

Postmodern urbanism has also altered the political landscape. This is a landscape in which formal politics has become largely irrelevant to the atomized worlds of peoples separated by race, class, gender, immigrant status, and sexual orientation. Los Angeles, the nation's second largest city, is still struggling with a deep recession and trying to rebuild after the social and physical devastation of April 29, 1992. Yet less than one quarter of all eligible voters turned out in 1993 to choose the first new mayor in twenty years. Why? Because it is so hard for people to see how a new mayor would have any impact on their everyday lives: their job prospects, quality of schooling, exposure to drugs and other environmental toxins, risk of victimization by street gangs or criminal elements, access to critical human services. As a result, informal politics, embodied in voluntary organizations, lobby groups, and neighborhood associations pursuing such causes as slow-growth, ethnic advancement, or gay rights, has become much more central to the local scene.[37]

Postmodern politics also in part explains the behavior of insiders toward outsiders. Already distanced by social class, often race/ethnicity, and by space itself, homed residents have lost all faith in the ability of local government to make good on promises or enforce laws in a consistent way. Thus worries about, for example, an increase in crime associated with a homeless shelter cannot be soothed by promises from city officials and police to protect the neighborhood. Rather, through an intense localism, neighbors band together and act autonomously to keep the outsiders out.

Social Justice and the Obligations of Community

Postmodern urbanism clearly constrains, but does not eliminate, our ability to solve the problem of homelessness. Rather, in developing solutions, powerful priorities are needed to create a new urban landscape. At the top of the priorities list must be an economic and industrial policy insuring that people who work earn a living wage. Next must be a major overhaul of the health and welfare system, so that indigent people unable to work can not only survive but improve their circumstances. Third, a major infusion of resources for affordable housing is needed, to offset the loss of a million-plus units over the past decade. And lastly, we need programs that assist homeless people in rebuilding their systems of social support, so that minor crises in the future do not send them right back onto the streets.

At base, the implementation of such policies and programs depends not only on well-crafted public and private initiatives and the availability of resources, but recalling Raban, on an honest rethinking of some of our fundamental societal values. Can we tolerate the gaps between the rich and the poor that grow wider each year? If not, we must renew a somewhat faded commitment to principles of social justice and redistribution. Part of this task involves reversing priorities that became so pervasive in the me-decade of the 1980s, that placed individual rights far above the obligations of community. Adhering to principles of social justice and community obligation would: (1) enable us to create resources for the wide variety of services and housing needed for homeless people to come inside, and (2) ensure that needed facilities for the homeless would be accepted and supported by a wide range of urban communities.

Ironically, the homeless themselves often show us how to take the first tentative steps toward meeting the obligations of community and redressing social injustice. For example, along a bike path that borders the beach between Santa Monica and Venice, a few homeless people have erected and maintain three or four small signs near some particularly sharp curves on the bike-path. On windy days, sand blown into the bike-path makes the curves especially hazardous for cyclists. A homeless woman, clutching a broom made of twigs, regularly sweeps sand off the slick corners, thereby making them safer for cyclists. By her selfless actions, this woman on the outside is making life easier for many on the inside. The effect of her altruism is to construct and maintain the beachfront community. She reminds us of the way people have confronted questions of social obligation for centuries: as a mixture of conscience and reciprocity.

A second example is contained in the signs held up at street corners and freeway on-ramps by homeless people seeking assistance. In simple, straightforward ways, they send messages about what life is like for those on the outside—about wartime experiences, children, joblessness and willingness to work, hunger and thirst. The signs give us a window through which to better understand the past and present of those who hold them, reminding us of their humanity, their individuality, their similarity to us. They also serve to initiate a long-overdue conversation, person to person, about social justice and the city, about what happens to society when fundamental needs are ignored and bonds of community are broken. These attempts at conversation often make us uncomfortable, bringing us abruptly face-to-face with unpleasant images and insistent demands. But these people are in most ways just like us. Do we have the courage to confront our discomfort, and to engage in conversations with the homeless?

Notes

Acknowledgment: Support for the research on which this chapter is based, provided by the National Science Foundation, Program in Geography and Regional Science, is gratefully acknowledged. Thanks are also due to Michael Dear, who reviewed an earlier draft and made suggestions that improved it immeasurably.

1. Maxene Johnson, Executive Director, Weingart Foundation, Los Angeles, as quoted in Jennifer Wolch and Michael Dear, *Malign Neglect: Homelessness in an American City* (San Francisco: Jossey Bass, 1993), p. 1.

2. Michael Sorkin, ed., *Variations on a Theme Park* (New York: Noonday Press, 1992), p. xii.

3. Joel Garreau, *Edge City* (New York: Doubleday, 1991), p.3.

4. The pedagogic importance of Los Angeles is cogently argued in Edward Soja, *Postmodern Geographies* (New York: Verso, 1989).

5. For an insightful discussion of the meanings of home and their changing patterns over time, see April Veness, "Home and Homelessness in the United States: Changing Ideals and Realities," in *Society and Space*, Vol. 10, 1992, pp. 445–468.

6. See Stacy Rowe and Jennifer Wolch, "Social Networks in Time and Space: Homeless Women in Skid Row, Los Angeles," *Annals of the Association of American Geographers,* Vol. 80, 1990, pp. 184–204; Jennifer Wolch and Stacy Rowe, "On the Streets: Mobility Paths of the Urban Homeless," *City and Society,* Vol. 6, 1992, pp. 115–140, and Jennifer Wolch, Afsaneh Rahimian and Paul Koegel, "Daily and Periodic Mobility Routines of the Urban Homeless," *Professional Geographer,* Vol. 45, 1993, pp. 159–169, for analyses of daily paths and mobility routines of homeless people.

7. For discussions of different sorts of homeless communities, see Carl Cohen and Jay Sokolovsky, *Old Men of the Bowery: Strategies for Survival Among the Homeless* (New York: Guilford, 1989), on bottle gangs in New York's Bowery; Marjorie Bard, *Shadow Women* (Kansas City: Sheed and Ward, 1990), on lone women in Los Angeles; Rowe and Wolch, op. cit., 1990, on sidewalk encampments in Skid Row, Los Angeles; Charles Hoch and Robert Slayton, *New Homeless and Old* (Philadelphia: Temple University Press, 1989), on Single Room Occupancy hotel communities; and L. G. Rivlin and J. E. Imbimbo, "Self-Help Efforts in a Squatter Community: Implications for Addressing Contemporary Homelessness," *American Journal of Community Psychology,* Vol. 17, 1989, pp. 705–728, on squatter camps in New York.

8. A recent survey of people living in street encampments in central Los Angeles found that the average size of encampments was around six persons. One half of survey respondents indicated that they lived in an encampment for economic reasons; another third reported that they did so because they felt secure and valued the sense of community provided by their camp mates. See Michael Cousineau, "A Profile of Urban Encampments in Central Los Angeles," Los Angeles: Los Angeles Coalition to End Homelessness, 1993.

9. Robin Law and Jennifer Wolch, "Homelessness and the Cities: Local Policies and Programs for the Homeless in Southern California," Los Angeles: Los Angeles Homelessness Project, University of Southern California, Working Paper #44, 1993, surveyed the almost 90 cities in Los Angeles County regarding their policies toward the homeless, finding a wide range of restrictive policing and zoning policies in force.

10. See Stacy Rowe, "Imagining the Victim: Documentary Photography and the American Urban Poor and Homeless," Los Angeles: Unpublished masters thesis, Department of Anthropology, University of Southern California, 1993; and Michael Dear and Brendan Gleeson, "Community Attitudes Toward the Homeless," *Urban Geography,* Vol. 12, 1991, pp. 155–176, for analyses of media images and accounts of homeless people, and the community attitudes revealed by these accounts.

11. For examples, Ellen Bassuk, "The Homelessness Problem," *Scientific American,* Vol. 251, 1984, pp. 40–45; Richard Lamb, ed., *The Homeless Mentally Ill* (Washington D.C.: American Psychiatric Association, 1984); Rodger Farr, Paul Koegel and Audrey Burnam, *A Study of Homelessness and Mental Illness in the Skid Row Area of Los Angeles* (Los Angeles: Los Angeles County Department of Mental Health, 1986); Peter Rossi, *Down and Out in America* (Chicago: University of Chicago Press, 1989); and James D. Wright, *Address Unknown* (New York: De Gruyter, 1989).

12. Examples include Jon Erickson and Charles Wilhelm, eds., *Housing and*

Homelessness (New Brunswick: Center for Urban Policy Research, 1986), Michael Dear and Jennifer Wolch, *Landscapes of Despair* (Princeton: Princeton University Press, 1987); Hoch and Slayton, op. cit.; Cohen and Sokolovsky, op. cit.; Irene Glasser, *More than Bread* (Tuscaloosa: University of Alabama Press, 1988); Stefanie Golden, *The Women Outside* (Berkeley: University of California Press, 1992); and Michael Lange, *Homelessness Amid Affluence* (New York: Praeger, 1991).

13. These sorts of studies include those focusing on substance abuse, criminal behavior, veteran's status, mental disability; for examples, see Marjorie J. Robertson and Milton Greenblatt, eds., *Homeless: A National Perspective* (New York: Plenum, 1992).

14. Louisa Stark, "Locational Conflict: The Service Provider's View," Paper presented at the Conference on Resolving Locational Conflict, Drachman Institute, University of Arizona, May 24, 1991.

15. Stefanie Golden, op. cit.

16. For discussions of Skid Row and its problems, see Farr, Koegel and Burnam, op. cit.; Hamilton, Rabinovitz and Alshuler, Inc., *The Changing Face of Misery* (Los Angeles: Los Angeles Community Redevelopment Agency, 1988); and Jennifer Wolch and Michael Dear, op. cit., 1993.

17. Garreau, op. cit.

18. An early study showing the relationships between socioeconomic status and community rejection is Michael Dear and S. Martin Taylor, *Not on Our Street* (London: Pion, 1982).

19. Law and Wolch, op. cit.

20. For analyses of the links between economic restructuring and homelessness, see Kim Hopper, Ezra Susser and Sarah Conover, "The Economics of Makeshift: Homelessness and Deinstitutionalization in New York City," *Urban Anthropology*, Vol. 14, 1985, pp. 183–236, and Jennifer Wolch and Robin Law, "Homelessness and Economic Restructuring," *Urban Geography*, Vol. 12, 1991, pp. 105–136.

21. Scott Lash and John Urry, *The End of Organized Capitalism* (Cambridge, United Kingdom: Polity Press, 1987).

22. For discussions of industrial restructuring, see Michael Storper and Richard Walker, *The Capitalist Imperative* (New York: Blackwell, 1989); Allen J. Scott, *Metropolis: From the Division of Labor to Urban Form* (Berkeley: University of California, 1988); Thierry Noyelle and T. M. Stanback, Jr., *The Economic Transformation of America* (Totowa, New Jersey: Rowman and Allanheld, 1984); Michael Piore and Charles Sabel, *The Second Industrial Divide: Possibilities for Prosperity* (New York, Basic Books, 1984); and Barry Bluestone and Bennett Harrison, *The Deindustrialization of America* (New York: Basic Books, 1982).

23. Barry Bluestone and Bennett Harrison, "The Growth of Low-Wage Employment, 1963–1986," *American Economic Review*, Vol. 78, 1988, pp. 124–128.

24. Susan Christopherson, "Labor Flexibility in the United States Service Economy and the Emerging Spatial Division of Labor," *Transactions, Institute of British Geographers*, Vol. 14, 1989, pp. 131–145.

25. Neil Smith, "New City, New Frontier: The Lower East Side as Wild, Wild West," in Michael Sorkin, ed., *Variations on a Theme Park* (New York: Noonday, 1992), p. 91.

26. Eligibility restrictions and bureaucratic disenfranchisement have forced large numbers of recipients off of the rolls. See Gary Blasi, "Litigation Strategies for Addressing Bureaucratic Disentitlement," *New York University Review of Law and Social Change,* Vol. 16, 1987–1988, pp. 591–603, and Woobae Lee, "Restructuring the Local Welfare State," Los Angeles: Unpublished doctoral dissertation, School of Urban and Regional Planning, University of Southern California, 1994.

27. Hector Tobar, "1 in 7 in County on Welfare Rolls," *Los Angeles Times,* March 3, 1992, sec A., p.1.

28. Woobae Lee, op. cit.

29. Kevin Phillips, *The Politics of Rich and Poor* (New York: Random House, 1990).

30. See Sheldon Danziger and Peter Gottschalk, eds., *Uneven Tides* (New York: Russell Sage, 1993).

31. This latter dynamic was all too evident when conflicts between African Americans, Latinos and Korean Americans boiled over in the wake of the April 29, 1992, Los Angeles uprising. These tensions reveal the stark contrasts between perspectives predicated on vastly different class standpoints and life-experiences linked to race, ethnicity and immigrant status, and are emphasized by the failure of the Rebuild LA effort, originally led by Peter Ueberroth.

32. Manuel Castells, "The Wild City," *Kapitalistate,* Vol. 4–5, 1976, pp. 2–30.

33. Mike Davis, as quoted on p. 60, Aaron Betsky, "Remaking LA," *Los Angeles Times Magazine,* December 13, 1992, pp. 58–64.

34. Jonathan Raban, *Soft City* (London: Harper Collins, 1974), p.9.

35. Michael Dear, "The Premature Demise of Postmodern Urbanism," *Cultural Anthropology,* Vol. 6, 1991, pp. 538–552.

36. Edward Soja, op. cit., p. 246.

37. Michael Dear, "In the City, Time Becomes Visible," in Allen J. Scott, Edward Soja and Richard Weinstein, eds., *Los Angeles: The Metropolis* (Berkeley: University of California, 1994).

6

Deviance and Human Nature

James Q. Wilson

The most controversial theory of crime and deviance is that differences among individuals may have some genetic basis. By a "genetic basis of deviance," I mean that the probability that a given individual who persistently breaks the ordinary criminal law will be influenced to a significant degree by dispositions that have been inherited. I wish to defend that theory, all the while acknowledging that it is not the whole story, not simply to convince you to believe it, but to persuade you to that there is nothing perverse, reactionary, or fatalistic about accepting the fact that most important forms of human behavior, including deviant forms, are influenced by our biological makeup and our evolutionary past. It is important that you be persuaded of this because it is impossible to carry on an intelligent discussion of crime prevention if for political or ideological reasons we rule out of consideration an entire set of possible causes.

Before proceeding, let me call your attention to certain key words or phrases in the proposition I have asserted. I am referring to people who "persistently" break the law by frequently stealing, fighting, or driving while drunk. Many of us will do these things once or twice; we cannot be said to have a disposition to do so unless we often act this way. The laws they break are the "ordinary criminal laws." By that I mean the rules, some variant of which exists in virtually every society, against theft, vandalism, and disorderly conduct. I omit rules defining what we call white-collar or political crimes, not because they are unimportant, but because the relationship between committing them and individual dispositions is not well understood. When I say that genetic factors "influence to a significant degree" the probability that someone will display a high degree of criminality, I do not mean that there is a "crime gene" or that genetic factors independently of all other considerations will determine people's behavior; I mean only that if you hold constant all observable environmental factors acting on two groups of people, one composed of frequent offenders and the other not, the differences in the rates of misconduct across the two groups will not be reduced to zero.

Before I summarize the evidence supporting my proposition, let me remark on how odd it is that anyone should even have to prove it. In every known society, past and present, there have always been certain individuals who have had a much higher average rate of law-breaking than anybody else. It makes no difference whether the society is primitive or industrialized, prosperous or poor, liberal or conservative, enlightened or traditional; essentially the same difference appears. This group consists of young males. If culture and environment were the sole causes of criminality, it is astonishing that nowhere can one find a culture in which young girls or old men commit crimes at a higher average rate than young men.

This example, convincing to some, is troubling to others. It immediately calls forth the rejoinder that gender is a socially determined phenomenon. In this view, if males are universally over-represented among those who commit crimes it is only because they are universally over-represented among those who wield social power and thus among those who create and perpetuate gender identifications. No doubt there is some truth to this. Evidence for it can be found in the fact that the biggest differences between the crime rates of men and women can be found in those societies where males enjoy the greatest social power. The male-female difference in Japan, for example, is much higher than it is in Sweden. But even in enlightened, emancipated Sweden, men are five times as likely to be arrested as are women. The cultural theory also predicts that as society expands opportunities for and reduces burdens on women they will become more criminal. Crime, in a truly free society, will become an equal opportunity employer. There is some evidence of a tendency in this direction. Between the 1930s and the 1980s, there was an increase in the United States in the proportion of arrests which were of women. But the increase was only from about 7 percent to about 15 percent, and most of that increase was concentrated in nonviolent property crimes such as larceny, fraud, and forgery. If one deletes from this historical comparison all petty property offenses, the female proportion of arrests rose over a half-century period by fewer than four percentage points.[1]

The male-female difference in reported crime rates parallels the male-female difference in aggression. As with crime, so also with aggression: some of the difference is under social and cultural control. But not all or even most of it. As Eleanor Maccoby and Carol Jacklin have reported, males are more aggressive than females in every society for which evidence is available and the difference appears very early in life before there is much differential socialization.[2] Julianne Imperato-McGinley and her colleagues studied males who were born with what appeared to be female genitalia and as a consequence were raised as if they were females. When they reached the age of puberty, these pseudo hermaphrodites underwent virilization: they developed male genitalia, deep voices, and male musculature. And they became more aggressive. A decade or more of being reared as girls did not prevent them from acting like boys after they went through puberty.[3] Daisy Schalling and her colleagues report that there is mounting evidence that this difference in aggressiveness is related to the effect of testosterone on the fetus; there is some evidence that the effect of testosterone continues after birth, such that different levels are associated with different degrees of aggressiveness.[4] Since I know that some people do not like to be told that women are different from men, even when the difference reflects well on women, I have gone to the trouble in the preceding few sentences of citing only women scholars as authorities for this view.

If women persistently differ from men in criminality and aggressiveness and do so beginning at a very early age, in every society, and even when the parents mistakenly think they are raising a girl when in fact they are raising a boy, then there are good grounds for thinking that whatever biological features explain male-female differences will also explain differences among males and among females. The evidence that this is the case comes from twin and adoption studies and it is remarkably consistent.

When we compare the criminal records of identical and fraternal twins, we find in virtually every study (and there have been over a dozen) that identical twins are much more alike in their criminality than fraternal twins. The studies work this way. We know that identical twins have identical genetic endowments and that fraternal twins are no more alike than any pair of siblings. If you find a member of a twin pair who has a criminal record, the chances of the other member also having a criminal record is about twice as high if the two are identical twins than if they are fraternal ones. Some may say that the greater similarity in behavior among identical twins arises out of the fact that their parents are more likely to treat them alike (and that the twins themselves wish to be more alike) than is the case with fraternal twins. But we have good reason for doubting that explanation. For one thing, studies of identical twins reared apart show similarities in personality that are about as great as what is found among twins reared together.[5]

For another, we know that boys put up for adoption have criminal records more like those of their biological parents than like those of the adoptive parents who have actually raised them. Again, one can imagine problems in making inferences from adoption studies; suppose, for example, that the adoption agencies tried to match boys from criminal fathers with similar adoptive fathers. But these are mostly imaginary problems. Adoption agencies don't engage in that kind of matching. One of the reasons is that they often do not know anything about the criminal records of the biological parents, either because the record is not available or because the parents have not yet started committing crimes. Adopted boys tend to have crime records more like those of their biological parents *even when those records began after the boy was adopted.* Furthermore, when two or more children of the same parents were adopted, their later criminality was correlated with that of their biological parents even when (as was usually the case) the children were raised in different adoptive homes.[6]

Taken together, twin and adoption studies provide hard-to-ignore evidence that some constitutional factors increase the probability that a person will be at risk for criminality. Moreover, the more crimes committed by a person's biological parents, the more crimes the offspring will commit, even though the child never knew his or her parents. The larger the number of parental crimes, the greater the probability that the offspring will be chronic or repeat offenders.[7]

These studies are consistent in finding a genetic effect on crime generally but inconsistent with respect to kinds of crimes. Some studies find a genetic cause for property crime but not violent crime, others for both property and violent crime.[8]

Twin and adoption studies permit us to make some estimate of the magnitude of the genetic effect. It is not trivial. Based on twin studies the heritability may be in excess of .6; based on adoption studies it is on the order of .3.[9]

We know more about the existence of a genetic effect than about its causes. Since criminals tend to have lower verbal intelligence quotients[10] and more impulsive and extroverted personalities than do non-criminals, it is likely that the heritable components of I.Q. and personality are the main explanatory variables. But it is one thing to believe this and another thing to show it by studies that rigorously measure the trait in advance of the appearance of criminal behavior. One study that has done this is quite suggestive. In England about one hundred boys were selected at random when they were age fifteen. Three of their physiological traits were measured: heart rate, skin conductance, and brain-wave activity. Ten years later the boys—now grown men—had their criminal records checked. Seventeen of the one hundred had one or more criminal convictions. Compared to those without such convictions, the criminal boys had earlier displayed a much lower heart rate, a much lower level of skin conductance, and a somewhat different pattern of EEG scores. These physiological traits have a high level of heritability. The authors of this study interpreted their findings to mean that boys likely to become adult criminals suffer from under-arousal: they do not respond to stimuli as readily as do non-criminals.[11] This has two implications. First, offenders are hard to train because they do not react strongly to rewards and punishments. Second, offenders need excitement because their own nervous system does not supply much them with much. Hard-to-train, easily distracted, hyperactive children are, of course, familiar to every school teacher. These are the boys most likely to become criminals.

A great deal of work is now underway trying to specify more exactly the biological mechanisms that make some people more likely to become offenders than others. Among the possibilities are these: Offenders seem to have lower levels of serotonin, a neurotransmitter, and lower levels of monoamine oxidase (MAO), and enzyme, than do non-offenders.[12] For example, incarcerated offenders who have abnormally low levels of serotonin are more likely than their fellow inmates to become arsonists and assaulters three years after their release from prison.[13] Moreover, sensation-seeking extroverts who have no criminal record also tend to have low levels of MAO and serotonin. The evidence with respect to hormones is conflicting, but the best studies suggest that aggressive boys have higher levels of testosterone.[14]

What Do Genetic Causes Imply?

Some of our best instincts lead us to rebel against accepting genetic explanations for behavior. We are optimists: we want to believe that everybody can overcome anything. We are egalitarians: we want to believe that there are no ineradicable differences among people. We are democrats: we want to believe that people who acquire power over other people will only do so if their claims are based on acquired merit and not inherited position.

There is little or nothing in genetic explanations for behavior that requires us to abandon any of these commendable instincts. The genetic influences on crime are not inexorable; as with all complex behaviors, criminality is the result of a complex interaction between biological endowments and social circumstances. For example, in Sweden a boy whose adoptive and biological parents are both non-criminal has a one in thirty chance of himself becoming a criminal. If only the adoptive parents are criminals, his chances rise to seven chances in a hundred. If only the biological parents are criminal, the chances increase to twelve in one hundred. If both biological and adoptive parents are criminal, the odds rise to forty chances in one hundred.[15] Obviously both environment and heredity are at work, though heredity seems to be doing more of the work.

Criminality is no different from other behaviors that have a heritable component. Consider learning. It is firmly established that certain learning disabilities have a genetic origin. But whether a person who is biologically at risk for school failure in fact fails will depend on whether his parents and teachers recognize the disability, understand that it is caused by biology and not laziness or stupidity, and provide special forms of instruction.

Crime is obviously a more complex case. A person who reads poorly does not break the law; a person who steals does. But in terms of treatment and prevention, the two cases are not that different. A boy who is at risk for delinquency because he is under-aroused, has a low verbal I.Q., and is hard to train because of poor response to stimuli or a very short time horizon can be taught in ways that emphasize achievement in nonverbal skills, closer controls on social activities, and motivation through the provision of immediate rewards.[16] It may turn out that it is precisely these aspects of preschool education that account for such reductions as have been observed in the later criminality of at-risk children. Understanding the biological bases of criminal dispositions strengthens, it does not weaken, the case for improving the care given to the very young. If environment were everything, we would expect to find more successes from rehabilitation programs aimed at teenagers and young adults. We find few such successes. This implies, I think, that the best time to intervene is when an at-risk child is only three or four years old and is still undergoing rapid neurological and behavioral changes.

In addition to early childhood helping programs, a better understanding of the neurochemical bases of the biological predisposition to aggressiveness and criminality will enable us to supply medical treatments. It is too early to speculate about what form such treatments might take, but in principle there is no reason, I think, to assume that enzyme or neurotransmitter deficiencies are beyond correction. We made far more progress in treating such mental illness as depression after we recognized their biochemical bases than we did by any form of purely verbal therapy.

Some people, worried about genetic explanations, urge us to concentrate on the social factors implicated in criminality. These factors, they argue, can be changed in ways that are easier and less threatening than is the case with any effort to cope with biology. They imply that nature is fixed, nurture is changeable and that paying attention to biology is "conservative," while focusing on the environment is "liberal."

There can be no doubt that environmental factors are deeply implicated in criminality. If they were not, we would not observe vast differences in the crime rates of different communities nor would we witness major changes in the crime rates of cities and nations. Crime rates change far faster than gene pools; crime rates differ across cultures more than do genetic endowments. We do not yet understand all the reasons why national crime rates change or why nations differ in those rates; in my view, we are witnessing highly complex and poorly understood gene-environment interactions.

But it is mistake to infer from the existence of cultural and historical factors in crime rates the lesson that culture or history can be altered easily or at a modest price in important human values. Cultures persist; that is why we call them "cultures" instead of fashions, tendencies, or choices. And as for history, recall Karl Marx's aphorism: history lies like a nightmare on the brains of the living. Let me be concrete. Suppose we were confident that a child's chances of becoming delinquent were increased by his suffering from both attention deficit disorder (or hyperactivity) and incompetent, neglectful parents. I believe that such suppositions are entirely reasonable. Over the next decade and making plausible assumptions about scientific progress, do you think we will be most likely to reduce the risks he faces by finding medical treatments for ADD or by inducing parents to be competent and caring? My bet is on the former. Making bad parents into good ones, and doing so by plan for tens of thousands of families, is, I think, beyond our power unless we are willing to take children away from their parents and raise them under state supervision. And doing the last requires us to believe that state-supplied child care would be tolerable and to accept the enormous costs in personal freedom and familial privacy that such an intervention would entail.

Family culture is almost beyond our reach. And culture more broadly defined is entirely beyond our reach. Suppose we were confident that crime rates have risen in almost every nation as a result of a vast expansion in the scope of human freedom and the celebration of individual autonomy. (Let me remind you that the rate of many kinds of property crime is as high in England and Europe as it is in the United States.)[17] People have more money, more mobility, and more choices and face fewer restraints from clan, tribe, village, or family. They do many things with these new opportunities: create new works of art, launch new social movements, start new industries—and commit more crimes. Only Japan seems to have achieved modernity without a great increase in criminality. What is there about this state of affairs that can be changed by plan? Nothing, I think. Nobody planned or caused it, nobody can un-plan or unmake it. America cannot become Japan; indeed, it is more likely that ultimately Japan will become America.

What uncompromising supporters of a purely environmental approach to crime prevention have in mind, of course, is neither remaking families nor reconstituting national cultures, but rather adopting conventional measures of social melioration—reducing unemployment and ending racism—or refashioning our social structure in ways that reduce inequalities. There is much to be said for doing all of these things, but large-scale crime prevention is not one of them. There is scarcely any evidence that rates of unemployment, the quality of intergroup relations, or the degree of economic inequality are strongly related to crime rates. And for a very good reason: high-rate, persistent offenders who, though few in number are responsible for most serious crime, emerge very early in life, long before they enter the labor market or become aware of economic inequalities.[18] Persistent, as opposed to episodic, criminality is more a cause of unemployment than it is an effect: high-rate offenders tend to be impulsive, restless, thrill-seeking young men who don't make good employees or who prefer the money to be earned from episodic criminality and drug sales than the same amount (or even more) to be earned from nine-to-five jobs.[19]

Let me be clear about my argument. I am not saying that all efforts to improve social conditions are useless or wrong-headed or that science is on the verge of inventing an anti-crime pill that will solve all of our problems at modest cost. I am only suggesting that one reason people have for taking the nurture side in the nature-nurture debate—that it is better, cheaper, easier, or nicer to change the environment—is probably wrong. Admitting biology onto our explanatory agenda is not the equivalent to saying that nothing can be done, that biology is destiny, or that every boy who wants to become an NFL linebacker should be given a prefrontal lobotomy.

But of course what the many relentless environmentalists are most concerned about, though of late they do not state it, is the problem of group differences. Carl Degler, in his informative history of Darwinian thought among American social scientists, shows quite clearly that beginning in the 1910s and continuing for a half century or more, there was a systematic and conscious effort to expunge biological explanations for human behavior because such explanations, it was thought, would provide ammunition to people who wished to subjugate women, ethnic groups, or other nations.[20] It is difficult not to sympathize with the motives behind these efforts. There are always tyrants and bigots around eager to seize on any evidence that might justify their repressive ambitions.

But despots will seize on *any* evidence, whether biological or cultural or environmental, and turn it to their grim purposes. Hitler preached racial superiority, and so he was ready to endorse selective breeding and race-based genocide. But Stalin preached environmental determinism, and so he was ready to use brainwashing, psychiatric reeducation, and class-based genocide. It makes no difference what scholars learn; tyrants will misuse and exploit it for their own ends. Hitler murdered Jews, Stalin murdered property owners. The understandable but wrong-headed effort of many American social scientists to rule out genetic explanations for behavior, whether it be intelligence, personality, or criminality, carries with it its own risks. If man is wholly the product of his environment, then he can be made into anything those who control his environment may desire. If every culture has equal merit, then any human practice can be justified provided only that it is culturally determined.[21]

Not only has the relentless environmentalism of the last few decades produced incomplete explanations of human behavior and provided a rationale for large investments in propaganda, it has also been based on an unfounded fear. That is the fear that somebody would show that group differences are both very large and wholly genetic, and so one group would come to be viewed as permanently inferior.

The Japanese, whether living in Japan or America, have lower rates of crime than do Caucasian Americans. They also have somewhat higher I.Q. scores.[22] Evidence may appear showing conclusively that a large part of these group differences involve genetic factors. Despite this, most Americans do not feel inferior to the Japanese or worry that the latter will oppress them. Caucasians look at the Japanese example and have, I think, two reactions. First, people should be judged as individuals. There are vastly larger differences among individuals within an ethnic group than there are between groups. Since individual differences are so great, it is sensible to judge people one at a time, as individuals. Second, even if group differences matter, there is no such thing as "group superiority." We may envy the lower Japanese crime rate and their higher scores on math tests, but the shared traits that may explain these differences have many complex consequences. For example, the lower Japanese crime rate may reflect a heritable tendency toward introversion, anxiety, and caution. But these traits may also lead to less individual risk-taking which, in turn, may mean lower levels of that kind of artistic, scientific, or economic creativity that requires solitary persons to pursue a private vision in the face of group hostility or indifference. Group differences that make the group "better" in some respects will make it "worse" in others.

Today, Caucasian Americans can live comfortably with Japanese-American group differences. But now suppose that the Japanese war lords had won the Second World War and occupied the United States, imposing on it a harsh regime in which all of the best positions in society were reserved for Japanese, and Caucasians were required to live apart, accept menial jobs, and suffer legal indignities. Suppose further that this state of affairs persisted for two hundred years, after which the Caucasians began to win back some of their lost freedoms. During that painful struggle and for many decades afterwards, I suspect that Caucasians would be highly sensitive to and quite upset about any claims, however scientific, about heritable differences between Japanese and Caucasians.

From this mental experiment one can easily understand why group differences can become a sore point in any society involving any groups that have been or are in a relationship of dominance and subordination one to the other. In the United States, the current sore point has to do with black-white differences in criminality, but in other societies it involves other groups and other characteristics.

How ought we to behave when science encounters sensitivities? The first requirement is to insist on scientific candor and precision. A candid and precise statement about black-white differences in criminality would, I think, go about as follows: There are large and real differences in the average rate of criminality between the two groups, and they cannot be explained away by reporting errors or system biases (though both exist).[23] We do not have adequate scientific grounds for asserting that these differences have a significant genetic component. We cannot test that possibility at all using twin studies since, by definition, the members of one pair of identical twins cannot be from different races. We can test that hypothesis by using a well-designed adoption study, but I know of none that has done so. We should remember that at one time, and for a long time, Irish Americans had a higher average crime rate than Yankee Americans. Some people thought that it was because the Irish were congenital drunkards and criminals. (Having an Irish-Catholic grandfather who was harassed by the Ku Klux Klan because of his presumed "racial" faults, I am quite sensitive to this charge.) Now we know that Irish-Yankee differences in criminality have largely disappeared. However, one cannot rule out the possibility that genetic factors can assist in explaining group differences, including black-white ones.

The second requirement is that we must reassert the proposition that individual differences will be vastly greater than group ones. A high-rate offender, black or white, may commit several hundred crimes a year; a law-abiding citizen, black or white, commits none. That difference dwarfs the average difference in criminality across the two racial groups, especially after controlling for age and gender.

The individualistic perspective on crime is not only scientifically correct, it is philosophically essential. To believe in a free and democratic society governed by the rule of law is to believe in the principle that all men are equal before the law and that no man should be punished or rewarded except for what he, as an individual, has done.

That commitment to individual justice and legal equality has of late come under heavy attack, however. Like the attack on genetic explanations for behavior in the 1920s, it is often well-intentioned. But however well-intentioned, it is misguided. That attack reflects one or more of two views: First, never give offense to the spokesmen of groups and, second, distribute the rewards of society explicitly on the basis of group claims. Scheduled to attend a recent conference were scholars who thought these factors were large and those who thought they were small or nonexistent. Panels were to discuss all of the scientific, ethical, and legal issues involved in this research. There was no reference to racial differences in the proposal. Peer reviewers had approved the plan. The grant had been approved. But when one psychiatrist criticized the idea on a television program, a few activists were moved to argue that even having a conference was "racist" and could lead to "genocide." Others said that it was an effort to "sedate" black youth. NIH withdrew the grant.[24]

Not only was this a politically motivated infringement of a serious and balanced scholarly endeavor, it gave credibility to complaints that were worse than wrong, they were silly. If there is any conspiracy to commit genocide or sedate youth or practice racism, it hardly needs a conference to do it or justify it. And if there is a conspiracy to deny to black children the benefits of a deeper knowledge of human behavior, then federal defunding of research in this area is the surest way to further it.

The second view that impedes clear thinking and decent action is that of group entitlements. To the extent that we judge existing social arrangements in terms of their disparate impact on groups and seek to remedy that impact by reallocating rewards on the basis of group membership, we call attention to group differences. Once such differences occupy front and center on the stage of public policy, there will be a debate on how to account for those differences and what, if anything, will reduce them. That debate will call forth the very issues that some advocates of group entitlements find most repugnant—nature versus nurture, evolution versus environment. Seeing society through the lens of group membership invites discussions of group characteristics, a discussion that I think is both scientifically unrewarding and emotionally unsettling.

One of the great strengths of the traditional commitment to individual merit and legal equality is that it relegates these issues to a subordinate position or makes them irrelevant altogether. When we judge an applicant for a job, a grant, or scholarship on the basis of his or her merits, we are reaffirming the truth that individual differences are more important than group ones and that recognizing individual merit is more important than explaining it. We may well wish to take note of group differences in accessing the rewards and privileges of society as a way of detecting the existence of racism or gender bias, but correcting such bias as exists is best done by enforcing fair and open procedures that individuals can take advantage of in proportion to their individual qualities.

It has taken three centuries at least for civilized people to accept science as a way of distinguishing between fact and prejudice and liberalism as a principle for giving dignity and autonomy to the individual. It would be a great tragedy and a great irony, if, in our desire to avoid offending anyone, in our preoccupation with removing the last vestiges of group prejudice, we—the liberalizing effects of free scientific inquiry—reinstated group rights over individual rights.

Notes

1. James Q. Wilson and Richard J. Herrnstein, *Crime and Human Nature* (New York: Simon and Schuster, 1985), pp. 104–112.

2. Eleanor E. Maccoby and Carol N. Jacklin, *The Psychology of Sex Differences* (Stanford: Stanford University Press, 1974), pp. 242–243.

3. Julianne Imperato-McGinley, R. E. Peterson, T. Gauthier, and E. Strula, "Androgens and the Evolution of Male-Gender Identity Among Male Pseudo Hermaphrodites with 5α-reductase Deficiency," *New England Journal of Medicine,* Vol. 300, 1979, pp. 1233–1237.

4. Dan Olweus, Dan, Ake Mattsson, Daisy Schalling, and Hans Low, "Circulating Testosterone Levels and Aggression in Adolescent Males: A Causal Analysis, *Psychosomatic Medicine,* Vol. 50, 1988, pp. 261–272; Felton Earls, "Sex Differences in Psychiatric Differences: Origins and Developmental Influences," *Psychiatric Developments,* Vol. 1, 1987, pp. 1–23.

5. Wilson and Herrnstein, op. cit., ch. 3; Thomas J. Bouchard, et al., "Sources of Human Psychological Differences: The Minnesota Study of Twins Reared Apart," *Science,* Vol. 250, 1990, pp. 223–228.

6. Sarnoff A. Mednick and Elizabeth S. Kandel, "Congenital Determinants of Violence," *Bulletin of the American Academy of psychiatry and the Law,* Vol. 16, 1988, pp. 105–106.

7. Ibid., p. 105.

8. Sarnoff A. Mednick, W.F. Gabrielli, and B. Hutchings, "Genetic Factors in the Etiology of Criminal Behavior," in S. A. Mednick, et al., eds., *The Causes of Crime: New Biological Approaches* (Cambridge: Cambridge University Press, 1987); and Mednick and Kandel, Ibid., in their study of Danish adoptees found no genetic effect on violent crime; C. R. Cloninger and I. I. Gottesman, "Genetic and Environmental Factors in Antisocial Behavior Disorders," in S. A. Mednick, et al., eds., Ibid., in their study of Danish twins found a genetic contribution to both. After a review of the evidence, a panel of the National Research Council concluded that genetic effects on violent crime were "weak," see Albert J. Reiss and Jeffrey A. Roth, *Understanding and Preventing Violence* (Washington, D.C.: National Academy Press, 1993), pp. 116–118.

9. Gregory Carey, "Twin Imitation for Antisocial Behavior: Implications for Genetic and Family Environment Research," *Journal of Abnormal Psychology,* Vol. 101, 1992, p. 22.

10. Terrie E. Moffitt and Phil A. Silva, "I.Q. and Delinquency: A Direct Test of the Differential Detection Hypothesis," *Journal of Abnormal Psychology,* 1988.

11. Adrian Raine, Peter H. Venables, and Mark Williams, "Relationships Between Central and Autonomic Measures of Arousal at Age 15 Years and

Criminality at Age 24 Years," *Archives of General Psychiatry*, Vol. 47, 1990, pp. 1003–1007.

12. Gerald L. Brown, et al., "Aggression in Humans Correlates with Cerebrospinal Fluid Amine Metabolites," *Psychiatry Research*, Vol. 1, 1979, pp. 131–139; Robert D. Coursey, M. S. Buchsbaum, and D. L. Murphy, "Psychological Characteristics of Subjects Identified by Platelet MAO Activity and Evoked Potentials as Biologically At Risk for Psycho Pathology," *Journal of Abnormal Psychology*, Vol. 89, 1980, pp. 151–164; Gerald L. Brown and Markku Linnoila, "CSF Serotonin Metabolite (5-HIAA) Studies in Depression, Impulsivity, and Violence," *Journal of Clinical Psychiatry*, Vol. 51, 1990, pp. 31–43; Daisy Schalling, G. Edman, M. Asberg, and L. Oreland, "Platelet MAO Activity Associated with Impulsivity and Aggression," *Personality and Individual Differences*, Vol. 9, 1988, pp. 597–605.

13. Matti Virkunnen, et al., "Relationship of Psycho-Biological Variables to Recidivism in Violent Offenders and Impulsive Fire Setters," *Archives of General Psychiatry*, Vol. 46, 1989, pp. 600–603.

14. Olweus, et al., op. cit.

15. C. R. Cloninger, S. Sigvardsson, M. Bohman, and A.-L. Knorring, "Predisposition to Petty Criminality in Swedish Adoptees: A Cross-Fostering Analysis of Gene-Environment Interaction," *Archives of General Psychiatry*, Vol. 39, 1982, pp. 1242–1247; Adrian Raine and Jennifer J. Dunkin, "The Genetic and Psycho-Physiological Basis of Antisocial Behavior: Implications for Counseling and Therapy," *Journal of Counseling and Development*, Vol. 68, 1990, p. 638.

16. Cf. Raine and Dunkin, Ibid.

17. "International Crime Rates," *BJS Special Report*, Bureau of Justice Statistics, May, 1988.

18. For a summary of the evidence, see Wilson and Herrnstein, op. cit., 1985, ch. 11, 12. For a recent demonstration of the stability of criminality over time, see Daniel S. Nagin, "The Stability of the Link Between Individual Differences at Childhood and Adult Criminality," Unpublished Paper, Carnegie-Mellon University, 1991.

19. James Q. Wilson and Allan Abrahamse, "Does Crime Pay?" *Justice Quarterly*, Vol. 9, No. 3, 1992, pp. 359–377.

20. Carl N. Degler, *In Search of Human Nature* (New York: Oxford University Press, 1991).

21. I explore this issue in James Q. Wilson, *The Moral Sense* (New York: Free Press, 1993).

22. On crime, see Wilson and Herrnstein, op. cit., 1985, pp. 452–457, and David H. Bayley, "Learning About Crime: The Japanese Experience," *Public Interest*, Vol. 44, 1976, pp. 55–68; on I.Q., see Richard Lynn and J. Dziobon, "On the Intelligence of the Japanese and Other Mongoloid Peoples," *Personality and Individual Differences*, Vol. 1, 1987, pp. 95–96.

23. From a review, see Wilson and Herrnstein, Ibid., ch. 18.

24. David L. Wheeler, "U. of Md. Conference that Critics Charge Might Foster Racism Loses NIH Support," *Chronicle of Higher Education*, September 2, 1992, p. A6; Philip J. Hilts, "U.S. Puts Halt to Talks Tying Genes to Crime," *New York Times*, September 5, 1992, p. 1.

7

Mothers at Risk:
The War on
Poor Women and Children

Alexis Jetter, Annelise Orleck, and Diana Taylor

We had this meeting with the Ways and Means Committee, so I'm standing here, and around this table was nothing but white men, silk suits, silk ties, silk socks, shiny black loafers and shoes. And I said, "You don't have money for welfare?" Senator Young burst out laughing at me. The tears started rolling down my face because I was totally sincere. I said: "Did you laugh at me?" And he said, "No, no, no." And I said, "You're the one I will never forget. I'll be back. You just inspired me to come back."

—Ruby Duncan, "Redefining Motherhood" Conference
Dartmouth College, May 15, 1993

We've all been fed the images: In a filthy tenement, the dull-eyed woman with a swollen abdomen reaches for a crack pipe and poisons her unborn child. Her mythic sister, the gold-toothed welfare queen, drives her Cadillac through the slums, craftily calculating how much money each new child will net her.

Why do these depictions resonate so powerfully in the national psyche? Because they are encoded with both conscious and inchoate fears about a social order in flux: Women having children without fathers to control them. The underclass, particularly people of color, multiplying without restraint, clamoring for bites of the middle-class taxpayer's hard-won sliver of the pie. The assumptions underlying these stereotypes are so familiar they hardly need to be verbalized: Everyone on welfare cheats. Everyone on welfare is black, promiscuous and lazy. And welfare doesn't work anyway, for the poor are genetically doomed to low test scores and high rates of criminality. This essay will challenge these myths and suggest political and economic reasons for their holding power.

Poor, single mothers are at risk for the same reasons that other poor people and people of color are. Many are stranded in decaying communities with high rates of violence, inadequate schools, and few opportunities for employment. As mothers, they have an additional burden: They must care for their children in a society that pays women less than men and provides almost no affordable daycare. Yet we are bent on seeing them as the agents rather than the victims of their predicament.

This essay explores the interplay between stereotyping of poor mothers and the real problems they face: high infant mortality, drug addiction, an irrational welfare system, and uncontrolled toxic dumping in their communities. We will argue that racism, sexism and fear of the poor not only exacerbate the dilemmas faced by these mothers and their children; they blind us to possible solutions. Poor mothers, the real experts on poverty, are kept out of all decision-making processes. Still, in communities across the nation, they are offering their own programs for breaking the cycle of poverty. They have exposed the deficiencies of a drug-treatment policy that consigns them and their children to the miseries of addiction. And they are leading the fight against the wholesale poisoning of their communities. Unless policymakers, scholars and politicians begin to listen to poor women's insights and solicit their participation, we will never make headway against these problems. And poor mothers and children will remain under assault and at risk in our society.

Let's look at the images and the story they tell about poverty, about responsibility, about victimization. This is how the story goes. She—the addict or the welfare queen—is the problem. Poverty results from personal choices; it is either self-inflicted or a cynical hoax. Thus, poverty is personalized and, specifically, feminized. Such a woman must be controlled or she will be a danger to everyone—society, her offspring, herself. She lurks in an underworld that educational psychologist Valerie Polakow calls "a zone of deviance and moral suspicion."[1] The addict and the welfare queen are both represented as transgressing the limits of legality and decency, suggesting that it is somehow criminal to be poor. Their dependence, either on addictive substances or on the munificence of the government, is a "bad habit" that borders on criminality. These women, the story goes, have a choice. They could "just say no" to poverty through either moral improvement or good hard work. But they don't.

For "they," the poor, are not like us. The discourse on poverty is an exercise in othering. Rather than explore poverty in terms of what creates it—lack of economic resources and opportunities—dominant ideology attributes poverty to a lack of moral character. By labeling them deviant, we define ourselves as responsible, hard-working, and morally righteous. The have-nots threaten the haves, depriving or cheating us out of everything from our hard-earned tax dollars to our sense of decency and well-being. The poor assault the social body both morally and financially: They rip off the system and add an enormous burden of welfare and health costs to already strained state and federal governments. Resources are available, the story goes, and although most poor women and children have only limited access to quality medical care, decent jobs, affordable housing, safe schools, or adequate child care, we blame them for not improving their lot.

The Roots of Othering

Negative images of the poor are so deeply rooted in our country's collective unconscious that they seem to have always been there. Indeed, the tendency to displace the problems generated by an unjust society onto marginalized women and children predates the founding of this nation. Political, economic and moral conflicts have long been played out directly upon the bodies of women. Poor mothers, especially single mothers, have been particularly demonized and attacked. In early seventeenth-century Somerset, England, where many early U.S. settlers came from, women were publicly stripped and whipped for having children outside of wedlock.[2] Some were taken from public marketplace to marketplace and beaten "til their bodies be bluddy." Others were placed in stocks to be publicly shamed, or locked up in local jails for short punitive terms.

Class, then as now, was the moral dividing line. While the rich routinely used wet nurses to extend their child-bearing years, parish officials fined poor, unmarried woman whose breast milk dried up and who had to turn to the parish for help. Such "unmotherly" women were deemed a burden on the community's land-owning ratepayers, who would have to pay for a wet nurse.[3] And because any child born in the parish was entitled to poor relief until it reached the age of seven, parish officials would go to great lengths to stop such children from being born within parish borders. Once a "base-born" pregnancy was detected, officials would load the mother—even if she was in the throes of labor—into a wagon and attempt to run her into a neighboring parish. Then, as now, the community felt some responsibility to care for marginalized women and children. But poor unmarried mothers were, by definition, "unworthy"—a label that approximates what we might now call the "undeserving poor." And so any help proffered to them was preceded by physical torture and public humiliation.[4]

The history of slavery and indentured servitude in the U.S. reveals another assumption about poor women and their children, the flip side of their depiction as social parasites: The idea that poor women and their children were destined for hard labor, a fate that superseded any mother-child bonds. This view was institutionalized in seventeenth-century Virginia laws that guaranteed male masters ownership of the children of both female slaves and female indentured servants. Such laws not only broke up families; they provided economic incentives for rape. Women servants and their children were seen under the law as property whose only value lay in their labor or breeding potential.[5]

As recently as the early twentieth century, women industrial workers had no illusions about the sanctity of their motherhood. They understood full well that romanticized notions about femininity and the mother-child bond were never intended to describe members of their class. As capmaker and labor leader Rose Schneiderman told a gathering of women garment workers in 1912: "I think the working woman ought to wake up to the truth of her situation. All this talk about women's charm does not mean working women. Working women are expected to work and [re]produce their kind, so that they, too, may work until they die of some industrial disease."[6]

The view that poor women and their children were meant for work dovetailed neatly with the American political mythology of rugged individualism and class fluidity. Late nineteenth-century Social Darwinists believed that, in a land of unparalleled opportunity, only the morally, culturally or intellectually flawed remained poor. Intractable poverty had to be explained in that way to sustain the core myth of U.S. political culture: unlimited class mobility. The only alternative would have been to confront the raw power dynamics of nineteenth-century industrial capitalism, which created far more economic losers than winners. And then, as now, a majority of those losers were women and their children.

Poor women in the U.S. have long been trapped in a vise. Caught in the myth of class mobility and the ideology of individualism, they were failures if they asked for public assistance. Judged by middle-class standards of feminine respectability and "good" motherhood, they were "deviant" if they did not have a man to support them and so had to work to feed and clothe their children. No matter what a poor mother did, her predicament was her own fault.

During the twentieth century, this gender-class vise was further tightened by the introduction of race into virtually all discussions of U.S. poverty. The sometimes spoken, often unspoken assumption that all poor Americans were people of color further distanced the poor "them" from what was conceived as a middle-class, white, patriarchal "us."[7] As historian Jacqueline Jones has argued, government pronouncements and news coverage of the last half century created the false but enduring impression that "all black people were poor and that all white people were middle class." Certainly, the last 50 years have seen the emergence of entrenched pockets of urban poverty occupied disproportionately by people of color. But the focus on inner-city destitution has obscured a central reality: Most poor Americans—and most welfare recipients—are white, and many of them live in small towns and rural areas. "Ultimately," Jones concludes, "the ethnic, regional, and cultural diversity of the poor population became lost in an exclusive focus—more rhetorical than substantive—on black people in the urban North. Americans in a postemancipation society thus continue to view poverty through a lens ground and polished in the days of slavery."[8]

From Welfare Queens to "Bridefare" and Orphanages: Back to the Future

At the end of the 1960s, when welfare rolls expanded to record levels, these gender, class and race prejudices combined to create a new national demon: the welfare queen, driving her pink Cadillac through the ghetto, taking public moneys out of the hands of "the truly deserving." In the aftermath of Lyndon Johnson's landslide victory in the 1964 presidential election, Republican governors from California's Ronald Reagan to New York's Nelson Rockefeller searched for a way to effectively attack him. The issue they settled on would become one of most powerful tools in the Republican Party arsenal. Turning Johnson's "War on Poverty" on its head, they declared a war on "welfare cheaters," whom they tied to every social ill from rising taxes to government corruption. Campaigning for governor of California in 1966, Ronald Reagan sounded the battle cry: "From now on, the able-bodied will work for their keep ... There'll be no more pay for play."[9]

During the past 30 years, Republicans and Democrats alike have played the welfare card. No political scapegoat has proven more reliable. The ubiquitous welfare cheat has helped catapult numerous local politicians to the national stage—most recently, House Speaker Newt Gingrich; most infamously, former Ku Klux Klan leader David Duke. In the 1990s, a new generation of politicians has discovered the political benefits of bashing poor women. In 1993, Wisconsin's Republican governor Tommy Thompson propelled himself into the national spotlight by calling for a "two years and out" welfare cap. In 1994, reflecting the New Victorianism—or perhaps the New Somersetism— Thompson inaugurated "Bridefare," which offered higher welfare benefits to teenage mothers who marry.[10]

Bridefare's success is yet to be measured. Critics point to two key drawbacks: one in two marriages ends in divorce; and most divorced fathers fail to pay child support after the first year. Since more than two-thirds of the men involved in teenage pregnancies are between the ages of 20 and 50, some experts suggest a different solution: Hold these men accountable for having sex with minors and for their failure to use birth control, which they as adults can legally purchase. Lost in this debate is the fact that only about 8 percent of welfare mothers are teen mothers, and less than 2 percent are under the age of 18. And the central moral question remains: Why should poor mothers be forced to marry— whether it's a butcher, a banker, or a batterer—when rich people aren't?

But by 1995, Thompson's programs looked downright indulgent. The Republican Contract With America called for ending welfare altogether for unmarried mothers under 18, without providing jobs or daycare, quashing any opportunity they might have to attend classes or learn job skills. The low intelligence of the poor makes such investments unwise, said conservative theorist Charles Murray, who correlated race, class and intelligence in his controversial 1994 best-seller, *The Bell Curve*. "There is nothing they can learn," he said, "that will repay the cost of teaching."[11] And if these mothers can't cut it, Murray suggested, why not simply place their children in orphanages? That idea was gleefully snatched and popularized by Newt Gingrich. "This city is going to be a mean, tough, hard city, and everybody better understand that coming down the road," he exulted.[12] And getting tough on welfare—that is, on poor women and children—quickly became the national pastime.

That get-tough posturing so consumed Democrats after their November 1994 electoral debacle that, while they condemned Gingrich and Murray's proposals, their own alternatives were scarcely less mean-spirited. Donna Shalala, Clinton's secretary of Health and Human Services, called Murray's solutions "Swiftian"[13] and "un-American." But she promptly unveiled a proposal that took a leaf out of his book. If able-bodied welfare mothers refuse to work, Shalala told Congress, they should lose their welfare benefits and their children, who would be placed in foster care, group homes or put up for adoption.[14]

The war over welfare has become one of the defining battles of U.S. politics during the last third of the twentieth century. Why should this issue, involving such a small slice of the federal pie, resonate so powerfully? Because the word "welfare" invokes unspoken anxieties about gender, race and class. The campaign for welfare reform has been waged at a particularly ugly crossroads in the American psyche where racism and sexism meet this culture's deep-seated fear of both women and the poor. Cracking down on welfare is about exerting control over recalcitrant and disobedient women. Indeed, Newt Gingrich, the leading proponent of the bully-poor-women-to-appear-manly school of politics, admits that he found parallels to his own life in the 1986 pop-psychology book, "Men Who Hate Women."[15]

Small wonder, then, that welfare recipients frequently call the system, "The Man." Johnnie Tillmon, the first chairwoman of the National Welfare Rights Organization, described the Aid to Families with Dependent Children program this way:

> The truth is that AFDC is like a supersexist marriage. You trade in *a* man for *the* man. But you can't divorce him if he treats you bad. He can divorce you, of course, cut you off anytime he wants. But in that case, *he* keeps the kids, not you. *The* man runs everything. In ordinary marriage, sex is supposed to be for your husband. On AFDC, you're not supposed to have any sex at all. You give up control of your body. It's a condition of aid. You may even have to agree to get your tubes tied so you can never have more children just to avoid being cut off welfare. *The* man, the welfare system, controls your money. He tells you what to buy, what not to buy, where to buy it, and how much things costs. If things—rent, for instance— really cost more than he says they do, it's just too bad for you.[16]

Once a woman is on welfare, the devil is in the details. For, while most of the rhetoric about welfare is on C-Span, the actual control over poor mothers is played out in the micro-management of state welfare programs, where women are humiliated and harassed to reinforce their already degraded position. As welfare-rights activist and author Theresa Funiciello has illustrated in *Tyranny of Kindness,* the confidence and dignity of poor mothers is systematically destroyed by a torrent of regulations that benefit no one. Women are forced to wait endlessly for welfare appointments. [NO MATTER WHAT TIME YOUR APPOINTMENT IS, IF YOU ARE NOT HERE BY 8:30 AM YOU WILL NOT BE SEEN, said a sign in one New York City welfare office]. They must do without any food or support for the first month until caseworkers can prove that they are poor. They are forced to line up with other welfare mothers outside the office of their children's school principal—in full view of their embarrassed children—to get a special letter proving that their children are not truants.[17] These exercises in humiliation serve more to break the spirits of women on welfare than to monitor eligibility, consumption or academic achievement. But that's precisely what they are designed to do.

For today's opinion-shapers are in agreement: Let's bring back shame. "A stronger sense of shame about illegitimacy and divorce would do more than any tax cut, or any new government program, to improve the life circumstances of children," says David Blankenhorn, author of a new book called *Fatherless America.* Conservatives in Congress say they want to restore the social stigma associated with "illegitimacy." That means, of course, that they want to stigmatize women who choose to bear and raise children even if the fathers disappear. This is nothing new. The notion that men are the answer, that forcing women to find and marry the fathers of their children will solve the social ills associated with poverty, is nothing more than a rehashing of Daniel Patrick Moynihan's infamous 1965 report on Black families, which implied that there is something pathological about the prevalence of female-headed families in the African-American community. Such fear-mongering politics fuel irrational policy measures that institutionalize social anxiety over loss of control and power. And public humiliation of poor women continues in the tradition of the Puritanical settlers. But, instead of stripping and beating them in the marketplace, our system dramatizes their "deviance" through degrading images and public policy.

The gendered nature of the welfare system is based on and reproduces the old stereotypes of male activity, independence and trustworthiness as opposed to female passivity, dependency, and untrustworthiness. In fact the welfare system creates the very women it claims to try to reform. The rules of welfare force women to "cheat" because they cannot support themselves and their children on their meager monthly checks. It makes women dependent by forcing them to submit to a hostile and irrational system. Given the lack of adequate jobs, medical and child care, they cannot afford to give up welfare in order to work. The system, not the women, destroys "family values" by making it impossible for men and women to live together. Thus, women are forced into the position of passivity and deviance supported by the stereotypes. They internalize prevalent images of themselves as useless, ugly and diseased. Welfare recipient Martha Maxwell recalled of her time on assistance: "I felt like I had a dreaded contagious disease. The bacteria from the disease spread slowly; it took the strength from my muscles causing me to feel ugly; it took the hope from my heart causing me to feel discouraged; it took ideas from my mind causing me to feel useless." [18]

AIDS Babies, Pregnant Addicts,
and The Culture of Character in America

The metaphor of disease becomes explicit in popular imagery of the HIV-positive drug-addicted mother. No one is more stigmatized in our society. That despised persona first entered the public consciousness in the mid 1980s, when crack-addicted and HIV-positive infants began to appear in the intensive-care wards of major urban hospitals. The epidemic was real—and its human costs terrible. But hysteria quickly replaced a sober examination of its root causes: homelessness, lack of drug treatment facilities for pregnant women, inadequate prenatal care, and economic destitution. Instead, "Children of the Damned" headlines screamed from New York City tabloids, and politicians started drafting laws to arrest pregnant addicts and charge them with crimes against their unborn babies.

New state laws were passed forcing physicians to report mothers of drug exposed infants. In 1991-92, 60 women were prosecuted for taking drugs during their pregnancies. In some states, babies born to addicts are forcefully removed from their mothers and placed in foster care. These punitive measures bespeak the gendered formulation of the problem and the solution. "At the heart of these punitive approaches," says Lynn Paltrow, senior staff attorney for the American Civil Liberties Union's Reproductive Freedom Project, "is the willingness to view pregnancy as a hostile relationship between two separate parties: the "innocent" fetus and the "bad woman" who does not care if she hurts the fetus. The fetus becomes the focus of attention while the problems the pregnant woman faces in getting help are ignored or neglected, as if somehow they had no effect on the fetus."[19]

The maternal body has long been the container of social fears and fantasies. The HIV-positive, crack-addicted mother furnished a powerful amalgam of older imagery: the female body as dangerous and diseased; and poor women as immoral and irresponsible. The addict functions simultaneously as the bad, promiscuous woman and the bad mother. She literally gives birth to disease, either through addicted or HIV-infected children. And, just as the welfare queen is seen as a "cheater" who sucks dry scarce social resources, so the pregnant addict or addicted mother is seen as undermining the health of the social body.

Such stereotyping eases greatly the work of conservative theorists, who prefer to neatly leap over the structural and economic bases of poverty to concentrate instead on the poverty of "culture" and "character." They attribute America's growing underclass to the breakdown of the family, the proliferation of drugs, and the failure of impoverished mothers to take advantage of existing resources. Social and economic inequality are not the problem, the Right maintains. People are the problem, especially poor people who lack "family values" and "character." As the 1990s began, George F. Will declared that "the reduction of poverty requires restoration of the moral environment in which poor people live."[20] Dr. Louis Sullivan, Secretary of Health and Human Services under George Bush, argued that today's alarming social statistics reflect a "poverty of parenting."[21] He cautioned that "we must not allow ... infancy and childhood to become merely a nostalgic relic of the past celebrated only in sentimental greeting cards [...] We must wage an all-out, unified effort for a culture of character in America." For pregnant addicts, "the bottom line is simple," according to Dr. Robert Harmon, former head of the Public Health Service's Health Resources and Services Administration. "Act responsibly, say 'No' to tobacco, drugs and alcohol during pregnancy, and seek care early and often."[22]

But seeking care is easier said than done. According to health analysts, it is obstetricians who have decided to "just say no" to poor women because of low Medicaid reimbursements and soaring malpractice costs. And few physicians are willing to work in poor urban or rural areas. As a result, health workers say, clinics for poor women are often so overcrowded and doctors so overwhelmed that the level of care isn't worth the trip. Judy Gallagher, executive director of the Bronx Prenatal Consortium, says that most women she works with want time to ask doctors about nutrition, health care, stress and exercise. "But," she says, "there simply isn't time to do that if one doctor has to see 40 women in one morning session." Geographic inaccessibility, in combination with impersonal and hasty care, make these programs unappealing to women. Says Gallagher: "We're asking women, many of whom are already seven to eight months pregnant, to climb down four flights of stairs with two other kids in tow, get on the subway, transfer to a bus, and wait several hours—all to be seen for five minutes to have her blood pressure checked and her belly pulled. We get into blaming women for not doing this, when any sensible person would question its usefulness."[23]

The problem with "poverty of character" stories is that they confuse cause with effect and obscure the underlying problem. Poverty is the symptom. Institutionalized sexism, racism and classism are the disease. Poor mothers, and especially mothers of color, are particularly vulnerable in the U.S. because they are positioned precisely where these three deadly *isms* intersect.

The surest way to debunk these stereotypes is to examine the realities for poor mothers, pregnant addicts, women on welfare, and the institutional agencies designed to serve them. Poor women are not reaping the benefits of increased welfare expenditures. A recent report issued by the Department of Health and Human Services points out that the cost of managing organizations such as food stamps, Medicaid and Aid to Families with Dependent Children (AFDC), is rising much faster than the number of people these programs assist. Indeed, the number of adult women on welfare has remained steady for the past 20 years. While critics of the "welfare state" blame poor women for ever-expanding welfare costs, it is actually those in mid-level management who are benefiting.[24]

But they are not safe either, for the programs designed to help poor women are themselves at risk. They are on-again, off-again operations that are always under budget attack. In 1991, New York City was forced to close all nine of its infant health centers, which target neighborhoods with Third World survival rates—all for lack of $7.1 million, the cost of

20 minutes of Operation Desert Storm. The centers were eventually reopened, but with only half the necessary funding. In 1995, they are once again faced with closure. Their vulnerability undermines their effectiveness and speaks volumes about government's lack of commitment to poor children.[25]

But the problem goes beyond dollars and cents. For it is true that many low-income women are not taking advantage of programs designed to assist them. One recent study estimated that only 60 percent of pregnant women and infants eligible for Medicaid are actually enrolled in the program. Why? Conservatives blame the "poverty of parenting." Health care providers blame a lack of community education and outreach, inaccessible clinics that are located far from the population they are meant to serve and programs that are insensitive to the needs and concerns of poor mothers.

Ava Ledford, a veteran social worker in Charleston, South Carolina, notes that backwater towns often have no doctors. Women who can scrape up the money or who are eligible for Medicare are forced to drive several hours for care. "You're talking about a two-hour ride and a three-hour wait," says Ledford. "That's an all-day situation." With a shortage of doctors in inner cities and rural areas, poor pregnant women who call for appointments in their first trimester are often told they have to wait until the second.[26]

The problems affecting the quality of medical care offered to "responsible" low-income women escalate when it comes to women who are "at risk." For the most castigated of all poor mothers—pregnant addicts—drug treatment and prenatal care are almost non-existent. While estimates of infants exposed prenatally to drugs range from 350,000 to 739,000 per year, the federal Institute of Medicine estimates that only 30,000 pregnant women who need drug treatment get it. In one New York City study, 87 percent of treatment centers turned down callers who said they were pregnant, on Medicaid and addicted to crack. Some residential treatment centers will take a new mother but only if she agrees to put her baby into foster care.[27]

Forcing a woman to choose between her baby and recovery is not only cruel, it eliminates her motivation for kicking drugs in the first place. Many pregnant addicts fighting to get into treatment are driven by a fear that child welfare agencies will take their babies from them, as they do in many U.S. cities when the child's urine shows traces of drugs. This same fear prevents pregnant addicts from seeking prenatal care.

But traditional drug treatment holds another danger. Methadone, the substitute drug most frequently administered in drug-treatment programs, powerfully addicts the unborn child. And while methadone blocks a craving for heroin, it does nothing for crack or cocaine addiction. When pregnant women take methadone and cocaine in combination, the result can be lethal. An infant exposed in utero to a combination of methadone and cocaine has an 8 percent chance of dying before its first birthday—a dramatically higher risk than if it were exposed to heroin or cocaine alone.[28]

So what can be done? "We know what works," says Gallagher. "The issue is that there isn't the political will to do what needs to be done. There is no mystery, really. It's as clear as the nose on your face why they don't get prenatal care." Health care workers say what's needed is community education, accessible and timely care, access to alternative drug treatments, continuing support to stay clean and to help addicted mothers develop their parenting skills. And finally, says Dr. Machelle Allen, Bellevue Hospital Ob-Gyn, more attention needs to be paid to treatment and less to judgmental attitudes: "Society condones brokers on Wall Street who use cocaine and condemns women in the ghetto who use crack. It's very telling about gender, economics and class. What's good for the goose is not good for the gander."[29]

But programs for poor mothers are a low priority, in part because there is far more political capital to be accrued through attacking poor women than by caring for them. The war on poverty becomes the war on poor women and children. And, since poor women, addicts and children often lack political advocates, few object when the programs designed to help them are cut.

Turning the "poverty of parenting" rhetoric on its head, we will examine the strength of character and parenting that marks some real women challenging the sexist and racist underpinnings of poverty in the U.S. today. What happens when women fight back? Here are two stories that haven't made it into the national discourse, that we believe should. For when poor women try to play by the rules, be "responsible" mothers—and in the process demand their rights—they cease being good mothers, and are assaulted politically, physically and discursively.

Ruby Duncan and Operation Nevada:
When Welfare Rights Hit the Las Vegas Strip

In December 1970, Nevada terminated or dramatically cut the benefits of more than half the welfare recipients in Nevada. It was a calculated political move meant to up the ante in the newly declared war on poor women and their children. State welfare administrator George Miller sent letters to the chief welfare officials of the 49 other states, trumpeting his determination to fight the growing menace of welfare cheating.[30]

A 20-year battle over welfare ensued in the state of Nevada that illustrates the hypocrisy behind many of the attempts to paint poor mothers as cheaters. The story of "welfare reform" in Nevada also makes starkly clear what happens when poor women are thrown off welfare for perceived or real transgressions: Their children go hungry.

It is worthwhile to step back here the definition of cheating that Nevada employed, for it sheds light on the economic and political realities underlying the rhetoric about welfare queens. In 1970, a statewide investigation had found that many Nevada women receiving Aid to Families With Dependent Children (AFDC) were working to supplement their welfare checks and had not reported this extra income to the state. Had they done so, their welfare checks would have been reduced accordingly.

At that point Nevada's monthly allotment averaged $144 per month for a family of four, the lowest benefits outside the deep South. There were no Food Stamps available in Nevada to stretch this meager check, just a surplus food program to which poor families could apply for moldy cheese, dried milk, Spam, Kool-Aid and rancid peanut butter. The only thing poor Nevada mothers could find in any abundance was low-paid, under-the-table work as maids and kitchen aides in Reno and Las Vegas hotels. This was the kind of work that many of Nevada's "welfare cheats" had been doing to provide better food for their children, along with clothes and shoes for school.

The Nevada case shatters one of the most pervasive myths about welfare mothers: that they don't work. The women cut from the rolls had never done anything but work. Almost all of them had grown up as fieldhands, "cotton choppers" and "bean-pickers" in the Mississippi Delta. The introduction of mechanized cotton pickers in the years after World War II created massive agricultural layoffs across the South. Women from the Delta were recruited to Las Vegas by agents for new hotels and casinos who were looking for politically docile and hard-working laborers.[31]

After cotton-field wages, the salaries offered by the hotels seemed fantastic. But even women inured to heavy labor found their new jobs backbreaking. Maids were expected to clean up to 50 rooms a day, kitchen aides to carry huge pots of water and cooking oil. Many of them ended up on welfare because their bodies broke down. But, because benefits were not enough to live on, they returned to the Strip to work off the books.

Nevada had an unusually high percentage of working welfare recipients, who worked intermittently to supplement their welfare checks. But the reality of welfare mothers working was by no means unique to Nevada. One early 1970s study of 5,000 AFDC recipients found that two thirds had been employed for some time during the previous three years. Still, most of them had been able to find only seasonal, unskilled and low-paid work—what economists have dubbed "the secondary market."[32] Poor education, inadequate child care, and limited job opportunities in poor areas made it difficult for most welfare recipients to find full-time jobs with health coverage for their children. And even when they did find work, they couldn't report it, because they would lose benefits and medical coverage.

The case of Nevada perfectly illustrates how states have shaped welfare policies with an eye toward creating a surplus labor supply for the secondary market. Nevada was the last state in the union to initiate an AFDC program, and it did not do so until 1955, when new hotels were rising daily from the desert floor. The state intentionally kept welfare grants low to insure a supply of cheap labor to the hotels. This was typical of the development of state welfare systems. Throughout the 1950s and 1960s, benefit levels and eligibility requirements fluctuated along with the demand of local secondary job markets for laborers.

In Nevada, as in the South, welfare payments were used to support workers during the seasons when there were no secondary-market jobs. That ensured that the poor mothers and people of color who usually filled those jobs would remain in the area even when jobs are scarce. Sudden tightening of eligibility requirements were used to drive wages down by flooding the market with desperate poor mothers who competed for a limited number of low-paying jobs. The fact that many Nevada legislators engaged in shaping welfare policies also owned stock in the state's big hotels forces the question of who benefits most from welfare.[33]

Nevada offers an unusually clear example of how a system that exploits and profits from the labor of poor women then manipulates popular perceptions so that those same women—rather than employers, legislators, and state functionaries—appear to be the parasites. Nevada, which depends on revenue from legalized gambling and prostitution, decided to lead the national charge against poor welfare mothers who "cheated" taxpayers. One Reno case-worker even admonished poor mothers to get "honest" jobs, reminding them that prostitution was legal in northern Nevada.

Ruby Duncan, then a 38-year-old former cotton picker, hotel maid and mother of seven, decided to expose the hypocrisy of the state's campaign. She led a protest that cast the conflict as one between mothers trying to feed their children and a state that based its economy on feeding the human appetite for vice. In March, 1971, 3,000 women and children marched on the Las Vegas casinos. They told reporters about families living on little more than $1,000 per year in the shadow of the Strip, where gamblers spent $600 million annually. Powerful images appeared the next day in *The Washington Post* and other national dailies: children standing by crap tables holding signs that said "Don't Gamble with Human Lives" and "Nevada Starves Children."[34] The Las Vegas mothers won more than headlines; they won their case in federal court.

In March 1971, a federal district judge ordered all families who had been cut reinstated with full benefits and condemned the state for "running roughshod over the rights of the poor."

But this victory was only the beginning of a 20-year pitched battle with state officials, many of whom exhibited deep personal animosity toward Ruby Duncan and other welfare mother-activists. One of the mothers' supporters, former state Assemblywoman Renee Diamond, said state officials were outraged that "these women just did not know their place." In Nevada, as in other states, the welfare system was used as a punitive tool to demand subservience of poor mothers. Blocked by the federal court from cutting women and children off the welfare rolls, state legislators and welfare officials found other ways to punish Nevada's poor women for their new-found militancy. They cut state and county food surplus food distribution. The women swiftly responded with another high-profile media campaign. They brought hundreds of children to an "eat-in" at the lavish Stardust Hotel. The demonstration, which was covered by CBS Evening News, dramatized the real result of state welfare cutbacks: hungry children. [35]

The mothers gradually developed a detailed analysis of what was wrong with the welfare system that was supposed to be serving them. They proposed an alternative: Let poor mothers become welfare administrators. Aided by Legal Services lawyers and middle-class women from the League of Women Voters, the welfare mothers moved from protest to institution-building. By lobbying, grantwriting and politicking within their county and state Democratic Parties, this group of African-American welfare mothers dragged Nevada—kicking and screaming—into the twentieth century, forcing it for the first time to accept federal programs aimed at insuring adequate nutrition and medical care for poor women and their children.

Between 1970 and 1976, Nevada's poor mothers brought to their state such federal programs as Food Stamps, Early Periodic Screening and Diagnostic Testing, and the Women and Infant Children nutritional supplement program. And they created jobs for themselves administering those programs. Says Mary Wesley: "I finally found a field I knew something about, poor people and kids." The mothers of West Las Vegas, not social service professionals, brought into their own community its first medical clinic, day care center, senior citizen housing, library, and job-training program to help women get off welfare. Operating out of an abandoned hotel, they created an alternative social welfare program they called Operation Life, administered by poor women for poor women. And as they grew more sophisticated in their understanding of federal and private grants, they created a community development corporation that drew millions of dollars into their community for construction and rehabilitation of low-income housing.

Duncan and the Las Vegas mothers argued that poor women were the real experts on poverty. As mothers, they knew best what their children needed. As former hotel workers, they knew which Las Vegas jobs paid well enough for them to be able to support their families, and they knew what training they needed to get those jobs. And they knew what their community lacked in terms of housing, medical care, senior citizen and youth services. Insisting that "we can do it and do it better," they attracted the allies and funding necessary to build and administer a community-run alternative to the traditional welfare bureaucracy, and they sustained it for almost 20 years. In 1976, President-elect Jimmy Carter hailed the women as examples to those who sought to break the cycle of welfare dependency.[36]

Then, during his 1980 campaign for the Presidency, Ronald Reagan reintroduced "the welfare queen" into national political discourse. Within a year, doors in Washington were no longer open to the likes of Ruby Duncan. Operation Life held on through the Reagan years, largely because Duncan and her allies had become very effective at raising private money to supplement federal funding. But, the former welfare mothers of West Las Vegas had to battle an array of powerful forces bent on seeing them fail. Some local politicians resented the women's encroachment on the lucrative turf of federal grant moneys. Powerful casino owners held lingering grudges against the women for the Strip march and the eat-ins which had been a public relations nightmare for the gambling industry. And several key state officials bitterly resented the women for outmaneuvering them in the courts and the media.

But their most powerful enemy was the Reagan-Bush department of Health and Human Services. And it is perhaps not coincidental that the women's old nemesis, George Miller, was handed the job of regional director during those years. Rather than reward the women for developing programs that both got them off welfare and provided much-needed services for the poor of Las Vegas, agency officials announced that the women must give up their jobs at Operation Life or lose federal funding for Operation Life programs. Ill-educated welfare mothers were not qualified, they argued, to manage social welfare programs. Hire credentialed professionals, the women were told, or federal funds will be discontinued. Former welfare mothers, who had pulled themselves off the dole by creating jobs for themselves as health-clinic, day-care, job-training and teen recreation center workers, were faced with little choice but to go back on welfare. "We were smart enough to bring those programs in," Mary Wesley says bitterly, "but then when they came we were too dumb to run them." Many of the women stayed on as volunteers because the program meant so much to them. But Wesley now calls that a mistake:

If I had it to do again I wouldn't volunteer. I would insist that they train us, give us an education ... That really hurt me when the government took the programs away ... I don't think Ruby knew that we wouldn't be able to keep those jobs after the money came in. Because that's what we would always tell ourselves: Soon we're going to be off of welfare, as soon as the money comes in ... That's why we worked so hard, worked our heads off and our hearts off—because we wanted to get off welfare.[37]

Mary Wesley, Ruby Duncan and many other Operation Life activists ultimately succeeded in doing for their children what they were unable to do for themselves: break the cycle of poverty and dependency. Duncan's children attended college. One is a lawyer and leading figure in Nevada politics. Another is a well-regarded union official in Washington, D.C. Wesley determined to put all of her children through college and was able to do just that. She also boasts of seven grandchildren on elementary and high school honor rolls. And now, with her eldest grandchild about to enter college, Wesley plans to accompany him, finally giving to herself what she had hoped welfare rights activism would bring her—education, meaningful work, a way out of poverty.

But for every one of these success stories there is a horror story. Without hope or anchor, sense of community in West Las Vegas began to dissolve in the late 1980s. Like so many poor neighborhoods in this country, the Westside came to be plagued by gangs who have made drug sales and drive-by shootings a regular feature of neighborhood life. One former member of Operation Life is now raising her grandchildren because her daughter—the children's mother—was shot to death through an open window while lying on the living room couch with her seven-month-old son.

In the furious aftermath of the first Rodney King verdicts, riots swept the poor African-American quarters of Las Vegas: Many commercial buildings were burned to the ground. But the Operation Life building and the senior citizen housing project it created, called Ruby Duncan Manor, were not touched. Ruby Duncan, still a symbol of hope in the community, was called out to calm the waters. She will never forget the way that even the roughest gang leaders came up and hugged her because, she says, they remember what she did for their mothers.

Some of the blame for this violence surely belongs with those public officials who destroyed a program that was working because they were angered by the women's audacity, and because there are many bureaucrats, experts, and politicians who have great investment in keeping the welfare system as it is. Welfare, as Theresa Funiciello has shown, is big business. So is poverty. "Countless middle-class people were making money, building careers, becoming powerful, and otherwise benefiting from poverty," Funiciello writes. "The poverty industry once again submitted its own interests for that of poor people and got away with it. To me, that's welfare fraud." [38]

These days, when Duncan speaks to young women who she hopes will pick up where she left off, she tells them: "Don't throw anyone away. Every gang kid on the corner has got a mother or a sister in the community. Make them see what they owe those that raised them." To hear Duncan tell it, the Westside suffers from neither "poverty of parenting" nor "poverty of values." It is being ravaged by plain old poverty of resources, poverty of hope, and the despair and frustration of young people who have been taught by society that they are expendable. The mothers of the Westside, unlike their pseudo-scientific adversaries who are now so much in vogue, don't see any of their children as expendable.

Still, no matter what welfare mothers like these have been able to accomplish, there are those who will dismiss them—they were, after all, on the public dole. End of conversation. We certainly do not agree. But to illustrate most vividly and dramatically the way that racism, sexism and disdain for the poor puts low-income mothers at risk, we would like to close with a brief examination of a woman who—even Newt Gingrich would concede—did everything "right." Patsy Ruth Oliver of Texarkana, Texas, was a poor, Black, divorced single mother who paid a terrible price for buying into the idea of a culture of character, for believing that she could give her family "what all other Americans have the right to enjoy" if she just worked hard enough. [39]

Oliver was determined to break out of the projects in Texarkana, to give her children a yard to play in, her mother a spacious home and herself a flower garden to tend. Chasing her vision of the American dream, the divorced mother of five worked three jobs: assembling detonators at an army munitions plant; waitressing at the army officers' club, and babysitting for the colonel's children. Her labors paid for a small, brick home in the only middle-class neighborhood open to Blacks in segregated Texarkana in 1968: Carver Terrace. After she moved her family into their new home, Oliver continued working to improve her situation. She studied at night to become a nurse so that she could get herself out of the munitions plant job, from which she bore numerous scars on her hands where explosives had blown away pieces of skin. "I never knew," said Oliver, "if my kids were going to greet me as a corpse or a person. But I took that chance to keep my children fed."

For a short time, it seemed that all the hard work was finally beginning to pay off for Oliver, and that life was getting better. "But then," she recalled, "my American dream turned into an American nightmare, because we were trapped in a prison of poisons." Carver Terrace had been built atop the remains of an old wood-treatment plant, and creosote had soaked through the soil and groundwater. The foul-smelling gunk bubbled up in their lawns after a rain, accumulated in their sinks and bathtubs, and its heavy odor rode on the evening breeze when they sat on their front porches to escape the fumes inside. "We had moved on top of a time bomb," said Oliver. "It was ticking but we couldn't hear it." Slowly, the residents started to get sick. It started with headaches and nosebleeds, spread to skin inflammations and respiratory problems, and gradually took a deadlier toll: cancer, kidney failure, aneurysms and heart attacks. "It got to the point where the hearse was here more often than Yellow Cabs," said Oliver.

In 1980, state health officials warned the families not to let their children play outdoors, but would not tell them why. It took four more years for Carver Terrace, which one reporter described as little more than a landscaped toxic-waste dump, to be declared a Superfund site. Even then the government refused to buy residents out of their homes so that they could move somewhere else. With their life savings sunk into poisonous homes, the people of Carver Terrace who, to use Bill Clinton's words, had "worked hard and played by the rules," were stuck. Oliver led her community in a decade of protest marches, lobbying, and coalition-building before the U.S. government finally agreed to buy their unsellable houses and release the residents of Carver Terrace from what Oliver called "the toxic Twilight Zone." The battle turned Oliver, in her words, "from a hysterical housewife to a committed environmentalist." She achieved national recognition for her work, becoming one of the first black women on the board of a Big Ten environmental organization and a delegate to the Earth Summit in Rio De Janiero.

Still, not until the summer of 1993 was Patsy Ruth Oliver finally able to move her family out of Carver Terrace. Similar cases of creosote poisoning in white Texas communities had resulted in much quicker government action. The cost of the delay for Oliver and her family was devastating. Twenty-five years of living on a toxic-waste dump had taken a terrible toll. Oliver's mother died of cancer less than a year before they were bought out. Oliver's daughter Stephanie died suddenly in 1993 of a brain aneurysm. She was 40 years old. And the night before the U.S. Army Corps of Engineers finally arrived to tear down her boarded-up old house, Patsy Ruth Oliver died in her sleep.

There are many lessons to be learned from the life and death of this hard-working family of Texas women. What stands out first is the cavalier attitude of the developers who built Texarkana's only decent housing for African-Americans on an abandoned industrial site. They knew that there would be plenty of applicants. "A lot of black people were desperate for decent houses," Oliver recalled. "They lived in dustbowls, shotgun houses, and shantytowns. They lived in the projects." They wanted out and they had nowhere else to go. The developers did not know quite how toxic the site was when they first began marketing those homes. But it is also true that no one questioned whether it was hazardous to build there because, given the people it was intended for, no one cared. "It never crossed my mind," says developer Sam Weisman. "I was just looking for a piece of property to develop for the colored in the area."

Secondly, the response to community complaints about health problems exemplified the blindness and deafness of government and the courts to people of color. When 64 Carver Terrace families filed suit against the Pittsburgh-based Koppers Company, which had owned the old treatment plant and knew about the dump, Koppers paid expert witnesses to testify that genes and diet , not creosote, doomed African-Americans to kidney failure, hypertension and diabetes. The largely white jury ruled against the plaintiffs. They received not a penny of compensation to help cover medical costs.[40]

A similar disregard was evident in EPA responses to community complaints. The EPA studied Carver Terrace for more than a decade. But, while it analyzed water, soil and air, it never tested the residents themselves, or even asked them what their experiences had been. Investigators wore white "moon suits," rubber gas masks and disposable gloves to inspect the soil that scantily clad children played in every day. And still they assured the residents that the neighborhood was safe for human habitation. When Carver Terrace residents finally located a Fish and Wildlife Service report done on their community, they found that the EPA was using a cancer-risk standard for them that was 30 times more lax than usual. "Is it not possible," an incredulous field supervisor for the Fish and Wildlife Service asked the EPA's regional director, "that ... the true cancer risk might exceed or closely approach the levels encountered at Love Canal?"[41] The only difference between Love Canal and Carver Terrace, Oliver noted, was the color of the victims' skin.

All this brings us back to the idea that drug-addicted mothers are responsible for poisoning their children and forces the question: Who is really poisoning the poor children of the U.S.? Who considers them expendable and who is really guarding their interests? The fact is that 60 percent of African-American and Latino communities in the U.S., and more than 50 percent of Native American communities, are located near one or more uncontrolled toxic-waste dumps. How simple for us to blame individual mothers when poor children are being poisoned by corporate greed in communities across the U.S.—and when it is mothers like Patsy Ruth Oliver who are forcing corporations and government agencies to deal with the wholesale poisoning of their children. Together, poor mothers of color and white mothers have created a new kind of environmental movement that foregrounds the issues of race, class and gender. As Oliver used to say: "Toxics do not discriminate. They are equal-opportunity killers." But who gets exposed to toxics, and how corporate and government officials respond to those endangered by toxic waste, has everything to do with race, class and gender. [42]

Poor women across racial divides are coming together to challenge the stereotypes and redirect demands of responsibility towards those who are literally poisoning their communities. In 1979, Lois Gibbs, a white, working-class mother organized the residents of Love Canal, New York, to fight for a buyout of their contaminated homes. Thirteen years after she helped found a new, grassroots, mother-led environmental movement, she told an interviewer how foolish she felt for believing in the culture of character argument:

> I did everything right. I prided myself on being a responsible mother, and then I found out about the dump. What really got me involved was the realization that my community and my family, specifically, could be sacrificed and that people who were in charge, whether they were health authorities or local government or state or federal authorities, all knew that my family was being poisoned and they still made a conscious decision that it was OK because of the cost involved in cleaning it up. That just totally flipped me out because I had always believed what was in your high school civics books ... I just got really outraged. Nobody can say that there is a price on my children's heads. Nobody can say that based on cost-benefit analysis ... that they can justify the killing, the murdering of people. [43]

From the deadly, tree-lined streets of Carver Terrace to the so-called "Cancer Alley" along the Gulf Coast and the "cancer cluster" of Fowler, California, [44] poor and working-class mothers—many of them African-American, Native American and Latina—are demanding that the rest of the nation acknowledge the poisoning of their children. One of the bases of the movement is central California, where uncontrolled use of pesticides has resulted in frighteningly high rates of birth defects and cancer among Mexican-American farmworker families. Marta Salinas, a leading activist in the fight against pesticides, says she decided to speak out after she found her six-year-old daughter making a coffin for her Barbie doll. The girl told her that Barbie had died of cancer and then asked: "My birthday wish is that I want clean water and dirt ... If I die of cancer I want to die with my kittens so I can die hugging them." [45]

Recounting what happened to the families of Patsy Ruth Oliver, Lois Gibbs and Marta Salinas, it is hard to imagine that there has not been a national outcry against such widescale poisoning. But neither the epidemic of cancer among Latino children in California's agricultural valleys, nor the untimely deaths of hard-working, African-American mothers and daughters like the Olivers of Texarkana, have received coverage comparable to the far-less prevalent problem of addicted mothers. Similarly, the campaigns by poor and working-class mothers to save their children from toxic contamination have received far less attention than the alleged irresponsibility of welfare mothers. (And it's worth noting that the same politicians who want to slash welfare plan to rewrite the Superfund law to let corporate polluters off the hook.)

The continued dominance of stereotypical images of poor mothers contributes to the invisibility of real mothers and their children. This obscures their needs, blinding us to potential solutions to the complex problems that put them and their children at risk. These days when Ruby Duncan sees a group of teenagers hanging out in one of the vacant lots that dominate the landscape of the Westside of Las Vegas, she raises her hand to her chest. "It makes my heart hurt," she says, "to think of all the potential that's there that might never go anyplace. We could reach them, if we still had our programs."

Maybe one way to lower the risk faced by poor mothers and their children is so simple that we can't quite believe it. Ask poor mothers what their children need. Let them suggest ways to fill those needs. And invite them to share the task of administering a new generation of social programs that get at the real sources of poverty, disease and despair in our nation. Of course, they're already working full-time at the task that we both expect of them and condemn them for: they're raising their children.

Notes

1. Valerie Polakow, *Lives on the Edge: Single Mothers and Their Children in the Other America* (Chicago: University of Chicago Press, 1993), p. 5.

2. We are indebted to Lynda Boose of the Dartmouth College English Department for giving us the following information:

(1614): Touching the base-born child of Margaret Adhames of Compton Dandow, of which she confesses that Thomas Ingham, Gent., is the father. Inprimis we order that Thomas Inham shall from the birth of the said child pay viii pence weekly to the overseers and churchwardens, until the child be bound apprentice ...

We do order that the mother shall keep the child without charging the said parish ... and if she refuse then she shall pay the viii pence weekly to the overseers ...

Item. We do lastly order that the said Margaret Addames (sic) shall be conveyed by the tithyng man of Compton to the town of Pensford on the next market day after the publication of this our order; and be stripped from the shoulders to the waist and whipped about the market for an example to others to avoid the like offense. And as there is no certain ground or vehement presumption to inflict the same punished on the reputed father, we therefore leave him to the judgment of the ordinary in that case to deal with him.

Somerset Quarter Sessions Records for 1614–1615. General Sessions held at Ivelchester, Rev. E. H. Bates, ed., Published by Somerset Records Society, Vol. 23, 1907.

3. On June 24, 1609, the court ordered a mother to pay for the "sustaination and myintenance of a child born in the parish of Kylmenton. The mother to pay iii d. a week, she having vnmotherly and most vunnaturally stopped and dried upp her brestes, by means whereof she has no milk to norishe, cherishe and breede vpp her said childe, but must be suckled and brought vpp by another Woman." The reputed father was to pay 9d. a week. From Somerset Quarter Session Rolls, op. cit.

4. We are indebted to Carl Estabrook of the Dartmouth College History Department for his explanation of the parish system in early modern England and how it treated poor unmarried mothers and their "base-born" children.

5. Warren M. Billings, "The Law of Servants and Slaves in Seventeenth-Century Virginia" in *Virginia Magazine of History and Biography*, Vol. 99, January 1991, pp. 45–62. We want to thank A. Alexander Bontemps of the Dartmouth College History Department for helping us locate this information.

6. "Senators Vs. Working Women," Transcript of Speeches at Cooper Union Mass Meeting, April 22, 1912, in the Leonora O'Reilly Papers, Tamiment Library, New York University.

7. Michael Katz, *The Undeserving Poor* (New York: Pantheon Books, 1989) is one of the most articulate and wide-ranging examinations of the practical consequences of a poverty discourse that sees the poor as "them" rather than "us."

8. Jacqueline Jones, *The Dispossessed: America's Underclasses from the Civil War to the Present* (New York: Basic Books, 1992), pp. 2–3.

9. *The New York Times*, September 10, 1966, p. 13.

10. "Governor Get-A-Job Tommy Thompson," by Norman Atkins, *The New York Times Magazine*, January 15, 1995, pp. 22–25. See also "Women Alone Will Bear Brunt of Welfare Cuts," Carol Delaney, Assistant Professor of Anthropology, Stanford University, in a Letter to the Editor, *The New York Times*, January 26, 1995, p. A20.

11. "The Most Dangerous Conservative," by Jason DeParle, *The New York Times Magazine*, October 9, 1994, pp. 48–79.

12. "Excerpts From House Speaker's Address to the G.O.P. National Committee," *The New York Times*, January 21, 1995, p. 8.

13. In his bitterly ironic pamphlet, *A Modest Proposal* (1729), Jonathan Swift suggested that the children of the poor be sold as food for the tables of the rich. Shalala noted that Murray's solution lacked Swift's satiric intent.

14. "Clinton Has Tough Plan on Refusal to Work," by Robert Pear, *The New York Times*, January 11, 1995.

15. "The Warrior," by Howard Fineman, *Newsweek*, January 9, 1995, pp. 28–34.

16. Johnnie Tillmon, "Welfare is a Women's Issue," Liberation News Service (no. 415), February 26, 1972, reprinted in Rosalyn Baxandall, Linda Gordon, and

Susan Reverby, eds., *America's Working Women* (New York: Vintage Books, 1976).

17. Theresa Funiciello, *Tyranny of Kindness: Dismantling the Welfare System to End Poverty In America* (New York: The Atlantic Monthly Press, 1993).

18. Ibid., Quoted by Funiciello, p. 3.

19. Lynn Paltrow, "Perspectives of a Reproductive Rights Attorney," in *The Future of Children*, Vol. 1, No. 1, Spring 1991, a publication of the Center for the Future of Children, The David and Lucile Packard Foundation, Los Altos, California.

20. George F. Will, "A Moral Environment for the Poor," *The Washington Post*, May 30, 1991. Quoted in Polakow's *Lives on the Edge*, op. cit., p. 46.

21. Remarks By Louis Sullivan, M.D., Secretary of Health and Human Services at the 38th National Health Forum, Washington, D.C., March 12, 1991.

22. Telephone Interview by Alexis Jetter with Robert Harmon, July 10, 1991.

23. Telephone Interview by Alexis Jetter with Judy Gallagher, June 24, 1991.

24. Jennifer Dixon, "Report Finds an Expensive Bureaucracy," *The Valley News*, (Associated Press), January 3, 1994, p. 1.

25. New York City Department of Health Memo, "DOH Efforts to Reduce Infant Mortality"; See also *The New York Times*, July 10, 1991, "Weapons Against Poverty Face Heavy Cuts," and Alexis Jetter interview with Karla Damus, Epidemiologist, New York City Department of Health, June 24, 1991.

26. Telephone Interview by Alexis Jetter with Ava Ledford, June 21, 1991.

27. "Bias Seen Against Pregnant Addicts," *The New York Times*, July 20, 1990.

28. From Damus Interview, op. cit.

29. Interview by Alexis Jetter with Dr. Machelle Allen, June 25, 1991, New York City.

30. *The New York Times*, January 12 and March 21, 1971.

31. For the most complete analysis of the African-American migration north after World War II, see discussion of the dramatic rise of African-American unemployment, the displacement of Southern agricultural workers, and discriminatory Southern relief policies after World War II in Nicholas Lemann, *The Promised Land* (New York: Alfred A. Knopf, 1991); Mimi Abramovitz in *Regulating the Lives of Women* (Boston: South End Press, 1988), pp. 320–321; and Richard Cloward and Frances Fox Piven in *Poor People's Movements: Why They Succeed and How They Fail* (New York: Vintage Books, 1979), pp. 267–269.

32. Joe R. Feagin, *Subordinating the Poor: Welfare and American Beliefs* (Englewood Cliffs, New Jersey: Prentice Hall, 1975).

33. Joe R. Feagin, op cit., Interview by Annelise Orleck and Alexis Jetter with Maya Miller, Carson City, Nevada, September 2–3, 1992.

34. *The New York Times*, March 21, 1971; *The Washington Post*, March 7 and 14, 1971.

35. Interview by Annelise Orleck and Alexis Jetter with Mary Wesley, Sept. 7, 1992, Las Vegas, Nevada; Orleck and Jetter interview with Renee Diamond, Sept. 5, 1992, Las Vegas, Nevada; Orleck and Jetter interview with Jack Anderson, former Legal Services attorney, Sept. 9, 1992, Oakland, California.

36. Anderson interview; Orleck and Jetter interviews with Ruby Duncan, Sept. 5–7, 1992, Las Vegas, Nevada.

37. Interviews with Duncan, Wesley, Anderson and Miller, op. cit.

38. Funiciello, op. cit., p. xix.

39. All quotes from Patsy Ruth Oliver taken from an interview by Alexis Jetter, July 27, 1993, Texarkana, Texas; see also Alexis Jetter "The Poisoning of A Dream," *Vogue Magazine,* November 1993.

40. Interview by Alexis Jetter with Dr. C. Jack Smith, M.D., July 26, 1993, in Texarkana, Texas. Smith, a specialist in nephrology and dialysis, was lawyer for Jeter Stegers, a former Carver Terrace resident who suffered kidney failure and sued Koppers corporation for his medical costs.

41. Robert Short, Field Supervisor, U.S. Department of the Interior, Fish and Wildlife Service, in letter to Robert Layton, Regional Director, Environmental Protection Agency, Dallas, Texas, November 3, 1988. Appended to the "Preliminary Natural Resources Survey for the Koppers Co. Superfund Site, Texarkana, Texas," U.S. Department of the Interior, Fish and Wildlife Service, 1988.

42. See Robert Bullard, *Confronting Environmental Racism: Voices from the Grassroots* (Boston, South End Press, 1993).

43. Interview by Giovanna Di Chiro for "Defining Environmental Justice: Women's Voices and Grassroots Politics," *Socialist Review,* Vol. 22, No. 4, October–December 1992.

44. Ann Misch, "Better Living Through Chemistry?" *Utne Reader,* November–December 1993, pp. 90–92.

45. Di Chiro, op. cit.

8

Successful Early Interventions for Children at High Risk for Failure in School

Craig T. Ramey and Sharon Landesman Ramey

Nearly one fourth of American children are growing up in poverty:[1] an almost incomprehensible fact in the midst of a country filled with tremendous resources and opportunities. Black, Hispanic, and other minority children are at elevated risk for growing up in poverty. Almost 50 percent of black children, for example, will live in a home where the income is below the federal poverty line in 1989. In our land of plenty, approximately 13,000,000 children lack the minimal resources essential to support normal growth and development. Poverty is defined by more than a family's income: *Poverty is synonymous with poor nutrition, poor health care, poor self-esteem, and poor educational and vocational opportunities*. Poverty contains no socially or personally desirable attributes. Poverty is a condition we universally wish to avoid. If unavoidable, during difficult times or transitions, we fight to reduce the experience to the shortest time possible. Tragically, when the condition of poverty cannot be kept brief and when poverty becomes *chronic*—especially the chronicity that emerges as intergenerational—then the ability to see horizons beyond the fences of poverty is impaired.

Poverty begins to take a developmental toll even prior to birth. For example, when poverty is accompanied by an unplanned pregnancy to a minority 13-year-old living in an increasingly isolated urban ghetto, perhaps in the midst of substance abuse and violence, one of the many scripts for developmental disaster has been written: developmental disaster with immediate negative consequences for both mother and child. The story likely to unfold includes an end to the mother's formal schooling, subsequent underemployment or unemployment, and a dramatic rise in the child's risk for poor intellectual progress. Such life scenarios contribute to the widespread *intergenerational pattern of dysfunction* characterized by:

1. delays in young children's developmental achievements, especially in their language, their independent reasoning abilities, and the quality of their social interactions with peers and teachers;
2. lowered aspirations and increased apathy among family members, sometimes accompanied by increased hostility toward the mainstream society that has excluded them from equal opportunities;
3. failure and ultimate withdrawal of many capable children from schooling and vocational education; and
4. extremely limited entry of adolescents and young adults into stable competitive employment and into sociopolitical groups that influence policy and the distribution of resources within the mainstream of society.

Despite some trends toward improvement in several indicators of children's overall progress in this country, the grim reality of intergenerational dysfunction—the leading cause of suboptimal development in children[2]—is on the increase. Exit from the entrenched underclass is more difficult today than ever before. Therefore, systematic intervention is called for to alter these dismal circumstances.

Intensive educational intervention has long been proposed as an important vehicle for social equity: a means for expanding the horizons of opportunities and benefits for children constrained by intergenerational poverty. What is our vision of quality? How can we focus on the positive value inherent in all children? Have we lost sight of the tremendous potential for growth in all children and inadvertently relinquished our commitment to providing the essentials of life to all children?

Universal free education, starting in kindergarten, has been the *cornerstone* that our country has established to maximize equality of opportunity. Yet we now have increasing evidence that a child's early years of development—the so-called preschool years—are vital in determining how well he or she will adjust to subsequent educational opportunities. This paper is concerned with describing projects that we have been conducting that are concerned with these issues.

The paper has three main purposes. First, we will present recent new findings showing that certain children and families benefit much more than do others from early educational interventions. Second, we will summarize new evidence of long-term positive effects of early intervention on I.Q. and academic achievement. Third, we will discuss why we think early educational intervention is beneficial for many children and propose key ingredients that are needed in the lives of all young children.

What Are the Recent Findings About Who Benefits the Most?

The new findings to be presented are from three inter-related studies conducted by Craig Ramey and colleagues: (1) the Abecedarian Project, (2) Project CARE, and (3) the Infant Health and Development Program. Each project will be described briefly below, followed by a presentation of recently published findings.

The first study, known as the Abecedarian Project,[3] was begun as an experiment to test whether mental retardation caused, allegedly, by inadequate environments could be prevented by providing intensive, high-quality preschool programs (along with medical and nutritional supports), beginning shortly after birth and continuing at least until children entered kindergarten. The findings from this research have confirmed that early educational intervention can significantly improve children's intellectual performance and academic achievement. New analyses, however, provide insights into *who* benefits *the very most* from this form of intervention.[4]

Traditionally, early educational interventions have been designed to serve "disadvantaged" children. The definition of "disadvantaged," however, varies from study to study. Most typically, children from economically impoverished families are those for whom early educational interventions are provided. Increasingly, it is recognized that the actual developmental quality of the home environment can differ dramatically even among poverty level families. This variation appears to be closely related to the parents' educational histories and their own intellectual and language abilities.[5] We thus decided to conduct additional analyses on the Abecedarian Project data set to answer the following questions:

1. Who truly is at the greatest risk for being cognitively delayed or mentally retarded among an extremely economically disadvantaged group of families?
2. Who shows the greatest benefits as a result of participating in a high-quality, intensive early educational intervention program?

Extensive background information was available on all families even prior to the children's birth. The information included family income, parental education, maternal I.Q. scores (from individual testing of the mothers), marital status, number of children in the family, mental health status of the mother, and other descriptive information indicative of the family's resources relevant to childrearing. As expected, this background information is predictive of children's developmental progress, especially in the area of intellectual development.[6] The single strongest predictor, however, is the mother's level of tested intelligence. For example, at age 3, for the mothers with I.Q.s below 70 points who were in the "control condition"—that is, the group whose children received supplemental medical, nutritional, and social services, but did *not* receive daily early educational intervention services from birth through age 3— all but one of their children also had I.Q. scores in the mentally retarded or borderline intelligence range (i.e., scores of less than 70 or from 71–85, respectively). In marked contrast, in the "early intervention" group (i.e., children who received a full-day, 5-day-per-week, 50-weeks-per-year early childhood educational program), *all* of the children tested in the normal range of intelligence by the age of 3. This new finding is consistent with a selection principle identified as "targeted intervention," which indicates that primary prevention of childhood disorders is more likely for certain sub-groups than for others.[7] Since the majority of children with mild and moderate mental retardation come from families with extremely low resources and with parents who have limited intellectual resources themselves, these families are the ones that are most in need of early intervention, and also are those that benefit the most in terms of outcomes valued by society.

Understanding of this new finding warrants consideration in light of the major findings from the Abecedarian Project. Figure 8.1, adapted from a report by Martin, Ramey, and Ramey,[8] shows the overall performance of children in the control and early intervention groups at 3 years of age on the Stanford-Binet intelligence test. The children who received the early education intervention had, on average, I.Q. scores that were 20 points higher than those in the control condition. Further, 95 percent of the children receiving early intervention scored in the normal I.Q. range (I.Q. score of at least 85) compared to only 49 percent of children in the control group. Thus, the majority of control children had I.Q. scores in the "borderline intelligence" category (I.Q.s of 70–84) or in the "mentally retarded range" (I.Q.s below 70). The relative reduction of mental retardation (I.Q. ≤ 70) via early educational intervention was by a factor of 9.8. The recent analyses reported by Martin, Ramey, and Ramey[9] also revealed that children whose mothers had the lowest I.Q. scores (below 70) were particularly vulnerable to low I.Q.s themselves if they did not receive intensive early intervention. For example, by 4-1/2 years of age, just before children enter the public school system (kindergarten), 86 percent had tested I.Q. scores below 85, which could seriously jeopardize their school progress unless special services were

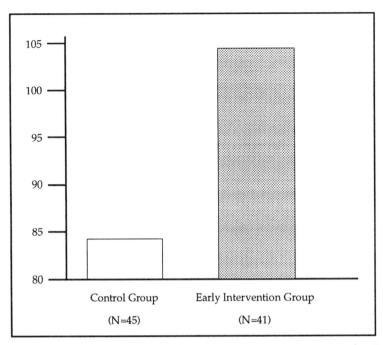

FIGURE 8.1. Mean Stanford-Binet I.Q. Scores at Age 3 Years for Early Intervention and Control Group Children from the Abecedarian Project. Adapted from data presented in Table 2 of the *American Journal of Public Health*, Vol. 80, 1990, p. 845.

provided. In contrast, none of the children of the low-I.Q. mothers in the early intervention group earned scores this low. Thus, intensive early intervention appears to have had a particularly powerful preventive effect on children whose mothers had low I.Q.s—while also benefiting other children from economically, socially, or educationally disadvantaged backgrounds.

The second study, the direct successor to the Abecedarian Project, is named Project CARE[10] and was designed to study home-based early intervention, where mothers learned more about how to provide good developmental stimulation for their infants and toddlers, compared to center-based early intervention, the same as that provided in the Abecedarian Project. Figure 8.2 presents the average I.Q. scores of the children at age 3 in the home treatment group, the center treatment group, and the control group. All children were randomly assigned to the treatment conditions, with children in the control group receiving free health and social services. The children who received the full-day, 5-day-per-week center-based program, supplemented by home visits as

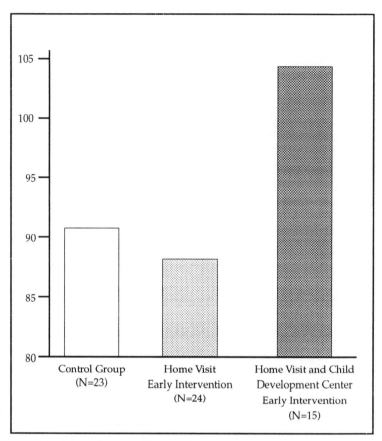

FIGURE 8.2. Mean Stanford-Binet I.Q. Scores at Age 3 Years for 2 Early Intervention Groups and a Control Group of Children from Project CARE. Adapted from data presented in Figure 2 of *Child Development*, Vol. 61, 1990, p. 1689.

well, showed much higher intellectual performance than did the children in the home-based only treatment group or the control group. The intellectual benefits associated with receiving both the center-based and home-based home treatment conditions are almost identical to those from the earlier Abecedarian Project. A disappointing finding, however, was that the home visit treatment—at least for this extremely economically disadvantaged population—was *not* able to improve the intellectual performance of these children. A noteworthy observation, however, is that mothers receiving the home visits expressed appreciation for them and continued to participate in the program for the first five years of their children's lives. The home-based treatment sought to teach mothers to carry out the same curriculum that the trained personnel in the center-based program used. Further, the home visitors (like the majority of the trained personnel in the center-based treatment) were women from the same communities where the study families lived and were of the same race as the mothers. One plausible interpretation of these results is that the home-based treatment was not sufficiently intensive, on a day-by-day basis, to produce the same benefits that occur when a more formally organized and monitored center-based program is provided year round. Whether other home-based interventions could become sufficiently intensive remains to be determined for this population.

The third and largest study is known as the Infant Health and Development Program.[11] This project built upon the techniques of the first two studies, but was extended to focus on infants who were born prematurely (< 37 weeks gestational age) and at low birthweight (< 2,500 grams or about 5 1/2 pounds), since these children are at higher than average risk for poor subsequent development, especially in terms of their intellectual performance.[12] In addition, this study was conducted in 8 different locations throughout the United States and enrolled nearly 1,000 children and families. Like the two earlier studies, the children and families were assigned randomly to receive either the early educational intervention or control services. As always, the control services involved free additional medical and social services that the families ordinarily would not have received. Unlike the two earlier studies in North Carolina which included only poverty-level families with multiple disadvantages in their lives, the Infant Health and Development Program included a much wider range of socioeconomic groups, although the majority of families had very low incomes and low educational resources.

In this project, the early intervention included home visits throughout the first three years and a center-based program modeled on the Abecedarian Program. In the Infant Health and Development Program, due to health considerations frequently associated with prematurity, the children waited until 12 months to begin attending the center and continued until they were 3 years old. The key findings from this project are presented in Figure 8.3 which summarizes the Stanford-Binet I.Q. results at age 3 for children who were in the early intervention and control groups.[13]

As can be seen, infants in the smaller low birthweight category (below 2,000 grams) and the larger category (between 2,000 and 2,500 grams) benefited from the intensive early intervention. What is clear is that the heavier low birthweight babies benefited approximately twice as much (13.2 I.Q. points higher than the controls) as did lighter low birthweight babies (6.6 I.Q. points higher than the controls). The 13-point I.Q.

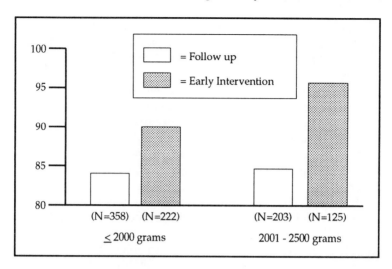

FIGURE 8.3. Mean Stanford-Binet I.Q. Scores at Age 3 Years for Early Intervention and Control Group Children for 2 Birthweight Groups from the Infant Health and Development Program. Adapted from data presented in Table 3 of the *Journal of the American Medical Association*, Vol. 263, 1990, p. 3038.

difference favoring the intervention group for the heavier low birthweight children is basically consistent with the general magnitude of differences in both Project CARE and the Abecedarian Project—a difference that across the three projects averages about 3/4–1 standard deviation at age 3 years. This finding also shows that even within the same high-quality intervention program, some children benefit more than others do. We interpret the findings that the lower birth weight children benefit *less* than heavier birth weight children as possibly indicating a difference in their biological status. The children who are closer to normal birthweight may be healthier and may have suffered less central nervous system damage than did the babies who were much smaller. Accordingly, they may have been able to benefit more from the general educational program that was provided for them.

Another new and striking relationship was found between how much children and families participated and the intellectual development of the children. Figure 8.4[14] displays the I.Q. results at age 3 years for control children and for low, medium, and high participants in the Infant Health and Development Program. The levels of participation were calculated on the basis of how actively the family participated in the three major educational components of the intervention: number of scheduled home visits completed, number of group parent meetings

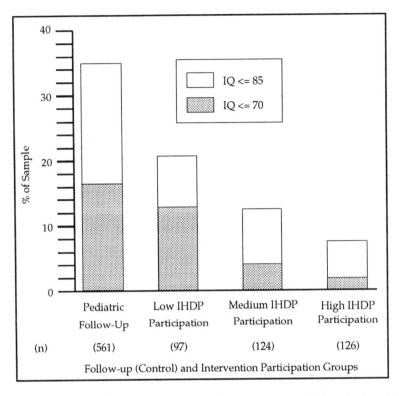

FIGURE 8.4. Percentage of Children at Age 3 Years with Borderline (I.Q. ≤ 85) and Retarded Intellectual Performance (I.Q. ≤ 70) in the Infant Health and Development Program. Data as presented in Figure 4 of *Pediatrics*, Vol. 3, 1992, p. 461.

attended, and attendance of the child at the center program. In the control group, 17 percent of the children scored in the mentally retarded range (I.Q.s below 70). In the intervention group, 13 percent of low participants earned scores in this range, compared to 4 percent of medium participants, and less than 2 percent of high participants. Thus, the most active participants had an almost nine-fold reduction in the relative incidence of mental retardation, compared to the control group. Interestingly, this relationship remained significant even after statistical adjustments were made for variations attributable to sex, race, birthweight, maternal education, maternal age, neonatal health, and variations across the eight sites. These findings support the general proposition that more active participation in intensive, high-quality early intervention programs is associated with improved developmental outcomes for vulnerable, high-risk children.

Another subgroup analysis using the mothers' Peabody Picture Vocabulary Test scores to estimate their verbal competence was conducted as a follow-up to comparable analyses on maternal intelligence in the Abecedarian Project.[15] Because the sample was of sufficient size, mothers were divided into verbal competence groups as depicted in Figure 8.5 and the performance of their children at 12, 24, and 36 months of age was plotted for the control and intervention groups separately. Figure 8.5 indicates that infants at greatest risk for functioning in the borderline intelligence or mentally retarded range at 3 years had mothers with scores below 70. Fully 47 percent of control group children had I.Q. scores less than 75 by 36 months. In contrast, only 23 percent of intervention group infants had scores that low. The downward trend of children's scores on the Bayley Mental Development Index and the Stanford-Binet I.Q. as they become older is particularly striking for children whose mothers scored in the retarded or borderline range and who did *not* receive the early intervention.

Long-Lasting Effects of Intensive Early Intervention

Health and education policy is being viewed with an eye toward the likelihood that early interventions will be a positive factor in leading to long-term benefits in developmental status, educational progress, and, ultimately, constructive participation in the social and economic life of our society. The long-term evaluation of the benefits is complicated due to the many factors that come to influence one's life course over the life span, and, of course, it takes long-term longitudinal follow-up to determine the outcomes of interest.

We have now followed all of the children in the Abecedarian Project through 12 years of age. Unlike many other earlier studies in which the early intervention was *not* very intensive, as measured by the amount of the program per day, the number of days per week, the number of weeks per year, and the total years the child received the program, the results from the Abecedarian Project are very encouraging and clear. A synopsis of these findings[16] is presented in Figure 8.6, which shows the average (mean) I.Q. scores on the Weschler Intelligence Scale for Children and for the Woodcock-Johnson Achievement Tests on reading and mathematics. All scores are on the same scale with a national average of 100 and a standard deviation of 15. All of the early intervention group means are above the control group means. The range of differences across the three domains is from approximately 5 to 10 points or, to put it another way, the "effect size" is between 1/3 to 2/3 of a standard deviation—an effect that in educational circles is generally regarded as of moderate to large magnitude.

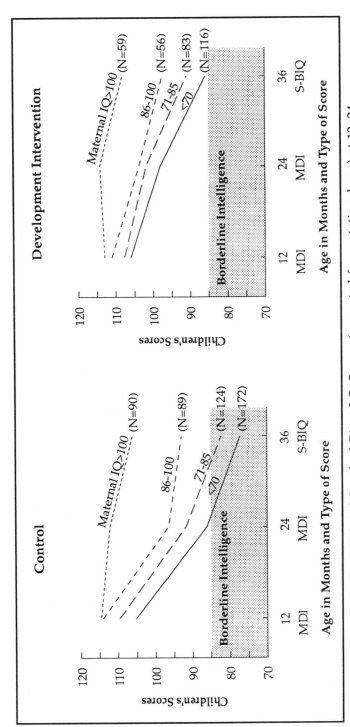

FIGURE 8.5. Mean Bayley MDI and Stanford-Binet I.Q. Scores (corrected for gestational age) at 12, 24, and 36 Months of Age as a Function of Maternal I.Q. Group (Infant Health and Development Program).

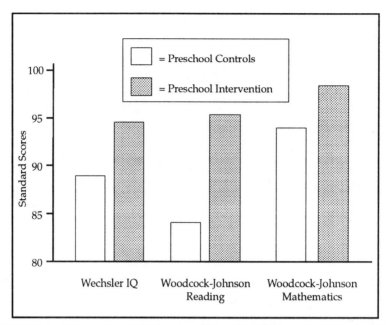

FIGURE 8.6. "Mean Age"–Referenced Standard Scores for I.Q., Reading, and Mathematics at Age 12 for Children in the Abecedarian Project

In Figure 8.7, the left panel shows that early educational intervention is associated with an almost 50 percent reduction in the rate of failing a grade during the elementary school years—55 percent for the controls versus 28 percent for those in the early intervention groups. In the right panel, evidence is presented for reduction in borderline intellectual functioning (I.Q. below 86) by a factor of 3.4, from approximately 44 percent in the controls to 13 percent for the intervention children. These findings support the proposition that *intensive* early educational intervention can produce *long-lasting* benefits in both intellectual performance and school achievement.

What is vital now is a more intensive analysis of different findings across different studies, especially in light of the new data indicating that (1) certain types of children are *more* in need of early intervention, and (2) the amount of program received relates strongly to the benefits for individual children. Also, the quality of the school programs children receive *after* early intervention must be considered in any comparison of effects across different studies. What can be done to improve disadvantaged children's everyday lives?

The scientific literatures on disadvantaged children, early learning environments, and basic learning strategies provide many clues about which facets of children's everyday environments facilitate (versus

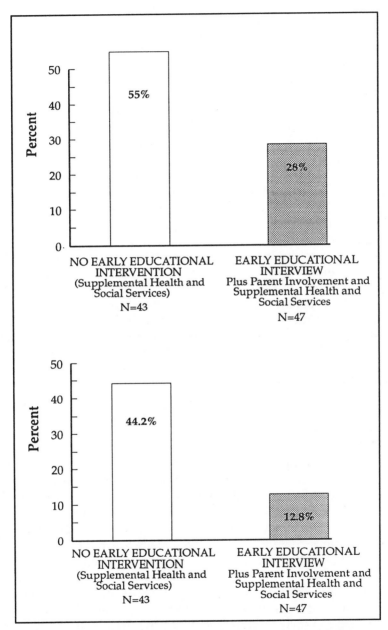

FIGURE 8.7. (Top) Percentage of High-Risk Children Who Repeated at Least One Grade by Age 12. (Bottom) Percentage of High-Risk Children with I.Q.s ≤ 85 (borderline intelligence or mentally retarded) at Age 12. Adapted from data presented in Figure 1 of *Applied and Preventive Psychology,* Vol. 1, 1992, pp. 131-140.

hinder) children's development. Although literally hundreds of variables have been correlated with children's developmental outcomes, we have endeavored to condense the empirical findings into a set of practical recommendations that inform policy planners, early interventionists, parents, and educators about how to enhance children's everyday lives. The focus is on those activities that (1) appear to be the most critical for learning and intellectual development, and (2) can be enhanced through the behavior of responsible, caring adults in the children's lives. Table 8.1 presents these as a set of suggestions for "essential daily ingredients" in young children's lives.

Collectively, these "essential daily ingredients" are hypothesized to operate in a mutually supportive fashion. Further, we think that there is a positive relationship between the amount of daily exposure to these activities and children's intellectual progress, recognizing that biological differences also influence initial and subsequent levels of performance. For very young children, the supportive environment needs to be predictable in terms of basic opportunities and patterns of interaction with those who are responsible for their everyday well-being. Not surprisingly, a content analysis of published early educational curricula[18] includes the elements listed in Table 8.1, although the activities and advice are presented differently in each curriculum and the importance of avoiding inappropriate punishment is not always mentioned. Our objective here has been to offer general guidelines that could improve the quality of a child's daily learning environment.

Conclusion

Our recent findings from three separate studies support and extend a large and growing 30-year, early intervention research literature that is consistent in demonstrating positive developmental outcomes for children of low-income and undereducated families. From new analyses, there is confirmation that maternal intelligence is a key factor in children's intellectual development, especially when these children are not provided with intensive daily stimulation related to learning. Fortunately, the children of low-I.Q. mothers respond positively to intensive, high-quality early intervention, leading to a dramatic reduction in their rates of mental retardation. Unresolved issues include: (1) how best routinely to identify children and families who will benefit from such programs, (2) how early to begin programs and for how long to continue them to produce desirable developmental outcomes, and (3) whether sufficient public and political will exists to scale-up early intervention efforts to match the magnitude of the problem in our society.

TABLE 8.1 What Young Children Need in Their Everyday Lives to Promote Positive Cognitive Development and Good Attitudes Toward Learning[17]

1. **ENCOURAGEMENT OF EXPLORATION**
   Children need to be encouraged by adults to explore and to gather information about their environments.

2. **MENTORING IN BASIC SKILLS**
   Children need to be mentored by trusted adults in basic cognitive skills, such as labeling, sorting, sequencing, comparing, and noting relationships between means and ends.

3. **CELEBRATION OF DEVELOPMENTAL ADVANCES**
   Children need to have their developmental accomplishments celebrated and reinforced by others—especially those with whom they spend a lot of time.

4. **GUIDED REHEARSAL AND EXTENSION OF NEW SKILLS**
   Children need to have responsible others help them rehearse and then elaborate on (extend) their newly acquired skills.

5. **PROTECTION FROM INAPPROPRIATE DISAPPROVAL, TEASING, OR PUNISHMENT**
   Children need to be spared the negative experiences associated with adults' disapproval, teasing, or punishment for behaviors that are necessary in children's trail-and-error learning about their environments (e.g., mistakes in trying out a new skill or unintended consequences of exploration or information seeking). This does not mean that constructive criticism and negative consequences cannot be used for behaviors which children have the ability to understand are socially unacceptable.

6. **A RICH AND RESPONSIVE LANGUAGE ENVIRONMENT**
   Children need to have adults provide a predictable and comprehensible communication environment, in which language is used to convey information, provide social rewards, and encourage learning of new materials and skills. Note: Although language to the child is the most important early influence, the language environment may be supplemented in valuable ways by the use of written materials.

Notes

The research reported in this document was supported by the National Institute of Child Health and Human Development, the Maternal and Child Health Bureau, the U.S. Department of Education, the Administration on Children, Youth, and Families, the Robert Wood Johnson Foundation, the Carnegie Corporation, the Spencer Foundation, the W. T. Grant Foundation, and the Pew Charitable Trusts.

1. M. Edelman, "A Children's Defense Budget FY 1989: An Analysis of our Nation's Investment in Children," Washington, DC: Children's Defense Fund, 1988.

2. S. Landesman, and C. T. Ramey, "Developmental Psychology and Mental Retardation: Integrating Scientific Principles with Treatment Practices," *American Psychologist*, Vol. 44, 1989, pp. 409–415.

3. Abecedarian means one who learns the fundamentals of something, such as the alphabet.

4. S. L. Martin, C. T. Ramey, and S. L. Ramey, "The Prevention of Intellectual Impairment in Children of Impoverished Families: Findings of a Randomized Trial of Educational Daycare," *American Journal of Public Health*, Vol. 80, 1990, pp. 844–847.

5. R. H. Bradley, B. M. Caldwell, S. L. Rock, C. T. Ramey, K. E. Barnard, A. Gray, M. A. Hammond, A. Gottfried, L. S. Siegel, and D. L. Johnson, "Home Environment and Cognitive Development in the First Three Years of Life: A Collaborative Study Involving Six Sites and Three Ethnic Groups in North America," *Developmental Psychology*, Vol. 25, 1989, pp. 217–235.

6. C. T. Ramey, K. O. Yeates, and D. MacPhee, "Risk for Retarded Development Among Disadvantaged Families: A Systems Theory Approach to Preventive Intervention," in B. Keogh, ed., *Advances in Special Education* (Greenwich, Connecticut: JAI Press, 1984), pp. 249–272.

7. Landesman and Ramey, op. cit.

8. Martin, Ramey, and Ramey, op. cit.

9. Ibid.

10. B. H. Wasik, C. T. Ramey, D. M. Bryant, and J. J. Sparling, "A Longitudinal Study of Two Early Intervention Strategies: Project CARE," *Child Development*, Vol. 61, 1990, pp. 1682–1692.

11. C. T. Ramey, D. M. Bryant, B. H. Wasik, J. J. Sparling, K. H. Fendt, and L. M. LaVange, "The Infant Health and Development Program for Low Birthweight, Premature Infants: Program Elements, Family Participation, and Child Intelligence," *Pediatrics*, Vol. 89, 1992, pp. 454–465.

12. S. K. Escalona, "Babies at Double Hazard: Early Development of Infants at Biologic and Social Risk," *Pediatrics*, 1982; M. Hack, C. Blanche, A. Rivers, A. A. Fanaroff, "The Very Low Birth Weight Infant: The Broader Spectrum of Morbidity During Infancy and Early Childhood," *Journal of Developmental Behavioral Pediatrics*, 1983; M. C. McCormick, "The Contribution of Low Birth

Weight to Infant Mortality and Childhood Mortality," *New England Journal Medicine,* 1985.

13. Infant Health and Development Program, op. cit.

14. Ramey, Bryant, Wasik, et al., 1992, op. cit.

15. C. T. Ramey and S. L. Ramey, "Effective Early Interventions," *Mental Retardation,* Vol. 30, No. 5, 1992, pp. 337–345.

16. F. A. Campbell and C. T. Ramey, "Effects of Early Intervention on Intellectual and Academic Achievement: A Follow-up Study of Children from Low-Income Families," *Child Development,* Vol. 65, 1994, pp. 684–698; C. T. Ramey, "High-Risk Children and I.Q.: Altering Intergenerational Patterns," *Intelligence,* 1992.

17. S. L. Ramey and C. T. Ramey, "The Transition to School: Why the First Few Years Matter for a Lifetime," *Phi Delta Kappan,* November, 1994, pp. 194–198.

18. J. J. Sparling and I. Lewis, *Learning Games for the First Three Years: A Program for Parent/Center Partnership* (New York: Walker Educational Book Corporation, 1981); D. Shearer and M. Shearer, "The Portage Project: A Model for Early Childhood Intervention," in T. Tjossem, ed., *Intervention strategies for high risk infants and young children* (Baltimore: University Park Press, 1976); J. J. Sparling and I. Lewis, *Partners for Learning* (Lewisville, North Carolina: Kaplan Press, 1984); S. Furuno, K. A. O'Reilly, C. M. Hosaka, T. T. Inatsuka, T. L. Allman, and B. Zeisloft, *Hawaii Early Learning Profile Activity Guide* (Palo Alto, CA: VORT Corporation, 1985).

9

Native Americans and the Demographic Legacy of Contact

Russell Thornton

1992 commemorated the 500th anniversary of the arrival of Columbus in the Western Hemisphere in 1492. This anniversary—the Columbian Quincentennial—was the cause of much celebration for many of the peoples of this hemisphere. They and the countries they formed ultimately trace their origins to the arrival of Columbus in the Caribbean. Certainly *most* of the hundreds of millions of people now populating the countries of North, Central, and South America had much cause to celebrate. *They* are the products of a remarkable population growth in this hemisphere which has occurred during the 500+ years since Columbus's arrival.

Another population history exists, however. It is the population history of the native peoples who first populated the Western Hemisphere, thousands and thousands of years before Columbus arrived. 1492 also represents a very significant date in their history. The date commemorates the beginning of a long demographic disaster: Following Columbus's discovery of his "New World," Native Americans, which include American Indians, Eskimos, and Aleutian Islanders, experienced a virtual decimation of their population. Their numbers declined sharply; many of their societies and cultures were pushed to the edge of extinction and beyond. Even today Native Americans are dealing with the demographic implications of contact with the Europeans and others who arrived on Native American lands.

As Paul Harrison noted,[1] the overseas expansion of European colonialism "was a vast upheaval of races, a reshuffling of genetic pieces on the chessboard of the globe. The arrival of the Iberian conquistadors depopulated large parts of Central and South America. The Indians who escaped their guns succumbed to their diseases, and only in the high Andes and the most inaccessible reaches of the jungle did they survive intact. Africans were uprooted from their native soil and shipped over to cope with the resulting shortage of labor. Asians were transported to East and South Africa and the Caribbean. Even the huge markets of the colonies were not big enough to employ Europe's expanding population in industry: Her surplus spread out into North America, Australia, southern Africa and South America." That this population expansion was detrimental to the indigenous populations of the Western Hemisphere is underscored by the fact that most of the world's 5.5 billion people today are descendants of the populations of the Eastern Hemisphere in 1492.

Population Collapse

There is considerable scholarly debate as to the size of the total native population of the Western Hemisphere at the time of Columbus's arrival. In my recent book, *American Indian Holocaust and Survival*,[2] I estimated that there were approximately 75 million Native Americans in the Western Hemisphere in 1492. At that time most of the native population was located south of the Rio Grande River, in what is today Central Mexico and some of the countries that form Central and South America. A significant portion of this population was concentrated in large urban areas. In the rest of the world, there were about 450–500 million people at this time. In the following centuries, the initial total Native American population declined to only a few million, after which some population recovery occurred. It is well documented that soon after European arrival, epidemic diseases—the primary reason for this decline—devastated American Indian populations in areas of present-day Mexico, the Caribbean, and Central and South America. Other important reasons for this tremendous population decline included enslavement and genocide as well as the destruction of native ways of life and subsistence patterns.

Considerable scholarly debate also exists as to the size of the native population of aboriginal America north of Mexico, i.e., present-day United States and Canada, including Greenland. Estimates have ranged from scarcely one million inhabitants to many millions. In *Holocaust and Survival*,[3] I analyzed these and other population estimates and concluded that the aboriginal population north of present-day Mexico numbered over 7 million people in 1492—somewhat over 5 million for the United States mainland and somewhat over 2 million for present-day Alaska, Canada and Greenland combined.[4]

Native populations north of the Rio Grande also experienced drastic declines following contact with European and African populations. Following 1492, the native peoples north of Mexico experienced a full 400 years of population decline. Not until about 1900 did their population reach its nadir and some population recovery begin. At the dawn of the twentieth century, when the population of the United States and Canada had grown to over 80 million, there were only about 250,000 Native Americans in the land area of the United States and another 100,000 to 150,000 to the north.[5] What accounted for such a population decline in the face of the remarkable population growth of the other peoples who colonized this hemisphere after 1492? Again, the primary reason for this Native American holocaust was the diseases the Europeans—and the Africans—brought with them to the Western Hemisphere; and again, war, genocide, and the destruction of native ways of life played an important role.

Populations change—grow or decline—over time according to increases or decreases in the three components of population growth: the total death rate, the total birth rate, and net migration (immigration into the area minus emigration out of the area). At this time, migration was not important in the overall picture of Native American population decline. Rather, diseases, war, genocide, and the destruction of ways of life produced population decline as ever numerically smaller generations of Native Americans were born, lived, and died. Each subsequent generation of the Native American population contained fewer people than the one preceding it due to an increase in the death rates and/or a decrease in the birth rates. Hence, Native American lives were either short-lived or unlived, and the total population declined accordingly.

Smallpox, measles, the bubonic plague, cholera, typhoid, pleurisy, diphtheria, scarlet fever, whooping cough, mumps, colds, pneumonia, malaria, yellow fever and various venereal diseases such as gonorrhea, chancroid and possibly syphilis came, sooner or later, with the newcomers.[6]

Native people here had few serious diseases prior to 1492. The reasons for this are not yet fully understood, but surely include the existence of fewer domesticated animals, such as horses, cows, or sheep, from which many human diseases may be traced, as well as the relative lack of large centers of population concentration, such as cities, which foster many diseases. The lower overall population density, a condition that hindered the survival of many diseases, may also possibly be a reason.[7] Europeans and Africans had degrees of immunity to the diseases which developed there, and some diseases had even become childhood diseases for them since many adults were immune. However, Native Americans lacked acquired immunity and perhaps natural immunity[8] to the new diseases the newcomers brought from Europe and Africa. Thus, the diseases often resulted in what are called "virgin soil epidemics," whereby a new disease becomes particularly virulent and spreads to virtually all members of a population.[9] Perhaps because of lesser natural immunity Native Americans were particularly susceptible to the new diseases. Moreover, the newly encountered diseases did not arrive merely once and then disappear; rather, they infected native peoples over and over again. Smallpox (Variola major), for example, was an especially deadly killer of American Indians, and epidemics of it among the native peoples of North America occurred from the early 1500s to the latter 1800s, although the latter epidemics were generally of a milder form (Variola minor). The overall effects were devastating. The newly encountered diseases caused increased death rates and, without doubt, decreased birth rates as well.

Although it was the primary reason for reducing the total Native American population, disease was not the only cause. Warfare with Europeans and Americans and, even more, outright genocide—the deliberate, state-sponsored mass murder of a people—at the hands of Europeans and Americans also reduced the native population, even to the brink of extinction for many Native American peoples. For example, tribe after tribe of California Indians was dramatically reduced in size following the arrival of miners and, particularly, of settlers in northern California during the gold rush of the mid-1800s.[10] The fate of the Yahi Yana of California and Ishi was but one instance of the racial genocide that occurred: Ishi was the last known survivor of the Yahi Yana, following a series of massacres of his people at the hands of the Californians.[11] Many other tribes suffered similar fates in the decades following the gold rush, as the California Indians were disposed of by the Euro-Americans. The massive population relocations and removals, as well as population concentrations on reservations, were also destructive demographically. In addition, the U.S. government sometimes broke tribes into different reservations, or threw tribes hostile to one another on the same reservation. Typically, reservations were land areas not desirable for farming by Euro-American methods, but Native Americans were generally encouraged to become farmers on them, even if they were not an agricultural people. At the hands of the Euro-Americans, Native Americans in the southeastern United States experienced particularly large-scale removals to Indian Territory (an area designated specifically for Indian relocation, now the state of Oklahoma) during the first half of the 1800s. The American Indian peoples involved named these removals "Trails of Tears" for good reason. The removals caused suffering, and death; hence, population decline.

Also, the overall destruction of native resources and ways of life must be added to any list of reasons, though the particular demographic effects are harder to ascertain. For example, how much American Indian population loss may be traced to the deliberate destruction of the North

American buffalo during the nineteenth century? We do not know, but American Indian population losses were likely substantial. Euro-Americans slaughtered buffaloes for the economic value of their hides and because they were in the way of westward expansion. The destruction was so great that the estimated 40 million buffalo in 1800 (down from an aboriginal population estimated at 60 million) declined to 20 million by 1850 and then to a mere 1,000 by 1895.[12] Such great American Indian peoples as the Arapaho, the Cheyenne, the Comanche, the Crow, the Kiowa, the Sioux, the Pawnee, and the Caddo were dependent on the buffalo for food, clothing, housing, tools, bedding, and other material necessities of life, but their societies and cultures—their ways of life—all but collapsed with its demise.[13]

Even today, epidemics of disease or geographical removals or war or genocide often stand as the most significant historical event in the collective memory of a particular American Indian people. What do the Cherokee of Oklahoma remember over and over again? "The Trail of Tears"—the thousands and thousands of Cherokees who died as a result. The Kiowa remember the cholera epidemic of 1849, and the remaining small number of Mandan remember when smallpox quickly struck them in 1837 and reduced their population from several thousand to a few hundred. Similarly, the Cheyenne remember the Sand Creek Massacre of 1864 and the Massacre at Camp Robinson, Nebraska in 1879. Only in 1993 did the Smithsonian Institution return to the Southern and Northern Cheyenne the skeletal remains of ancestors killed at Sand Creek and Camp Robinson! Will any American Indian ever forget the massacre of Sioux men, women and children on Wounded Knee Creek in 1890? Probably not. Also significant and also mourned today are the destructions of many native resources and the life-styles that accompanied them. Dispersed on reservations or concentrated in urban ghettos, many, but certainly not all, Native Americans have not yet achieved integration into American society, economically or otherwise; they live in poverty, with little hope that their children may have better lives. Many native people have been at risk virtually since their first contact with Europeans or Euro-Americans; most are at risk today, in one way or another.

Scholars who study population use the term "demographic regime" to refer to the determinants of fertility (for example, age at marriage and patterns of breast-feeding), mortality (for example, occupations and health-care practices), and migration (for example, movement to urban areas from rural areas) in a population, which, as they interact together, produce growth, decline, or stability over a particular period of time. These patterns are typically more or less stable, and influence the population's ability to respond to disturbances such as those caused by episodes of a disease.[14] Disturbances such as episodes of a disease may result in only short-term population decline as populations may also return to their previous levels of population growth, decline, or stability.[15]

Similarly, the historian William H. McNeill noted: "the period required for medieval European populations to absorb the shock of renewed exposure to plague seems to have been between 100 and 133 years, i.e., about five to six human generations."[16] Societies in Western Europe during the sixteenth, seventeenth, and eighteenth centuries were able to withstand severe demographic shocks, in large part because of the particular nature of their demographic regimes. By contrast, other populations have surely been driven to extinction by a series of relatively mild shocks because their demographic regimes were not capable of coping with the exogenous disturbances. All Native American populations in 1492 had previously experienced exogenous biological shocks of one form or another to one degree or another. Be they the shocks from disease, war, or natural disaster, the Native Americans who were here in 1492 had dealt with these shocks and had survived them. Such shocks were so commonplace elsewhere in the world that it is hard to conceive of the Western Hemisphere being free of them. The arrival of the Europeans, with their weapons and their diseases, was yet but another shock to the Native American demographic regimes, albeit one of a magnitude until then not experienced. We know from history that some Native American demographic regimes survived European contact, although in changed form, while others did not. McNeill[17] also noted that the 100 to 133 year period it took European populations to recover from the plague was about the same length of time the "Amerindian and Pacific island populations later needed to make an even more drastic adjustment to altered epidemiological conditions."

Thus, depopulation may have been followed by population recoveries, though not necessarily total ones, and epidemics may not reduce a population permanently or even for an extended period of time. A zigzag pattern of population growth, loss, and growth again seems more realistic for many groups than a downward stair-step pattern of population loss, loss and further loss.[18]

All Native American groups were subjected to similar forces of depopulation following European contact; however, similar tribal experiences did not necessarily have similar results. As I have stated elsewhere, the *"differential survival of American Indian tribes does not seem to have been a straightforward result of depopulation experience.* Consequently, tribal social and cultural factors may have influenced survival."[19] For example, I did a comparative study of the differential survival of the Tolowa and the Yuki Indians of California after both were depopulated during the gold-rush period, and found that the Tolowa were able to survive as a distinct tribal people to a greater extent than were the Yuki.

The study suggested three factors which might account for their differential survival: one, the relative magnitude of the depopulation (the Yuki were larger and experienced greater relative loss, though both were reduced to small groups); two, the different reservation experiences (the Yuki were placed on a reservation with other tribes, and intermarried with them); and, three, patterns of social organization (Tolowa kinship patterns allowed for the easy incorporation of outsiders into the tribe).[20] Hence, the depopulation experience per se was not the only factor determining tribal survival. Similarly, I tried to illustrate in *Holocaust and Survival* that Native American populations actually exhibited an exceedingly wide range of responses to the shock and aftermath of European contact.[21] Many of these responses may be seen as attempts to establish ways of surviving and adapting to the European presence and its implications. In this sense, then, Native Americans can be seen not only as victims but also, at least in part, as actively involved in attempting to shape (if not actually shaping) their own destinies.

Twentieth Century Patterns and Adaptations

The Native American population north of Mexico began to increase about the turn of this century. In part, this population recovery was a result of lower mortality rates and increases in life expectancy as the effects of "Old World" diseases and other reasons for population decline lessened. The population recovery also resulted from adaptation through intermarriage with non-native peoples and changing fertility patterns during the twentieth century, whereby Native American birth rates have remained higher than those of the average North American population.[22] The census enumerations indicate a Native American population growth for the United States that has been nearly continuous since 1900 (except for an influenza epidemic in 1918 that caused serious losses) to 1.42 million by 1980 and to over 1.9 million by 1990. To this may be added some 740,000 Native Americans in Canada in 1986 (575,000 American Indians, 35,000 Eskimos [Inuit], and 130,000 Metis, a group of individuals of Indian and white ancestry who are not legally recognized as Indian) plus some increase to today and perhaps 30,000 Native Americans in Greenland. The total then becomes around 2.75 million in North America north of Mexico—obviously a significant increase from the perhaps fewer than 400,000 around the turn of the century.[23] However, it remains far less than the estimated over 7 million circa 1492. It is also but a fraction of the total populations of the United States (250 million in 1990) and Canada (over 25 million in 1990).[24]

Native Americans occupy a demographically and socially disadvantaged place within contemporary American society. For example, infant mortality rates and age-adjusted mortality rates are higher for Native Americans than for others in our society; life expectancies are lower for Native Americans than for others; and Native Americans continue to face serious health threats from poor nutrition, alcohol and cirrhosis, diabetes, trachoma and tuberculosis as well other diseases.[25] Also, Native American housing does not equal the housing of the majority population; their educational levels are below those of whites and blacks; their rates of unemployment are exceptionally high; and their income is below that of the larger American population.[26]

Native Americans today are distributed unevenly throughout North America, a reflection more of events following European arrival than of aboriginal patterns (although they were certainly not evenly distributed at the time of European contact). The 1990 census enumerated the largest number of American Indians in the states of Oklahoma, California, Arizona, and New Mexico. The 1990 census also indicated that slightly over one half of Native Americans live in urban areas. As Table 9.1 illustrates, only 0.4 percent of American Indians in the United States in 1900 lived in urban areas. This percentage increased gradually during the early decades of the century. At mid-century some 13.4 percent of American Indians in the United States lived in urban areas. During the past few decades, more rapid increases in urbanization have occurred. Cities with the largest Native American populations are New York City, Oklahoma City, Phoenix, Tulsa, Los Angeles, Minneapolis-St. Paul, Anchorage, and Albuquerque. Around one fourth of American Indians

TABLE 9.1. Percentage of the United States
Indian Population Who Were Urban: 1890–1990

Year	Percentage
1890	0.0
1900	0.4
1910	4.5
1920	6.1
1930	9.9
1940	7.2
1950	13.4
1960	27.9
1970	44.5
1980	49.0
1990	50.0 +

in the United States live on 278 reservations (or pueblos or rancherias) or associated "tribal trust lands," according to the Bureau of the Census. The largest of these is the Navajo Reservation, with 143,405 Native Americans and 5,046 non-Indians living there in 1990. Around 60 percent of the Native American population of Alaska live in "Alaska Native Villages."[27]

The increase in the twentieth century in the Native American population reflected in successive censuses of the United States was also due to changes in the identification of individuals as "Native American." Since 1960, the United States census has relied on self-identification to ascertain an individual's race. Much of the increase in the American Indian population from 523,591 in 1960 to 792,730 in 1970 to 1,366,676 in 1980 to over 1.8 million in 1990 resulted from individuals not identifying as American Indian in an earlier census but identifying as such in a later census. It has been estimated, for example, that as much as 60 percent of the population "growth" of American Indians from 1970 to 1980 may be accounted for by these changing identifications![28] The political mobilization of American Indians the sixties and seventies along with other ethnic pride movements may have lifted some of the stigma attached to an American Indian racial identity. This would be especially true for persons of mixed ancestry who formerly may have declined to disclose their American Indian background. Conversely, however, individuals with only minimal American Indian background may have identified as American Indian out of a desire to affirm a "romanticized" notion of being American Indian.

Today over 300 American Indian tribes in the United States are legally "recognized" by the federal government and receive services from the U.S. Bureau of Indian Affairs. (There are a few tribes recognized by states but not by the federal government.) In addition, there are some 125–150 tribes seeking federal recognition and dozens of others who may do so in the future. The Bureau of Indian Affairs uses a "blood quantum" definition—generally a one-fourth degree of American Indian "blood"— and/or tribal membership to recognize an individual as American Indian. However, each tribe has a particular set of requirements— typically including a "blood quantum"—for membership (enrollment) of individuals in the tribe. Requirements vary widely from tribe to tribe. For example, some tribes, such as the Navajo, require at least a one-half Indian (or tribal) blood quantum, many tribes require a one-fourth blood quantum, some tribes, generally in California and Oklahoma, require a one-eighth or one-sixteenth or one-thirty-second blood quantum; and many tribes have no minimum blood quantum requirement but only require some degree of American Indian lineage.[29] (See Table 9.2.) Typically, those tribes located on reservations have higher "blood quantum" requirements for membership than those not located on

TABLE 9.2. Blood Quantum
Requirements of American Indian Tribes

Blood Quantum	Number of Tribes
5/8	1
1/2	19
3/8	1
1/4	147
1/8	27
1/16	9
No Minimum Requirement	98
Information Not Available	17

reservations (see Table 9.3). This pattern of requiring low percentages of Indian "blood" for tribal membership and dealing with the federal government to certify it also may be seen as a result of the demographic legacy of contact. As the numbers of American Indians declined and American Indians came into more frequent contact with whites, blacks and others, American Indian peoples married non-Indians at an increasing rate. As a result, they have had to rely increasingly on "formal" certification as proof of their "Indianness."

In the early 1980s, the total membership of these approximately 300 tribes was about 900,000. Therefore, many of the 1.37 million individuals identifying themselves as American Indian in the 1980 census were notactually enrolled members of federally recognized tribes. In fact, only about two thirds were. In the late 1980s the total membership was

TABLE 9.3. Blood Quantum
Requirements by Reservation Status

Blood Quantum	Reservation Based Number	Percent
1/2 or more	21	85.7
1/4 or less	183	83.1
No Minimum Requirement	98	63.9

around 1 million; hence, only about 55 percent of the 1.9 million people identifying themselves as Native American in the 1990 census were actually enrolled. Such discrepancies varied considerably from tribe to tribe. Most of the 158,633 Navajos enumerated in the 1980 census and the 219,198 enumerated in the 1990 census were enrolled in the Navajo Nation; however, only about one third of the 232,344 Cherokees enumerated in the 1980 census and the 308,132 enumerated in the 1990 census were actually enrolled in one of the three Cherokee tribes (The Cherokee Nation of Oklahoma, the Eastern Band of Cherokee Indians [of North Carolina], or the United Keetoowah Band of Cherokee Indians of Oklahoma).[30] Thus the Navajo Nation is the American Indian tribe with the largest number of enrolled members, but more individuals identifying as Native American identified as "Cherokee" in the 1980 and 1990 censuses than as any other tribe.

Similarities and differences obtain with the situation in Canada. Officially, to be an Indian in Canada one must be registered under the Indian Act of Canada. A person with Indian ancestry may or may not be registered, and categories of Canadian Indians include: "status" or registered Indians, individuals registered under the Act; and "non-status" or non-registered Indians, individuals who either never registered or who gave up their registration and became enfranchised. Status Indians may be further divided into treaty or non-treaty Indians, depending on whether their group ever entered into a treaty relationship with the Canadian government. Of the 575,000 American Indians in Canada in the mid-1980s, some 75,000 were non-registered and some 500,000 were registered.[31] The Metis are a group of individuals of Indian and white ancestry who are not legally recognized as Indian.

Canadian provinces with the largest number of registered Indians are Ontario, British Columbia, Saskatchewan, and Manitoba. In 1986, some 40 percent of the 740,000 Native Americans in Canada lived in cities. This was a significant increase from the preceding decades: in 1971 only about 30 percent lived in urban areas, and in 1961 only about 13 percent lived in urban areas. Wide variations in urbanization exist among the different groups of Canadian Native Americans: in 1981 some 70 percent of Canada's non-status Indians lived in urban areas, while some 60 percent of the Metis did and only about 30 percent of the status Indians and 20 percent of Eskimos [Inuits] did. Cities with the largest American Indian populations were in Vancouver, Edmonton, Regina, Winnipeg, Toronto, and Montreal.

Many Canadian Native Americans live on what are called "reserves," however: about 70 percent of the registered Indians live on one of 2,272 reserves.[32]

In the early 1980s, there were 578 organized bands of Canadian Indians. Most bands contained fewer than 500 members; only eight bands contained more than 3,000 members: the Six Nations of the Grand River (11,172); the Blood (6,083); the Kahnawake (5,226); the Iroquois of St. Regis (4,098); the Saddle Lake (4,020); the Wikwemikong (3,493); the Blackfoot (3,216); and the Lac La Ronge (3,086).[33]

Urbanization and intermarriage are bringing about new threats to Native Americans in the last half of the twentieth century. Urbanization has brought about a decreased emphasis on American Indian tribalism. For example, overall about 25 percent of American Indians enumerated in the census report no tribe, but only about 10 percent of those on reservations report no tribe while about 30 percent of those in urban areas report no tribe.[34] Similarly, urban residents are far less likely than reservation residents to speak an Indian language or participate in tribal cultural activities.[35] Urbanization has also increased the intermarriage rates of American Indians with non-Indians. Today, over 50 percent of all American Indians are married to non-Indians.[36]

If these trends continue, both the genetic and tribal distinctiveness of the American Indian population will be greatly lessened. It will perhaps make sense at some point in the future to speak only of people of American Indian ancestry or ethnicity. Taking into account the high rates of intermarriage, it has been projected that within the next century the percentage of American Indians of one-half or more blood quantums will decline to only 8 percent whereas the percentage of American Indians with less than one-fourth blood quantum will increase to around 60 percent.[37] Moreover, these individuals will be increasingly unlikely to be enrolled as tribal members. Even if they are tribal members, the traditional cultural distinctiveness of tribalism may be replaced by one of mere social membership if language and other important cultural features of American Indian tribes are lost. Certainly American Indians as a distinctive segment of American society represent a population at risk in the twentieth century.

Conclusions

Native American peoples north of the Rio Grande survived four hundred years of depopulation following 1492, and experienced some population recovery during the twentieth century. Although many specific tribes were "wiped from the face of the earth" during this "holocaust," many others managed to survive as distinctive tribes. That native peoples were able to survive both demographically and tribally is a tribute to their perseverance and adaptability. Native Americans are demographically and socially deprived within American society; this will likely continue well into the twenty-first century. New demographic and tribal dangers must be faced during the twenty-first century, however. Intermarriages with non-Indians will continue to undermine the basis of a distinctive, racial Native American population. The key in the next century to who is distinctively Native American may very well be tribal membership, irrespective of how that may be determined. Tribes with high "blood quantum" requirements may find themselves with a shrinking population base unless they manage to control marriages between tribal members and non-Indians (or even Indian non-tribal members). Continued urbanization will produce not only more intermarriages as more and more Native Americans come in contact with non-native peoples, it will also further weaken Native Americans as distinctive tribal peoples.

Native Americans need to find new ways to adapt to these challenges. Certainly tribal membership as the defining characteristic of Native Americans is a way of retaining their distinctiveness vis-à-vis other Americans. New definitions of tribalism are perhaps needed for urban Native Americans. There is no reason why "new" Native American tribes or branches of existing tribes cannot develop in urban areas. Already pan-Indian urban centers and associated activities such as powwows are firmly established in many cities. In the next century, with the cooperation if not the help of U.S. government policy makers, perhaps the next step might occur whereby these pan-Indian groups coalesce into new, distinctive Native American tribes with their own membership requirements as well as distinctive social and cultural activities.

Notes

1. Paul Harrison, *Inside the Third World: The Anatomy of Poverty* (New York: Penguin, 1981), p. 41.

2. Russell Thornton, *American Indian Holocaust and Survival: A Population History Since 1492* (Norman: University of Oklahoma Press, 1987).

3. Ibid.

4. For a somewhat higher nadir population figure, see Douglas H. Ubelaker, "North American Indian Population Size, A.D. 1500 to 1985," *American Journal of Physical Anthropology*, Vol. 77, 1988, pp. 289–294.

5. Thornton, op. cit.

6. Tuberculosis was seemingly present in both hemispheres by this time, as were other diseases, including treponemal infections, but probably not syphilis which is caused by *Treponema pallidum*.

7. It has also been argued that the "migration" of *homo sapiens* across cold, inhospitable Beringa "filtered out" certain pathogens causing human diseases. See Thornton, op. cit., p. 40.

8. According to Francis L. Black, "Why Did They Die?" *Science*, Vol. 258, 1992, Native Americans lacked genetic polymorphism in the MHC alleles; that is, they are able to present fewer pathogens to T cells for destruction.

9. Alfred W. Crosby, Jr., "Virgin Soil Epidemics as a Factor in the Aboriginal Depopulation in America," *William and Mary Quarterly*, Vol. 33, 1976, pp. 289-299.

10. Thornton, op. cit., pp. 107–109.

11. Ibid., pp. 109–113.

12. Today, there are well over 50,000 buffalo. Ibid., pp. 52–53.

13. Ibid., pp. 51–53, 123–125.

14. Various other scholars have also discussed the demographic regimes of historic European and other populations, and I have discussed those of American Indian populations. See Russell Thornton, Tim Miller, and Jonathan Warren, "American Indian Population Recovery Following Smallpox Epidemics," *American Anthropologist*, Vol. 93, 1991, pp. 28–45.

15. Even the effects of depopulations can produce spurts of population growth thereafter. See Thornton, Miller and Warren, op. cit.

16. William H. McNeill, *Plagues and Peoples* (Garden City, New York: Anchor Press, 1976), p. 150.

17. McNeill, op. cit., p. 150.

18. Thornton, Miller, and Warren, op. cit.

19. Russell Thornton, "Social Organization and the Demographic Survival of the Tolowa," *Ethnohistory*, Vol. 31, 1984, p. 188.

20. Russell Thornton, "History, Structure and Survival: A Comparison of the Yuki (Unkomno'n) and Tolowa (Hush) Indians of Northern California," *Ethnology*, Vol. 25, 1986, p. 129.

21. Thornton, op. cit., 1987.

22. Russell Thornton, Gary D. Sandefur, and C. Matthew Snipp, "American Indian Fertility History," *American Indian Quarterly*, 1991, pp. 359–367.

23. Douglas Ubelaker, op. cit., suggests the Native American population of North America exceeded 2.5 million in 1895.

24. Russell Thornton, "Population," *Native American in the Twentieth Century: An Encyclopedia* (New York: Garland, 1994), and Russell Thornton, "Urbanization," *Native American in the Twentieth Century: An Encyclopedia* (New York: Garland, 1994).

25. Thornton, op. cit., 1987, pp. 168–173.

26. Russell Thornton, "He Loves His White Children Most," *Contemporary Sociology: An International Journal of Reviews*, Vol. 19, 1990, pp. 575–577.

27. Thornton, op. cit., "Population," 1994.

28. The 1980 United States census obtained information that some 7 million Americans had some degree of Native American ancestry. Native American ancestry ranked tenth in the total United States population in 1980. In descending order, the ten leading ancestries were: English, German, Irish, Afro-American, French, Italian, Scottish, Polish, Mexican, and Native American. See Thornton, op. cit., 1987, pp. 220–221.

29. Thornton, op. cit., 1987; Melissa L. Meyer and Russell Thornton, "The Blood Quantum Quandary," Unpublished paper presented at the 1991 Annual Meetings of the American Historical Association (Pacific Coast Branch), Kona, Hawaii, 1991.

30. Russell Thornton, *The Cherokees: A Population History* (Lincoln: University of Nebraska Press, 1990).

31. Thornton, op. cit., "Population," 1994, p. 224.

32. Ibid.

33. Ibid.; The largest "group" of Canadian Indians, in terms of language and culture, are the Chippewa-Ojibwa. Adding the over 100,000 Ojibwa enumerated in the 1990 U.S. census to them would make for a total population (registered and non-registered) that rivals the 220,000 self-declared Navajos in 1990, if not the over 300,000 self-declared Cherokees.

34. Thornton, op. cit., 1987, pp. 237–238.

35. Ibid., p. 238.

36. Ibid., pp. 236–237.

37. *Indian Health Care,* OTA-H-290 (Washington, D.C.: Congress of the United States, Office of Technology Assessment, for Sale by the Supt. of Docs., U.S. G.P.O., 1986), p. 78.

10

Sites of Danger and Risk: African Americans Return to the Rural South

Carol B. Stack

My intent in this essay is to pivot the center of our concerns, indeed, to move us off center from a particularized definition of our subject as urban. I hope to entangle rural spaces within urban dichotomies, ultimately re-defining the subject of our inquiry. My comments are based on my own ethnographic observations of diverse, multi-generational, African-American families and communities in the United States—studies that chronicle nearly fifty years of a population in motion bounded by an uninterrupted commitment to group survival.[1] The migrations of African Americans along well worn paths between urban and rural locations in the North and South provide a fulcrum for constructing connections between rural and urban. Moreover, the perspectives of migrants themselves offer a window of vision on the language we are using and the discourse that has framed our conceptualization of populations at risk.

In this paper I call attention to the decidedly urban focus in the debate in the U.S. about endangered populations. To the contrary, I hope to reveal connective tissues and the tensions between rural and urban places, and convey how both are "thoroughly penetrated and shaped in terms of social influences quite distant from them."[2] Center-periphery political categories create borders that negate intersections of power and difference. "Borders," as anthropologist Anna Tsing writes "are a particular kind of margin; they have an imagined other side."[3] The other side in this matter is the rural South, a place which has become a site of creative political and cultural production for the people whose narratives inform this essay. From a book that is being completed on this topic, I selected the narratives of four African Americans who left the North for rural southern home communities.[4] They are returning with a mission: hoping to improve economic and political circumstances for African Americans in the South—providing alternatives to the contradictions of urban life. Their narratives, which document both the political and personal risks of their return journey stand in contrast to social theories built around center-periphery paradigms. In particular, I refer to Anthony Giddens' conceptions of the dangers of modern, urban places, which he compares to the safety of the hinterlands. In striking contrast to the image of a protected refuge in far away places, I argue the dangers of local cultures and domination.[5]

The South, which held untold grief and suffering for African Americans, has become a new promise to many urban dwellers. However, in contrast to the Great northbound Migration of preceding decades, people returning south are no longer placing hopes in promissory notes. They are moving back south to rural as well as urban communities, and appropriating a history filled with ancestors, land, and memory in modern ways. Those who return to rural southern communities encounter a vexed alternative. Bringing home a consciousness of race constructed out of their participation in the Civil Rights/Vietnam Era of the 1960s and 1970s, they are returning to create African American citizenship back home. What this requires, along with the sentiment of a symbolic journey home, is an awareness that they must treat "time and history back home as something to create rather than accept."[6]

African Americans in the United States are participants in this unexpected twentieth century drama. Their return back South from northern cities and other urban centers outside the South began in the 1970s, picked up in the 1980s, and is a dramatic reversal of a fifty-year-long migration trend.[7] Why African Americans are returning to rural southern communities is an exploration linked to many larger issues and global trends that seed the contradictions facing urban industrial sectors.[8]

Post-industrial transformations have altered industrial composition and the nature of work and opportunity in metropolitan regions. While goods production shifted to peripheral areas (both to non-metropolitan locations within the United States and to foreign countries), large metropolitan areas came to depend on their ability to function as service centers. One of the main stories in the postwar economy of the United States, especially as it affects African American working men and women, has been the decline in importance of goods production, especially in the regions of the North that were traditionally manufacturing-intensive. This adversely affected blacks, especially men living in the North who had always been heavily employed in this sector of the economy. In 1950, there were 26.5 million manufacturing jobs nationally, making up 49 percent of all jobs. This figure grew by only 5 million over the next 30 years, and, proportionately, the manufacturing sector dropped to 33 percent.[9] For blacks in the Northeast during the 1970s the displacement was particularly acute. In a decade when total black employment grew by 15 percent in the Northeast, with one-quarter of a million non-manufacturing jobs added, blacks lost 10,000 jobs in manufacturing, a 2.5 percent decline.[10]

In 1960, nearly two thirds of all manufacturing jobs were located in the Northeast and the North Central regions of the country. Over the next 25 years, the net decline in manufacturing jobs for the two regions was close to 1 million, while the net gain in the South was 2 million.[11] Since World War II, the focus of industrial growth shifted dramatically, first to the West and then to the South. The rise to economic power of many large- and intermediate-size southern cities with economies driven by a tremendous growth in producer-oriented services, coincided with this turnaround in basic employment growth.[12] The term "Sunbelt" coincides with this turnaround, and is most appropriately associated with these booming, urban-based, post-industrial economies.

The pattern of long-distance African-American migration in the United States since the 1970s stands in marked contrast to those in previous decades. For the first time more African Americans were moving to the south than leaving. And they moved to isolated rural settlements and non-metropolitan locales as well as to the region's largest cities. In contrast to the popular media and scholarly focus on Sunbelt migration to southern cities such as Atlanta, Georgia, this essay chronicles a return of people from northern cities back to rural southern homeplaces.

After decades of depopulation, a doubling of the number of people moving into rural areas between the 1960s and 1970s represents a dramatic turnaround and positive population growth in most non-metropolitan areas as they were defined in 1970. At some point in the late 1960s, population losses were replaced by gains. After losing almost 9 percent of the black residents during the 1960s, the non-metro South grew by 7 percent during the 1970s. Instead of losing a half million blacks as in the 1960s, the non-metro South grew by over 300,000. By 1990, the non-metro South had regained the black population lost since the 1960s. At the same time, black population growth outside the South slowed dramatically, especially in the Northeast.

The Dangers of Redemption

The following narratives follow dust tracks that are often erased by census migration streams. In the voices of Donald Hardy, Joella Fountain, Earl Henry, and Doris Moody—all returnees from the northeast to rural Carolina hamlets—there is evidence of personal and political power expropriated to rural homeplaces. Each of the conversations on the following pages are a collage of field notes, informal conversations, and deliberations that took place over long periods of time, as well as verbatim taped interviews. They are also a commentary on my own observations during our conversations, including the setting, mood, and the tone of our exchange. It is difficult to reconstruct the humor, whim, and vagary of the moment, as well as what I noticed or felt, or the ways I spurred on or encumbered communication. However, I have tried to present these conversations in order to bring to the reader the depth of thoughtfulness people brought to this study. These are discussions are with experienced travelers; some are highly educated, some have lived in poverty all their lives, but all are seasoned and wise.

The narratives below convey the passion and frustration of people longing for social change and empowered by a hope that they could partake in racial progress. They bring diverging perspectives and overlapping agendas from locations that cross the margins of north and south, past and present. Donald Hardy, Joella Fountain, Earl Henry, and Doris Moody come face-to-face with the dangers of local cultures and domination. Their act of going home implodes the tension between belonging and exile within one nation. Their encounters expose national culture as indivisible; from either the centers or the peripheries, national culture is reenacted. Emancipatory politics become risky business.

Donald Hardy. Sam Butler opened The New Yorker Diner, where he sold fresh fish, hot meals, and repaired small engines, after he returned south from Brooklyn in 1980. The tin-roofed cafe was dwarfed by several tall pin oaks providing summer shade and a winter shield. No hours were posted, and as far as I could tell the business was always open. Many of the Vietnam Veterans who returned to Harding county hung out in the front yard of the cafe under the teetering neon sign on what passed for a street corner in the countryside.

Pointing to the assembly of outdoor inhabitants, Sam told me, "Any of the local Vietnam Veterans who aren't in the county jail are to be found at the corner, that is with the exception of my nephew, Donald Hardy." Donald, whom I knew by reputation and had wanted to meet, did the books for a local non-profit organization and was studying evenings for his CPA exam.

"Donald survived both Vietnam and the corner, but not without cost,"

Sam said. "Come by the New Yorker tomorrow morning about 7 a.m. He'll be here and I'll cook you both an early breakfast."

The next morning Sam brought grits, bacon and eggs, coffee, and an anthropologist to Donald's table. He managed at one and the same time, with his hands full, to introduce us, sit me down, serve us breakfast, and fill in folks around us with the information that we hadn't met before. As soon as we sat down people in the cafe passed by our table, joined us, or chimed in, telling Donald to "tell it straight."

I am always torn about when to meet the formidable sages, as they are characterized, in a community—early on, or after I've been around awhile. I had been shy about meeting Donald until it got perfectly awkward. After an hour of attention and interruptions from regulars at the cafe—and constrained talk between the two of us, with Donald interviewing me about Vietnam, my study, whom I knew in the county—he changed the pace of the conversation.

"I don't know what took so long for you to show up," he said chiding me, "but since you circled 'round before you got your nerve up, I've had time to serve up some thoughts about those of us who came back. You may be on the right track. My talking to you is a way of checking it out. But we can't really talk here. Come by my Aunt Vivian's place. You know where it is, fenced in across the yard from Sam's. Drop by sometime tomorrow evening if you can."

I cautiously approached Vivian Doyles' home, where she lived alone but within earshot of relatives, with some caution about the old hound dog. Her rusty trailer was surrounded by a fence confining a few grunting hogs and occasionally, I heard the sound of crickets. The trailer had a sturdy wood porch and safe stairs with banisters built by her grandson for her to grasp. Vivian sat with us on the porch and, although hard of hearing at eighty-one, she nodded and echoed many of our phrases. But occasionally she shook her head and murmured in disagreement.

"Vietnam gave me a new freedom, a new perspective on life," Donald resumed the topic he questioned me about at breakfast. He pointed his index finger out in space to other men in the cafe as if saying, "You, and you, could tell your own similar stories." "I was fighting to determine once and for all where do I stand, what do I believe in? I knew if I could fight for what others believed in when I was in Vietnam, I could come back home and stand up for my own beliefs." His eyes held mine in a somber gaze.

Because it did not occur to me to do otherwise, I pressed directly into what I had been told already, and said, "I understand that you didn't prepare mentally for your return."

"No one should have to prepare for indignities," Donald answered abruptly, looking at both of us.

"I hope you don't mind talking to me." I sensed his anger.

He carried on without comment. "I have felt my life coming to a head since I came back. It's been terribly difficult, but I am determined to stay. When I got back south I got a job at the phone company. It is a fact and you could check it out that I was probably the most experienced, most knowledgeable person working there because of my training in the army. I was one of the few who could read a wiring diagram, but they put me in the warehouse. Despite the insult, it wasn't that bad at first."

He turned away refusing for the moment to bring memories forward, but then said in a flat voice, "they complained that I was trying to incite the workers."

"Yes, I've heard."

"I wouldn't laugh at the supervisor's jokes—coon jokes," he said, uneasily. "I would walk away. One day the supervisor came over to me as I walked away and said, "What's the matter, you don' fit in."

"I began to hate the all-black crew because they did not know they didn't have to laugh. They resented me because I wouldn't laugh. Something had to happen. Most of my friends—some you already know— knew that something was not right with me. After a while I couldn't function, I couldn't deal with whites. I would actually sweat—almost like a phobia. It was a hatred so intense it manifested itself physically."

I was feeling uneasy, but kept quiet. Vivian stopped rocking. She had raised Donald after his mother died and remembered the months that Donald had seemed half-alive.

"I went back up north for awhile. I wanted to assert myself and I did not know how. My rage was built partly on my impetus to control my own life, my own destiny. I could have gone elsewhere to start over, but I came back and dropped out. I spent my days on the front porch counting cars—how many passed by the street, 20, 30, more. For months I was paralyzed. A friend of mine came by and would sit for hours. Sometimes we would talk if I wanted to, but otherwise he would just sit there. Many folks sat with me."

Donald's voice hardened. But others would say, "Hey, he's back from Vietnam and he's not normal."

"I was not normal in the sense that I could not accept the status quo any longer."

Donald got up. He took a deep breath. The lines of his face appeared to deepen. He sat down again. "Slowly, after many months, with the help of those who sat by me, I was able to speak. During those months of silence, I had been speaking in my head to the whites I scorned. I had not been speaking to myself. Slowly, and surrounded by the love of those who sat by my side, I became assertive again."

~ ~ ~

Joella Fountain. The mosquitoes were thick and I thought I never wanted to fish again. But Joella Fountain loved Heckert's pond, the hike to it, crawling through the hole in the barbed-wire fence which she enlarged at each passage, the red-checkered napkins I brought with our sandwiches, and the catch. She was much less jittery away from folks at the house, despite the dangers of trespassing. It seemed to me that the air stood absolutely still by the pond in between her long silences. And then, like the soft, sweet breath of a whirlwind before a southern tornado, she would unexpectedly begin speaking. It was part of our agreement that the pace of our conversation was hers.

"I fell in love with old Jives who came down home sweet talking me. That's why I went north."

"I'm surprised."

"I just had to have him so I moved to New York in 1973. I was raised in a church and my whole life was nothing but church, singing in the choir, and teaching Sunday school. I never dated. I stayed upstairs in my room, read books and took walks. I was spiritual. Believe me, when I went to New York at eighteen it was a whole different ball game.

"It must have been traumatic."

"Yes, I was scared to death. I was trapped inside of myself. Everything I did, I wondered if I was doing it right. After my mother died I was raised by my Aunt, and everything I did wasn't good enough for her. If I expressed myself, I was wrong. I wasn't good enough. I could never do anything right. I grew up thinking that I am not going to be anything. I was believing it. I had to do it all on my own. I had to learn how to cook on my own, how to clean. I was just thrown out there. I wasn't taught anything.

"You were taught not to be heard."

"I was taught how to sing in the choir and go to Church and Sunday school. I wasn't taught anything about the facts of life. Anything about men. Half of the time some beat me up, shit like that. I was taken advantage of. But I made it. In New York I was getting severe headaches and getting depressed. I went to the Doctor and he told me I had to start living for me and stop worrying about what people think. When I was twenty-five I started opening up a bit."

"What did it?"

"Like I said, by then I was depressed and living alone in a little old dinky basement apartment. The cockroaches, the rent, all that was going on my nerves. I went to work for a Jewish lady and she had one of the finest homes I had ever seen in my life. I worked for her for a couple of years and got to know her well. She was so depressed she said she was going to commit suicide. One day I couldn't believe my ears. She got on my nerves so bad I took action. I screamed at her and said, 'Lady, you is a fool. You are living in all of this luxury, this beauty. Here I am trying to help you, reaching out to you, and my apartment is rich in cockroaches.' I said, 'You have to be a fool. You want to commit suicide—you go ahead!' I yelled at her. I stayed by her side. I kept yelling, keeping quiet, and yelling. I yelled at her, and then I stayed with her for what seemed like one hundred hours of tears. I prayed, I cried, I walked around, and I talked to god. I told her exactly what I thought!"

"How long did this go on?"

"I don't really know, Somehow I reached her. The last evening of the ordeal her son came in my room where I was taking a short rest. He told me, "Joella, you were fantastic. I don't know what you did to my mama, or what you told her, but mama has come out of it. You turned her around.""

"You turned her around," I echoed.

"When I got home it scared me to death. Like something just clicked inside of my body. Like a spring went off. I started thinking, oh my god, what have I done. I just told this white woman this. And she is going to fire me. She could fire me or kill me or something. I don't talk to white people like this."

"Where did that fear come from?"

"Who am I too say? I laid in bed for two weeks after that. I was speaking to myself and a voice came out of me that I did not know was there. I was hearing this voice for the first time. I was speaking with my own voice. Before that I walked around in silence, scared to speak. A lot of experiences happened to me and I couldn't tell nobody. I carried them around on the inside. I use to cry to myself. Scared to death to talk about what was bothering me. When this voice came out, I was speaking for the first time. It scared me to death. It was the beginning of my growth, of my realizing that I was losing my fear—losing my fear of whites. I quit a month later. Whatever I did—it was out of concern for her and for me. But at the time I didn't realize it. I was scared to death. I do not want to ever live that experience again. I learned for the first time how to speak. I moved back home in 1983 not long after that."

~ ~ ~

Earl Henry. The midsummer's humidity of the previous day reversed quickly to chilly fall air and rolled into the small trailer as Earl Henry Webb opened the front door. Looking out through the early morning sunlight, I could see the footpath that I had so much trouble finding the night before from the road. A thickly clustered stand of sugar pines and dogwoods surrounded the trailer disturbed only by a clearing where Earl Henry and Cora had a sizable garden of corn and okra. As usual Earl Henry addressed me from the podium of the large over-stuffed couch that nearly filled the living room.

"I'd better advise you now," he said, already dressed for the day in his blue suit at 8:00 a.m., "I have plenty to do. But I've been mulling over last night's conversation. You were right when you said we were talking about religion and politics and home all at once. Try to think about it this way. The good Lord sent me back home to my proving ground."

"That sounds religious," I said.

"There you go again," he reproved.

"One more time?" I requested, "What is the proving ground?"

"It's where you first were hatched, had that first cry, and gave that first punch you had to throw in order to survive. You go back to the proving ground to check on your own progress. You say, well I'll-be-damned, I have bettered myself—but more important, you go back to see how things are, and what you can do to better things for others if at all possible."

"The other day you called it soul-searching," I said.

"Look at it this way, if I can succeed away from here, I can do it here. This is the proving ground. We call it soul searching. Soul searching is looking inward to what you're putting outward. Think about elderly folks who come home to die—to make things right with their kinfolks."

"But people your age, in their late thirties and early forties?"

"For them the proving ground becomes a test—a test and a half, hear me! It's a hell-of-a-lot tougher task to come back at my age with my dreams. When I came back I looked up and told the Lord, 'There's got to be something better than this away from here for me.' But the Lord brought me back. There's a bigger task ahead."

I met Earl Henry Webb weeks earlier at what turned out to be an all-night work session for his cousin, Clyde Webb, who was running for School Board. Everyone at the house was edgy because Earl Henry was pushing Clyde to bring his campaign to white peoples' houses. "If you want to win this thing you have to knock on white doors," Earl Henry argued. Clyde resisted and an argument started.

"Mr. Charlie loves us fighting over this," Earl Henry announced to the group. As long as we keep fighting among ourselves, Mr. Charlie has a powerful form of social control." This was not the first disagreement of the long evening, and like other on-going debates, the heat of the moment dropped as well-intentioned folks managed to steer the conversation in another direction. This time, Clyde's wife, Bernice, changed the subject. She told Earl Henry about my study. From the expression on his face when Bernice specified "coming home," it was clear that Earl Henry had a lot to say.

"Quite frankly," he said to me, and straightway to others around the table, "This place leaves a lot to be desired. I probably have more than most folks to say on the subject."

"But not now," I protested. It was already 2:00 a.m. I didn't want my project to intrude on the work at hand. A small group of us were sitting close to one another around the kitchen table—Clyde and Bernice, Bernice's sister Sarah, and Earl Henry—writing campaign slogans and still debating the key points of Clyde's speech for the coming rally. Squeezed together on a hard bench at the rally the following Saturday afternoon, I met Earl Henry's wife, Cora. She commuted four hours a day in a van pool to Newport News, Virginia, to teach school. After teaching in Los Angeles for seven years she reasoned that she would get one of the advertised positions in the county. A two-year job hunt led nowhere. Although she was angry at the results, she searched for work further away, as did many of the local workers. Sixty-eight percent of the students in the local district were black. There was not one black administrator in the school district, and very few black teachers— a campaign issue close to home for Clyde Webb.

Cora invited me for supper at their home after the rally. Still shackled in his attempts to start a business—not one bank loan had ever been given to a black business in the county—Earl Henry cooked for the family, took care of their daughter, and kept a critical eye over political matters in the county. Their trailer was crowded, but both generously insisted I stay with them while I was in Harding County. Born on the two acres surrounding the trailer, Earl Henry made all concerns in the county since his return his business. Amid laughter and a savory cook-out, some neighbors dropped by. Together, we dissected every angle of the rally.

Over the next couple of weeks Earl Henry and I talked nearly every morning. In the afternoons he made his rounds in the community while Cora was at work. Their daughter, Sophia, whose friends nominated the trailer an after-school "teen-center," occupied the space vacated by Earl Henry in the living room.

One morning when I was going over my notes, Earl Henry seemed preoccupied. "Don't worry," I told him, "I have things to keep me busy if your have other things on your mind." It was near election time, he was dressed up, and I expected he needed to leave. But instead he picked up on a conversation we had begun the previous afternoon when a man he had known since childhood dropped by the house. As if assigned the task, the visitor teased and called Earl Henry down for being too hard on Clyde and trying to move too fast. He brought this to Clyde's attention carefully by humorously imitating a shy expression that, he said, could have belonged to Earl Henry in younger years.

"He didn't have it altogether wrong," Earl Henry said, "I was once a shy man." He relaxed and spoke softly. "I was eighteen when I left home to serve in Vietnam. The man I took over to Vietnam, he was a man, but he was a quiet man, scared and reserved."

And then in a voice from which rage sprung, he said, "The man I brought back ain't a bit more reserved than a man in the moon. You ask him what color something is, he gonna tell the truth—'cause he almost died for it before. He almost died for somebody else's beliefs. You understand where I'm coming from?"

"Yeah."

"Now I'm back here. I know what's right for me now, so if I could die for somebody else saying what's right for me, why can't I speak up for what I know is right for me and my family, that's what I'm saying. I brought a different man back from Vietnam all together. And look around you. Some of the other men back from Vietnam, they's hurting just like me. We've gone over to Vietnam. We've put our lives on the line. But we come back home and we can't get a damn job."

"You come back with a different feeling," I repeated.

"You come back home with a different feeling, and you got animosity in your heart. No sooner than you step off the boat somebody's telling you get to the back, and then you say, 'Wait a minute sucker, I just come from the Vietnam fighting for your butt, and you been on your clean white sheets for the past two years. I been out there eating rice and bugs. You better kiss my ass. And then you ready to kill him because Uncle Sam taught you how to. That's wrong. But how in the hell can you relate to what I'm talking about—how can you understand when a vet comes back and tells you—'I lived off of bugs and rice during the monsoon, I didn't have nothing to cover up with,' and you look at him and maybe even say, 'What's a damn monsoon?"

"You're right." I felt as removed from the Vietnam experience as he guessed.

"So I got to come and pour my heart out to you!"

"And I don't know a damn thing!"

"Yeah, and then they call in some physician, Dr. Charlie, who don't know or care half as much as you. I have to turn around and pour my heart out to him, and he says, 'We ought to put him on Codeine 2000.'"

"I saw Codeine in your kitchen and in the bathroom."

"Give me a job and let me feel like a man. Forget about the goddamn Codeine."

"Black men coming south—is it worse here for them?"

"It depends, and I'm dead serious. Men who left the south and served in Vietnam, they need to stay away a while, several years, to be able to come back. I worked in California and I know there is a better life. I know how I'm supposed to be treated. After I finished college in Los Angeles, I received bank loans and owned concessions in several bowling alleys in the late 1970s. It was a difficult process of trial and error, but I waged my goals and hard work against the bank loan and I had some success. If I had come back south immediately after Vietnam I would have worked my way right back into the fold again. Either that or I would have left immediately. Most people ain't got them guts."

"Didn't I meet your brother?" I said, remembering a brief visit from Clarence who had turned around and gone north just a month after he moved home in the late 1970s.

"Yes, damn him, one insult and he was gone. His bags were packed before they were unpacked. That was about the time they put a cop in prison. You read about it."

"Yes, it's in the stack of papers over there you gave me to go through."

"Do you know what the cop told the detectives?"

"What?"

"He told them, 'Down here we don't get no time for killing a nigger.'

"So if a cop kills a white person," I asked?

"They gonna do a year, six months, somebody gonna raise all hell about them smaking you, but kill my ass, ain't gonna say nothing."

"And this is in 1986," I said.

"And this is in North Carolina. You saw all those young black men prisoners doing road work in the county?"

"Yeah."

"I worked at the prison. Don't you remember the last time you were here I was working at the prison?"

"That's right!"

"I quit, I couldn't take the way they were treating people there. But you should go over there and try to talk. Many of those prisoners have been somewhere else, and then came back and got very frustrated. They are in there for pennyante crimes, and by them being black, they got more time than anybody else too."

The conversation was intense. I had been sitting on the edge of the straight-backed kitchen chair across from the couch, and Earl Henry had not moved since he started speaking. But after his comment on men in the prisons, I broke in, provoked at the never-ending orbit of this study—and in an attempt at wit.

"That's a new one on me," I said. "All I need to do this study is go to the local prison."

Earl Henry laughed. He knew that over that past weeks he had opened my eyes in many directions that sent me spinning, and I was both grateful and exhausted. His comeback cautioned that my luck might not be that good at the prison.

"What makes you think they'll talk to you," he said. "Look at me! Why do you think that I am sitting here conversing with you right now? Why do you think that I can sit here and converse with you the way I am?"

I stiffened, not sure of what his answer would be.

"Because I have gone somewhere else and smelled the roses. Now I come back here and I get thorns again."

"And people say to you, I've heard them, 'Why are you hostile?'"

"Yeah, they say, 'I've given you a slice of bread.' Don't give me a slice when you can let me make money and I can buy the whole goddamn loaf."

"And you know what a loaf is," I said.

"I can see that you are beginning to understand where I'm coming from. Don't give me the slice no more. Some of the guys in prison, they are used to the whole loaf, and then they come back and get nothing but a slice."

"Perhaps I should look at the local prison records," I said.

"You would find that half of them are in because Mr. Charlie told them do something and they said no, and Mr. Charlie slapped one of them or called them a nigger, and then he hit Mr. Charlie in the mouth."

"If they were men who had never left here, never gone north?"

"They would know how to play the game and they would be still playing it. Yesam, boss!"

"But by leaving?"

"They don't want to play the game no more. I used to walking tall, I don't mind working, but give me an honest wage. Don't give me 75 cents when my co-worker in California is making at least $6.00. I done smelled the roses, don't bring me back and give me the thorns again. That puts hostility right back in my heart again. I know that I can go and buy a gun. I've been trained to use this gun. So I'm not gonna take but so much pushing."

"Do many of the guys in prison—"

"Feel the same damn way?"

"Have they been to Vietnam?"

"A lot of them have been in the military, and others haven't been nowhere."

"It's just that life played them a cruel trick."

"You see Carol, I'll do anything that I can for people, but I remember an old saying my mother use to tell me, 'Don't piss in my face and tell me it's raining.' 'Cause then you show me you think I'm ignorant, because I don't know piss from rain, and that makes me hostile. Don't try to make me ignorant. I'm not!"

"Everything's twisted everything around."

"That's what makes people hostile, black or white, even a poor white person has what my mother use to call 'mother wit,' which is common sense. He hurts when you try to make him look stupid. So give me my due."

~ ~ ~

Doris Moody. Doris Moody shook her head. "Everybody is scared of the system. I don't have anything to be scared about. If I lose this one I believe I'll win another one." A small group of us sat long after the meeting in the basement of the Mt. Zion Baptist Church in New Jericho dismayed that all attempts to map out an aggressive political campaign for black candidates had crumbled into conflict. Doris lamented, the first black candidates to run for office in the country since Reconstruction may be defeated by "those folks who are addicted to tradition." A committed community worker in her early forties, Doris returned home after working for a tenants organization in public housing in New York. She brought back organizing skills, tenacity, and a hard-earned understanding of public bureaucracies. As people began to leave the Church I turned to Doris and said, "To my knowledge, the white candidates campaign in the Black Churches, why not try for reciprocity?"

"I was very disappointed when I moved back," Doris answered indirectly. "There was really not that much difference from the way it was when I left. To tell you the truth, and the reason why it has been different for me, is because I am different. There are things I know I don't have to accept. I know what's right and wrong. But many folks, after they come back, they lose their nerve."

"But in what ways are your experiences different from Clyde Webb's," I asked, recalling his caution at the meeting, and that he and Bernice moved back south in the mid-1980s about the same time as Doris.

It was getting late. Doris pushed her palms towards me bringing a stop sign to the conversation, grabbed a pen from her basket of papers, and sketched a map to her house on the back of a small campaign poster—a genuine invitation for me to visit her. The next afternoon I followed the map from the town center, a point of reference in those rural parts I always needed to find my way down long reaches of dirt roads. I recognized feeble signs of economic growth, for example, the small brick houses build by successful black workers and professionals who had returned from the North.

Once at the farmhouse Doris started up the conversation where we had left off the previous evening. "That meeting last night," she said, "It was another example of caution, fear, and trauma. There are great human costs for those who come back and see every challenge as a personal test. Some folks who came back lost their patience before they even arrived."

"Some people are ebullient about their hopes for social change back home," I reminded Doris, "but I also understand that returning home can be a terrible, self-imposed test. "

"They are unable to personally survive the anguish of defeat," Doris said, "especially defeat of their dignity."

Neither of us specified, but as if we were both heading on the same collision course, Doris brought it up.

"Last night," she said, I was too tired to talk any more, and what you asked about Clyde, really about some of the men at the meeting, well it took me a long time to realize," she said, meeting my eyes, "and then again, I don't know if you have ever met anything like this. Some things I don't have together yet, so what's to expect that you could understand."

Doris hesitated, and then went on. "You will find some differences, at least in my view, in how men and women make themselves at home as they return to these communities. How they settle in—and I don't mean whether they sell out—but how and where they rest their bodies, and what they look out upon when they see home."

"I think that what is at stake may be where home is in peoples' minds," I said. "I've wondered at times if home can be vested in different localities—I would go so far as to say home may occupy different spiritual spaces."13

"That has a lot to do with who we are and how we change over the years. I'm only now beginning to understand. You watched me last night as hurt feelings flew around the room?"

"Yes, and I wondered how you held it together."

"As I told you earlier, I am different now. I can find home close around me, sometimes closing in around me—inside my insides. There's some safety inside."

Doris paused, took a long breath, and led me across the room into her large farm kitchen where she had started water for hot tea. The kitchen, which appeared larger than the living room where we had been sitting, functioned as a workplace with desks, files, and papers piled high, as well as a place to cook and eat. I helped bring a fine porcelain tea pot and cups to the table while Doris sliced the peaches I had brought.

For a moment we were both distracted. As if to acknowledge the juncture we had reached in our discussion, Doris began again. "We'd better finish this up soon before the school bus arrives or I'll lose my train of thought. You must watch and listen carefully to the ways people work out who they are when they return."

"From what I have observed," I said, "it's a difficult negotiation. It's not easy. People need to bring a different part of themselves to different situations."

"It's the lucky ones, who can switch and deal," she quickly added, "but it takes the ability to let some things go, to believe in yourself so deeply so that they can't rock the very ground on which you stand."

From what I had observed Doris did not take defeats personally. But, she worried about the people who came back south and wore their hearts on their sleeve, people who could not separate personal from political challenges. After I had known Doris several months, and seen her both challenged and esteemed, I asked her directly how she managed to maintain her balance, and she responded.

"As a leader in my community organization I have met with both support and resistance for my positions. To sustain myself I go to the well, I ask for help, I communicate with the spirit, and it tears me to pieces. But I am strong. I have an eight-room house in my soul. I only let them tear down five rooms; that leaves me three to rebuild on. As long as you can keep two to three rooms of self-esteem to build on, you are okay. You can rebuild. Some people aren't as strong. They can only keep one line open. It's a thin line between sanity and insanity."

Much of modernist thought fastens a power base in the Diaspora to the cities, and leaves the footsteps facing one way, as if they stop there. This has rendered invisible cycles of return migration and the resources carried home on people's backs, in their heads, and in their hearts. Why are African Americans leaving northern cities and returning to rural southern communities? Who is returning, and what does it mean to them and to the rest of us? Looking back to a history filled with tales of their own victimization, how do people manage the collision between belonging and identity and the almost mythic racial geography of home? What happens when the landscapes of contemporary capitalism, carried by the movers themselves, spill over bringing yet another aspect of capitalism into rural southern enclaves?

These questions are about people who left the past behind and those who did not, and about a world system that is becoming de-centered, rendering modernism more complex than we ever imagined. The twentieth century has witnessed shifting geographies and radical changes in the movement of people from rural to urban places, and now back again. Symbolic of fundamental changes in Western capitalism, these migrations of people uprooted, two and sometimes three times, may indeed be the latest stage in twentieth century migrations.

As scholars we have not concerned ourselves with the implications of these shifting geographies, nor the consequences for migrants themselves. Such issues get lost in "center-centered" theory. Nor have we asked what it means in practice to people who are extricating themselves from one hazardous place to another. The migrants to U.S. cities from the rural southern communities who comprise the focus of underclass debates, moved north, historically, by way of the underground railroad. Migrants returning to rural homeplaces, are now negotiating what I might call the overground railroad as an underclass strategy.

We have been led to believe that the great migrations that formed the modern states thoroughly dislocated migrants, and that with mobility, people abandoned meaningful ties to places of origin, and separated themselves from the power of kin, land, and ancestors.[14] The return movement of African American individuals and families escaping urban conditions and urban poverty is a form of resistance to modernism that is a re-working of traditional relationships between rural blacks and whites, between men and women, among those who never left the south and those who returned, and across generations. It is a return that is emancipatory, gendered, and dangerous.

The political actions and social practices of African-American return migrants present a challenge to notions of modernity. We have assumed that people in the modern world, once torn from tradition, become diffused, fragmented, self-motivated and self-interested, and that they are thoroughly emancipated from moral or collective purpose. Most significantly, they never look backwards. If however, they look back, it is seen as a sentimental journey, a reunion, that collapses time into communities of memory. From this perspective, modern industrial centers are symbolically juxtaposed to places of origin. The urban centers are viewed as sites of danger and risk. Out of the way places on the other hand have come to represent safety in the context of a timeless past. To the contrary, the people in this essay enact emancipatory politics back home in the hinterlands; multiple agendas and sites of power inform their actions. They meander through, and within political agendas that transcend borders; in doing so they must negotiate an array of dangers.

Notes

1. Carol B. Stack, "The Kindred of Viola Jackson: Residence and Family Organization of an Urban Black American Family," in *Afro-American Anthropology: Contemporary Perspectives*, N. Whitten, Jr., and J. Szwed, eds., *The Free Press*, New York, 1970; *All Our Kin: Strategies for Survival in a Black Community* (New York: Harper and Row, 1974); *Holding On To The Land and The Lord: Essays on Kinship, Ritual, Land Tenure, and Social Policy*, Robert L. Hall and Carol B. Stack, eds. (Georgia: University of Georgia Press, 1982); "The Journeys of Black Children: An Intergenerational Perspective," in *Noneconomic Migration*, P. Jobes and W. Stinner, eds. (University Press of the Americas, 1992); Carol B. Stack, *Call To Home: African-Americans Reclaim Rural Places* (Basic Books, 1995).

2. Anthony Giddens, *The Consequences of Modernity* (Stanford: Stanford University Press, 1990), p. 19.

3. Anna Lowenhaupt Tsing, *In the Realm of the Diamond Queen* (New Jersey: Princeton University Press, 1993), p. 21.

4. Carol B. Stack, op. cit., 1995.

5. Anthony Giddens, *Modernity and Self-Identity: Self and Society in the Late Modern Age* (Stanford: Stanford University Press, 1991).

6. David Harvey, *The Condition of Postmodernity* (Oxford, Massachusetts: Basil Blackwell, 1989), p. 204.

7. Gladys T. Bowles, Calvin L. Beale, and Everett S. Lee, *Net Migration of the*

Population, 1960–1970, by Age, Sex, and Color (Athens, Georgia: University of Georgia Printing Department, 1975).

8. African-American return migration occurs in both metropolitan and non-metropolitan regions of the South. The focus of this study is on urban to rural migration which is more characteristic (but not entirely so) of low-income people who follow their own paths back home.

9. David Clark, *Post-Industrial America: A Geographical Perspective* (New York: Methuen, Inc., 1984), p. 22.

10. Kevin E. McHugh, "Economic Restructuring, Social Ties, and Black Migration to the American South," Paper presented at the 1988 Annual Meeting of the Population Association of America, New Orleans, 1988.

11. John D. Kasarda, "Population and Employment Change in the United States: Past, Present, and Future," Paper prepared for the National Research Council Transportation Research Board, 1988.

12. Rebecca S. Roberts and Lisa M. Butler, "The Sunbelt Phenomenon: Causes of Growth," in *The Future of the Sunbelt: Managing Growth and Change*, Steven C. Ballard and Thomas E. James, eds. (New York: Praeger Publishers, 1983), p. 6.

13. I am reminded of Marshall Berman's definition of modernism in *All That Is Solid Melts Into Air*. He writes, "I define modernism as any attempt by modern men and women to become subjects as well as objects of modernization, to get a grip on the modern world and make themselves at home in it," Preface to the Penguin Edition, 1988, p. 6.

14. Anthony Giddens, op. cit., 1991.

About the Book and Editors

As this century draws to a close and the new one approaches, the United States is still struggling with serious and persistent social problems. These troubling dilemmas, including poverty, homelessness, discrimination, and severe inequity, afflict some subgroups of the population more than others, and it is the plight of these at-risk groups—children, growing numbers of homeless families and individuals, people of color, poor mothers—that this timely volume explores.

Contributors to this forward-looking book include some of the most respected and distinguished social scientists in the United States. They provide keen and powerful insights into the problems affecting the "disadvantaged" populations of this nation. Their informed perspectives are critically important if we are to comprehend the scale and complexity of the obstacles to achieving an "equitable society" in the twenty-first century, and the observations and prescriptions they offer make a significant and much-needed contribution to the literature on these urgent national issues.

George J. Demko is professor of geography at Dartmouth College, and **Michael C. Jackson** is a practicing psychoanalyst and is a member of the Board of Visitors of the Rockefeller Center for the Social Sciences at Dartmouth.

Index